玉見生机

傅熹年書

the Natural Wonders of Jade

Ancient Chinese Jade Exhibition of Animal and Plant Themes

玉見生机

中国古代动植物题材玉器展

北京市颐和园管理处
中国人民大学清史研究所 编

五洲传播出版社

特别鸣谢

北京居然传世文化艺术发展有限公司

《玉见生机——中国古代动植物题材玉器展》编辑委员会

CONTENTS

目 录

Preface I

Throughout nearly the last seven thousand years of Chinese history, jade has been a very profound cultural accomplishment. It is also exceptionally unique in the history of human culture.

As early as 4000 BCE, ritual jade objects had already appeared in the Hongshan Culture in Northeast China and also in the Liangzhu culture along the Yangtze River in Eastern China. Subsequently the Shijiahe culture in the middle course of the Yangtze River and the Longshan culture along the Yellow River further enhanced the rich and exquisite beauty of ritual jades. The Shang dynasty craftsmen in the 16th Century BCE had already been producing very striking ritual and imperial display objects using jade. Many scholars also believe that these jade objects were utilized as amulets portraying the sacredness of jade and also emanating the harmony between man and nature. The Shang jades were usually made in flat and plane shapes with patterns almost similar with those of the bronze vessels of the period. The "chicken-bone white jade tiger" in the current exhibition is a good example of the Shang jade emanating the ruling class's revelation of jade and attached importance to cultural unity.

The Western Zhou period (1046 BCE–771 BCE) inherited the Shang's jade culture without many new developments in jade producing technique. However, the jade patterns and craftsmanship were rich and more exquisite. Jade had already become very important ritual objects among the ruling classes and also later accommodated the Confucian values and beliefs. However, in the later Eastern Zhou period (770BCE–256BCE), Confucian thinking and values were challenged and this led to the rise of the many schools of thought in the Spring and Autumn and the Warring State periods (770BCE–221BCE). With a more diversified society, jade became more circulating and fashionable among the aristocracies.

During the Warring State period (475BCE–221BCE) where new thoughts and culture were flourishing, jade represented a human-centered world affiliating virtue and moral concepts to the wearer of jade. Jade also proliferated to a high degree of development during both the Western and Eastern Han periods. The use of jade as ritual objects gradually diminished as the slavery society transformed itself towards a feudal society. Jade objects were primarily seen as emanating the power of the ruling classes in the Han periods. The jade objects of the Han period (206 BCE–220 CE) were later acting as optimal source models to be copied and revered in later periods.

In the Southern and Northern Dynasties period (also called the Six Dynasties period) (420–589), the rise of Buddhism had further impacted Confucian thoughts. The rituals in feudalism were also being replaced by those minority ethnic cultures that valued more freedom. Jade also gradually turned into embellishment and ornamental objects in the life of the gentry. In the Sui and Tang dynasties (581–907) the aesthetic values of jade and the inherent value of jade materials were highly treasured. This had further faded away jade's affiliation with religion and deities.

The jade objects of the Sui and Tang periods emanated a big metropolis culture with open, prosperous and multi ethnicities. The Tang jades were also highly influenced by foreign cultures reflecting multi regional, ethnicity and religious styles. These jades are usually ornaments accompanied with gold, such as hair pins, belt ornaments, and clothing embellishments. Compared with those of the Warring States and Han periods, the ruling classes of the Tang paid less attention to jade burial culture. As such, jade objects were less excavated and the quality of jade also declined. The Tang period paid more attention to gold and silver wares than jade reflecting the great change in attitude and taste of the ruling class.

The Song period (960–1279) was a pivotal stage in Chinese jade history. While inheriting the profound jade culture of the earlier generations, it also blended in its own unique characteristics of the period. The eminent scholar Zhao Ruzhen of the late Qing period commented in his book *Guwan Zhinan* (A Guide to Antiques) that the Song jades were great revivals in Chinese jade with exquisiteness comparable to those of the earlier Zhou and Han periods. Song period jades were heavily influenced by the literati culture in venerating the ancient forms and styles while also improve on skills and techniques of jade production. Song jades were said to be more commercialized to suit the refined and popular aesthetic tastes.

The Song period was also a period governed by the culture of the Han ethnicity taking jade culture to a new level. With the uphold of new Confucianist thoughts, the people of the Song also took the collection of ancient objects and antique relics to a new height. The jade objects and ornaments were a much welcome acquisition and a form of accomplishment. Many *fanggu* jade objects (jade imitating the ancient forms and styles) such as the sword ornaments, *bi, cong* and auspicious beasts appeared. The Song period usually imitated the Han jade objects in style and form but also with its own added distinctive characteristics.

Other than the *fanggu* jades, the Song period also produced an abundance of realistic jade carvings under the aesthetic influence during the reign of Emperor Song Huizong (1100–1125). This was particularly true for those jades of animal and plant themes influenced by the realistic Song period imperial paintings. It can be said that both the *fanggu* and realistic jade objects represented the main stream of Song jades. Ornamental and embellishment jade objects reached its most prosperous during the Song period with both the rise in the demand together with the flourishing jade trade.

The Liao, Jin and Yuan (907–1368) jades possess a strong northern grassland nomadic style with previously unseen scenic compositions. These intricate and realistic northern nomadic "Spring and Autumn hunting" (*chunshui* and *qiushan*) compositions became the chief characteristics of the Liao, Jin and Yuan jades. They also heavily influenced the later Qing period imperial jade boulders (*shanzi*), jade brush pots and jade table screens. Many scholars inadvertently neglected the importance of Yuan jades within the context of Song, Liao and Jin jade objects. In actual fact, the Yuan jades are a fusion and continuation of the Song, Liao and Jin jades, exercising a profound influence over the jades in the later Ming and Qing.

In the Ming and Qing periods (1368–1911), jade became the imperial decorations in a large scale. It was also being collected and worn by the aristocrats and the gentry. Jade became the first-choice material for imperial seals in the Song and Yuan periods signifying the supremacy of imperial power and wealth. With the Northwestern Territories under Chinese rule in the middle of the eighteenth century, jade materials from the Kunlun Mountain range came incessantly into Central China. The Ruyiguan in the Forbidden City and the Jiangnan Zhizaoju became the designated jade manufacturing production center for the imperial jades. During the middle to the late Qianlong period, the quantity, quality, variety and the innovations of jade objects had reached unprecedented heights. The collection of Qianlong period jades in the Palace Museum exceeds the sum of all jades in all the other previous periods. Emperor Qianlong's achievement in jade collection and production had surpassed all his predecessors and successors.

There were three very outstanding achievements in the Qianlong jades. Firstly, it was in the field of *fanggu* jades (jades imitating the ancient styles and forms). The Qianlong *fanggu* jades covered almost all the forms and styles from the bronze wares of the Xia, Shang and Zhou periods with a variety of no less than a thousand forms including many ancient auspicious beast patterns such as the *taotie*, phoenix, and *panhui* patterns.

Secondly, in the field of realistic carving of nature, the Qianlong jades in a way had surpassed the achievements of the Song period in variety, styles, and realist carvings. Other than the auspicious beasts and birds such as the dragon, phoenix, lion and *qilin*, the Qianlong jades also included patterns and shapes such as plants, fruits, and flowers. Others such as deities, immortals, religious figures and ordinary human figurines also became common

subjects of jade carvings. Many of these were very realistically carved.

Thirdly, the Qianlong jades utilized many of the paintings and illustrations from the imperial collection to render into jade carvings. Scenic carvings of grandeur such as jade boulders, brush pots and table screens were made. Throughout history, the Qianlong Emperor's endeavor in the innovation, continuation, and promotion of jade has reached the highest peak of achievements in the history of Chinese jade culture. They were at the top in terms of variety, volume, genre, innovation and even in sizes. The Qianlong Emperor even named his sons with names of jade. This is a unique phenomenon in the history of China.

Chinese jade artefacts appeared as early as the Neolithic period. The historical influence and cultural significance of jade continued up to the Wei and Jin dynasties and even into the Sui and Tang periods playing the role as ritual and religious objects. Starting from the Sui and Tang periods, jade has morphed into a work of art and gradually losing its aura of ritual vessels. People began to appreciate jade's inherent natural beauty and its intricate craftsmanship. After the Sui and Tang until the Ming and Qing periods, the role of jade underwent momentous changes transforming itself from being ritual objects in high places to beautiful and artistic objects appreciated and collected by the ordinary populace. The ups and downs of the development of jade aptly reflect the historical changes in the Chinese culture. This is, however, also where the magical charm of jade lies.

Shan Jixiang

Chairman of the China Cultural Relics Academy

May 2023

序一

纵观浩瀚的中国历史，玉石作为重要的文化载体，已经与华夏文明相知相伴了近七千年，形成了中国独特的玉文化，被誉为人类文明史中最璀璨的艺术形式之一。

过去一百年的出土文献资料证明，早在公元前 4000 年，辽河流域的红山文化以及长江流域的良渚文化就拉开了礼玉时代的帷幕。之后的一千年里，长江中游的石家河文化以及黄河流域的龙山文化揭开了礼玉的神秘面纱，让玉器有了更加精美和丰富的呈现。公元前 16 世纪，商朝的玉石工匠们已经可以用玉石制作精美的礼器与宫廷陈设器。值得一提的是，除了一些常规的玉璧、玉璜以及玉琮，动物题材在商代玉器中广泛出现。有学者认为它们多被当作护身符，既有礼玉神圣的一面，亦有与大自然天人合一的精神体现。商周时期的玉器大多是片状平面呈现的，纹饰大多与同时期的青铜器相类似，如展品“商代鸡骨白玉虎”便是典型的例子，彰显出这一时期统治阶级对玉器这一珍贵资源的高度重视与文化的高度统一。

西周时期（前 1046—前 771）的玉器发展与殷商一脉相承，受复杂的礼仪制度的限制，玉石的制作和生产工艺并没有突破性的发展，但做工和纹饰较商代都更加精美，品类也更加丰富。据出土西周青铜器上的铭文记载，玉器在当时已经开始作为重要的礼器流通于统治者之间，多用于稳固政治和社会秩序。同时儒家以玉比德的哲学思想，将玉比作士大夫应有的五种美德——仁、智、礼、义、信，也给玉注入了儒家的思想价值观。然而到了东周后期，礼崩乐坏动摇了儒家思想的统治地位，迎来了百家争鸣的春秋战国时期，社会主流价值观的多元化使玉器这一帝王神明独有的珍宝更广泛地流通于王侯将相之间。

天地、神明、人伦品德都在玉中得到体现，在东周之后的一千年里，战国作为新思想和新文化极其活跃与兴盛的时代，赋予了玉器特别是佩玉人性化的世界观和道德观。玉文化在两汉近五百年的历史里也得到了空前的发展。随着社会的发展，奴隶制社会逐渐向封建社会过渡，玉器作为礼玉的重要职能逐渐淡化，饰玉作为统治阶级的重要象征在汉朝得以长足的发展，其深度和广度都是空前的。汉朝（前 206—公元 220）玉器作为后世历代宫廷玉器的摹古蓝本对中国玉器史有着不可替代的历史地位和艺术影响力。

魏晋南北朝（六朝）时期（220—589），佛教以及外来文化的兴起，冲击了儒家思想的影响力，封建礼制被崇尚自由的少数民族文化所替代，玉器作为封建帝王财富与权力的神物，在六朝之后逐渐以饰玉与佩玉的形式走入了士绅阶级。特别是隋唐时期（581—907），玉器会因其本身的艺术价值和材料价值而得到广泛的重视，但与宗教和神明之间的密切联系已渐行渐远。

从目前的出土文献可以总结出，隋唐时期的玉器呈现出了繁荣、开放、多民族混合的大都会文化特点。唐朝的玉器深受外国文化的影响，反映了许多不同地区、民族、宗教的风格特点，大多是与黄金相配的饰玉，如发簪、带板、衣饰等。唐朝的艺术美学是多元文化形成的浪漫主义基调，玉石的柔美配以金银的华丽与此种艺术风格相得益彰。与战汉时期相比，唐代的统治阶级已经不再重视葬玉文化，因此出土的玉器数量大大减少，质量也大大降低。从唐代的出土玉器来看，对金银器的重视程度远大于玉器，反映出了统治阶级对玉的态度正在发生巨大的变化。

宋代（960—1279）是中国玉器史上传承与发展的关键时期。宋人克己复礼，对前朝古物深入研究、穷理尽性，延续历史传统的同时，还注入了独有的时代特征。清末著名学者赵汝珍在《古玩指南》一书中如此评价宋代玉器："中国玉器以周汉宋清四朝之物最为精妙……宋代有国，承大乱之余，极力崇文抑武，以与天下休息。虽国势衰微，然文艺兴隆，古代典章文物多有恢复，故玉器又得复兴……好玉之风遍行全国，其做工之精巧，直可上追周汉。"宋代玉器一方面深受士大夫文化的影响，讲究形神兼备、格调高雅，崇古复古；另一方面，在制作工艺上不断精进，在商品经济的作用下更具市井气息，贴近大众生活，所以宋代玉器可以说是雅俗共赏，既具文人崇尚的金石味，又有百姓钟情的市井气。

宋代作为一个以汉文化治国的朝代，无疑将玉文化推向了一个新的高度。随着新儒家思想的确立，宋朝的统治阶级鼓励古籍典学，并试图通过儒家教育让整个社会恢复礼仪制度。因此，这一时期的贵族士绅对编修古籍、研究古代思想，特别是对古器物研究与收藏的热情达到了空前的高度。古代玉器一时间成为上流社会最为津津乐道的玩物。宋代涌现了很多仿古玉器，特别是玉剑饰、玉璧、玉琮、神兽等。宋代多仿汉玉，虽与汉玉一脉相承，但亦有自己明显的时代特征。除了仿古玉器之外，在宋代宫廷，尤其是宋徽宗时期（1100—1125）现实主义审美的影响下，宋代玉器出现了十分逼真的作品。特别是在动植物题材上，以宋代院体书画为蓝本的写实作品，成为宋代传世玉器的显著特点。从已知的世界各大博物馆馆藏来看，仿古和写实作品基本代表了宋代玉器的风貌。宋代玉器也为后来的元明清玉器建立分类体系，开创了艺术品类的先河。魏晋隋唐以来，玉器逐步成为士绅贵族的标志。赏玉与饰玉文化到宋朝达到了空前的繁荣，玉器贸易也随着需求的提高而盛极一时。

继宋代玉器之后，辽金元（907—1368）玉器有着浓郁的北方草原民族风格，场景化的构图方式开创了中国玉器史的先河。玉质选料上乘，雕工大刀阔斧，风格浩然磅礴，又不失天真趣味，是辽金元玉器的主要特征，如著名的春水玉（天鹅海东青）与秋山玉，描述了北方游牧民族春围秋猎的场景。这一题材的玉雕，动物刻画生动活泼，常巧用籽料的皮色来表现落日、秋林、虎斑等纹饰，可谓传神之至。辽金元场景化的构思对后世，特别是清代宫廷的玉山子、玉笔筒以及玉插屏都有着非常深远的影响。在辽金玉器之外，学者们经常忽视元朝玉器的重要性。元玉既是宋辽金玉器的延续和融合，又对明清玉器有着深远的影响。

明清时期（1368—1911），玉器大规模地成为了宫廷陈设的重要组成部分，也进一步在贵族士绅阶级广泛流传。自宋元开始玉也成为了宫廷玺印的首选材质，玉玺同时象征着至高无上的皇权与财富。另一方面，从宋代开始兴起的江南玉作坊已经逐步形成了可观的商业规模。随着清朝康雍乾三代帝王不断地征战，西域各部特别是新疆昆仑山沿线地区于十八世纪中叶逐步归顺清廷。源源不断的玉料以进贡的形式抵达中原。紫禁城如意馆玉作以及江南织造局指定的玉作工坊成为了主要的宫廷玉器创作和生产场所。到乾隆中后期，玉器无论从数量、质量、品种以及创新等各个方面都达到了前所未有的高度。据不完全统计，故宫博物院所藏乾隆玉器的数量，已经超过了历史其他时期玉器的总和。除各色和田玉外，乾隆玉器在材料上也是博采众长，选材丰富，如青金石、绿松石、玛瑙、寿山石、孔雀石等等。乾隆皇帝在玉器方面的成就无论是收藏还是制作，都可谓前无古人后无来者。

乾隆玉器主要有三个较为突出的成就。首先在仿古方面，乾隆玉器几乎涵盖了所有夏商周青铜器皿的样式。其中大多以宋徽宗的《宣和图谱》为蓝本，以及清内府所藏的商周至唐的青铜古器图录《西清古鉴》为借鉴，加以乾隆自己和文臣巧匠的创新。品类不下千余种，其中不乏许多上古的动物神兽纹饰，如饕餮纹、凤鸟纹、蟠虺纹等，无不体现了中国古代能工巧匠的奇思妙想。其次乾隆在“师法造化”方面也是超越宋人的，他的自然写实主义比宋代同类玉器更加逼真传神，在各色玉材的运用方面竭尽所能，通过利用不同玉材的特点因材施工，使得题材构思变得非常广泛。除龙、凤、狮、兽、麒麟等吉祥神兽之外，《山海经》中的动物、十二生肖、各色蔬果花卉都成为常见的玉器题材。人物作品也变得十分多样化，各路神仙、宗教人物、老少妇孺为主导的人物玉雕，通常都有十分写实的开脸。许多花卉蔬果的逼真程度令人叹为观止，如白玉“蝶恋花”纹鏨扣，叶脉和花蕊的刻画真切细腻、栩栩如生。乾隆玉器的第三个成就，便是以宫廷内苑珍藏的历代书画为蓝本，所制的各类玉山子、玉笔筒以及玉插屏，场面宏大，细节突出，故事情节性强。如北京故宫博物院所藏的清乾隆“大禹治水山子”，人民大学清史研究所征集的“松鹤延年笔筒”以及颐和园所藏的清乾隆“《岁朝村庆》碧玉插屏”都是十分典型的作品。纵观历史，乾隆皇帝在玉器的创新、传承、推广方面都做到了极致。乾隆玉器作为重要的宫廷陈设器，几乎占据了所有的历史制高点：品类最全，品种最丰富，体量最大，数量最多，创新最多等等。从乾隆的御制诗集以及宫廷造办处档案中可以发现，乾隆一生痴迷玉器，就连他的皇子们也都以玉石为名。乾隆皇帝在中国玉器史上旷古绝今的成就可谓一骑绝尘。

早在新石器时代就出现的中国古代玉器，其历史影响力及文化内涵一直延续到魏晋甚至隋唐时期。这份传承性来源于玉器作为礼器的特殊职能，它被赋予了浓重的宗教色彩。自隋唐时期起，玉成为了一种艺术品。逐渐褪去了礼器的光环，不再是仪式的象征，人们开始欣赏玉的天然之美与雕琢后的工艺之美。隋唐之后直至明清两代，玉石的作用发生了翻天覆地的变化，从束之高阁的礼器转变为世俗大众都可欣赏把玩的美物。玉器跌宕起伏的发展史，正映射出了中国文化的历史变迁。这也是玉的神奇魅力之所在。

中国文物学会会长

2023 年 5 月

Preface Ⅱ

The significance of jade in the history of China's culture cannot be overstated, and the true understanding of its importance in the West is, in historical terms, very recent. It was gold in the West that was appreciated and valued most highly but in China that position was held by jade and for over seven thousand years it has been central to the culture of China.

One of the earliest Western contacts with jade was in the form of the gift of a jade ruyi sceptre from the Qianlong Emperor (1736–1795) to Sir George Staunton, who was second in command of the unsuccessful British Macartney Embassy to China in 1792. The sceptre entered the collection of the South Kensington Museum (the forerunner of the Victoria and Albert Museum) in London in 1852 (V&A:A17–1925). It was little understood by the British and Macartney described it as " a whitish agate-looking stone about a foot and a half long, curiously carved, and highly prized by the Chinese, but … [which] does not appear in itself to be of any great value" (Wilson, Ming; Chinese Jades, London 2004, p. 90).

Serious understanding of jade, its significance and status in Chinese culture only began to develop in the West in the 20th century, beginning with the famous International Exhibition of Chinese Art at the Royal Academy of Arts (London, 1935–6). Chinese academics such as Cheng Te-k'un and then James Watt, and Western scholars such as John Ayers and Jessica Rawson, among others, began the process of exploring and writing about the material. Collectors and scholars in Hong Kong and Taiwan had always understood jade's position in their history and studied and collected it. However, our knowledge and understanding of Chinese jade works of art still has some way to go and now the focus is on controlled archaeological excavations, similarities to Spirit Road sculptures, and comparisons with comparable objects in other materials, such as bronze, and to related images in paintings. In the absence of reliable scientific resources to be precise about when the stone was worked, one must fall back on comparisons to known genuine examples, the colour of the stone and design elements.

It must be remembered that from early times, and particularly from the Song dynasty (960–1279) onwards, and throughout the Ming (1368–1644), copies of works of art – not just in jade – were made in homage to the past. The Qianlong Emperor was ardent in his need to uphold his position as the rightful ruler of China, asserting his Chinese credentials by the creation of jades in traditional forms.

In this latest publication, we are overwhelmed with an abundance of treasures and thought-provoking works of art that stimulate both appreciation and understanding of the subject. It is rare to have so many fine examples gathered in one place, and this is a great achievement and contribution to the subject.

I have selected just a few for comment – others speak for themselves and have such merit they need no contribution from me.

Fig. 003 This *gui* is a rare bronze-form vessel and incites one to consider not only its archaic bronze inspiration but also the jade craftsman Lu Zigang who was active in the Jiajing (1522–1566) and Wanli (1573–1619) periods. Resident in Suzhou, Lu Zigang is celebrated for his skill and in particular for his beautiful plaques, hairpins and refined scholarly subjects. Jades with the Zigang mark have been excavated from tombs, and inevitably in later times copies of his work were produced. This *gui* commends itself for its quality, colour and size and is a rare larger example of Lu Zigang's workshop.

Fig. 007 This large vessel is a magnificent example of the jade worker's art. The original boulder has been well

hollowed and then worked in high relief with vigorously curling dragons amid waves and clouds, the flaws of the stone skilfully enhancing the composition. The more subtly worked base has beautiful low-relief swirling waves. Several of these vessels exist in all forms and sizes but this example is a *tour-de-force* of its type and relates – as do all other such vessels – to the Yuan dynasty (1206–1368) example now in Beihai Park, Beijing. S. Howard Hansford, the English scholar, relates the story of its discovery in *Chinese Carved Jades* (London, 1968) "the great vessel … [was] rescued by the Ch'ien-lung emperor from a temple where it was used as a receptacle for pickled vegetables. The emperor composed three poems in its honour, and caused them to be inscribed in the interior" (p. 89).

Fig. 013 This white jade plaque is a superb example of craftmanship, being finely pierced and cut. Its proportions are unusually large for such a plaque and it relates to similar items in the Imperial collections with Kangxi (1662–1722) reign marks. The Qianlong Emperor spoke against decadent over-elaboration in his poems but he must surely have been impressed by this very fine plaque. Also to be noted is the very fine wood and ivory stand.

Figs. 023 and 024 These plaques are useful in illustrating the continuing evolution of the small curling dragon over many years as fig. 023 is from the Qianlong period and fig. 024 is Yuan in date. The feline dragon, already fully formed in the Han dynasty (206 BCE–220 CE), continued to be popular and evolve over the next 2,000 years.

Fig. 040 This delightful rendition illustrates the continuing desire to refer to the past and in this case the curling dragon and phoenix have evolved into a Manchu rococo-style jade reminiscent of, but very different to, its archaic original.

Fig. 068 The fangding is another reminder of the Qianlong Emperor's instruction to create jades in the style of ancient bronzes. The colour of the stone is chosen to complement the robust, simple design of ancient bronzes. The inscription "Da Qing Qian Long Fang Gu" exemplifies the Emperor's resistance to vulgarisation and elaborate decoration, and it was always his endeavour to recall ancient ideals. Such jades were sometimes placed in the palaces juxtaposed with ancient works of art and deployed in such rooms as the Hall of Fragrance in the Forbidden City.

Fig. 086 The subject of boys and elephants in jade was a favourite over many years during the Qing dynasty (1644–1912) and, due to its popularity, was produced in other mediums such as cloisonné enamel and lacquer. This is a superb example as the stone is skilfully used and the high relief ribbon is particularly well done. This theme is depicted in a more subtle way in fig. 087, worked from a small pebble that fits well in the hand. The essence of the stone is retained in its rugged form and the composition is delightfully composed.

Fig. 107 These two goose-form boxes and covers exhibit the ultimate achievements realised in 18th-century jade working for the Imperial household. There is a very similar grey jade goose-form box dated Song dynasty in the collection of Tianjin Art Museum. Well rounded and finely incised with good detail, the eyes and feet are typical of the best detailed work of this period, and the fine white stone is enhanced by the russet markings.

Fig. 149 This brush pot reaffirms the skill employed by the best craftsmen in drawing the most pleasing compositions from the stone available to them. In examining the composition, the design elements remind us of earlier scroll paintings and brush pots in other mediums such as bamboo, popular in the 17th and 18th centuries. Fig. 158, a charming water pot, is a further reminder of designs popular in bamboo being recreated in jade.

Finally, I end my appreciation of these jades with fig. 225, the superb white jade ruyi sceptre, worked with peaches and bats. Ruyi sceptres were celebrated and appreciated as important gifts in the 18th-century. In this collection of jades and hardstones it could perhaps be suggested that many wishes have come true.

It is most unusual to see such an important collection of jades in one group and it affords an opportunity for all those fortunate to observe them to reflect on and consider the best of the jade workers' skills.

Roger Keverne

Former President of the British Antique Dealers' Association and

Former Chairman of Asian Art in London

The Renowned Chinese Jade Expert

June 2023

序二

玉器在中华文明的历史长河中占据着无可取代的重要地位。然而在西方世界里，人们真正从历史的角度去重视玉器与玉文化，还要从近代说起。正如在西方世界中，黄金的地位最为重要与尊贵，玉器在绵延七千多年的中华文明中一直占据着核心地位。

西方世界最早与玉石的结缘可以追溯到乾隆皇帝（1736—1795 年）送给乔治・斯汤顿爵士的一把玉如意。1792 年，乔治・斯汤顿爵士时任英国麦卡特尼驻华大使馆的副使，在向乾隆皇帝祝贺八十大寿时，获得乾隆皇帝所赏赐的一柄玉如意。这把玉如意于 1852 年被伦敦南肯辛顿博物馆（著名的维多利亚与阿尔伯特博物馆前身）纳入收藏（收藏号 V&A: A17–1925）。当时的英国人对它知之甚少，麦卡特尼将其描述为"一块形似白色玛瑙的石头，大约一英尺半长，雕工奇特。中国人对它极其珍视，但是……它看起来并没有什么特别之处"（威尔逊，明，《中国玉石》，伦敦，2004 年，第 90 页）。

西方世界对玉石及其在中国文化中非凡的意义与地位的认知，始于 20 世纪初。当时英国皇家艺术学院（伦敦，1935—1936 年）举办了一次国际著名的中国艺术展。之后研究东方学术的中国学者如郑德昆，西方学者如詹姆斯・瓦特、约翰・艾尔斯和杰西卡・罗森等人，开始对玉石这种矿石进行探索研究并展开论文编纂。香港和台湾的学者与收藏家自始至终都了解玉器在中国历史中的重要地位，因此他们一直致力于研究和收藏玉器。然而，现阶段我们对中国玉器艺术品的了解和认知还有很长一段路要走，当今的重点聚焦在有限度的、保护性的考古发掘；与皇家陵园前神道碑、神道雕塑的对比；与其他材料如青铜器的实物对比；以及与绘画中的相关形象进行比较。在当前科学技术手段受限，缺乏精确确定玉石雕刻制作年代的情况下，人们必须通过把已知的确切时期的真品作为标准器来进行对比和研究，其中主要比对的元素包括玉质、雕工和时代审美特征等。

值得注意的是，从中国早期，特别是宋代（960—1279 年）开始，贯穿整个明代（1368—1644 年），艺术品的仿古之风盛行，这不仅仅表现在玉器上，而是在各种艺术类型上。好古、慕古、仿古表现了人们对前朝高超艺术造诣与繁荣国力的向往与致敬。到了清代，尤其是乾隆时期，乾隆皇帝为了彰显和巩固他在汉民族中的统治地位和无上皇权，十分热衷于制作各种仿古玉器。

在本书中，大量精美绝伦、引人入胜的玉器艺术品被收集于此。它们再一次激发了人们对这一领域的欣赏与探究热情。一次性汇集这么多优秀的中国古代玉器艺术精品十分难能可贵，这本书注定将为玉器研究领域做出巨大的贡献。

在此，我甄选了一些我个人非常喜爱的玉器精品做一个简短的赏析，希望能抛砖引玉，与诸位读者分享。

第一件是白玉“子冈”款兽面纹龙耳簋（图 003）。这是一件罕见的仿青铜簋的玉器精品。不仅让人缅怀古老的青铜器，也更让人追忆活跃于明代嘉靖至万历年间的苏州玉器巨匠陆子冈。子冈制作玉器，无论是玉牌、玉发簪还是文房用品和摆件，都可谓得心应手，技艺高超绝伦。带有“子冈”款的玉器常见于墓葬出土。由于陆子冈制作玉器的声望之高，在他之后的各个历史时期不可避免地出现了一些仿“子冈”、伪“子冈”款的玉器。这件白玉“子冈”款兽面纹龙耳簋工艺精湛，玉色和器型都属于陆子冈作坊制作之中少见的比较大型的作品。

“青玉乾隆御题云龙纹瓮”（图 007）是一件巨大的玉雕作品，无疑是制玉工匠们巧夺天工之作。巨型的玉料内部被精细地掏膛打磨。外腹部以高浮雕技艺娴熟细腻地饰于卷龙云纹。玉石的一些细小瑕疵被细腻的雕刻技术掩盖并加以美化。腹底部则配以构思精妙的浅浮雕海水纹。虽然存世尚有多件大小不一的同类玉雕，但是此青玉龙纹瓮无疑是其中的上乘之作。这些大型玉雕都不约而同的和北京北海公园团城承光殿前的元代渎山大玉海有着微妙的联系。英国学者 S• Howard Hansford 在《中国玉雕》（伦敦，1968 年出版，第 89 页）一书中讲述了这个巨型大玉海被发现的故事：“这个巨大的器皿……被乾隆皇帝从一座寺庙中发现。在寺庙中它被僧侣们用作腌菜的容器。乾隆皇帝喜得此大玉海，并为它赋诗三首，雕刻于该大玉海内壁。”

白玉雕龙纹佩（图 013）：此玉佩是极具特色工艺的玉雕精品。以减地阳起镂空技法雕琢。玉佩体型较其他同类玉佩相比较为硕大。它和带有康熙年款的同类型清宫旧藏玉器有着相似之处。乾隆皇帝曾在他的诗中极其反对过分的奢华和繁琐，但他肯定会被这块精致的龙纹佩所打动。放置这枚龙纹佩的硬木与象牙屏架也是十分引人瞩目。

碧玉仿汉鸡心佩（图 023）以及青玉双螭衔灵芝纹饰件（图 024）：这两件玉器彰显了螭龙纹长期以来的演变过程。碧玉仿汉鸡心佩是乾隆时期的器物，而青玉双螭衔灵芝纹饰件则是出自元代。螭龙这类讨喜的玉器纹饰在汉代已经完全成型。在接下来的两千多年里持续演变并且一直深受欢迎。

白玉鱼化龙纹佩（图 040）：这也是一件惹人喜爱的玉器作品，充分地展示了当时的怀旧慕古情怀。远古的卷龙纹与凤凰纹已经演化为满族人的新式洛可可风格的玉器，让人一面怀念其古老的原型，一面又欣赏着时代演变产生的不同之处。

青玉“大清乾隆仿古”款兽面纹方鼎（图 068）：这件硕大的玉雕方鼎向我们展示了乾隆皇帝在玉器上的仿古情怀，尤其是对仿古青铜器的偏爱。以青玉来制作方鼎，更衬托了远古青铜器粗旷简洁的设计，也从色彩上更接近青铜器。“大清乾隆仿古”的款识更是体现了乾隆帝抵制庸俗繁复的纹饰和对慕古仿古的提倡。这类大型方鼎玉雕大多数时候和一些古物一起陈设于紫禁城的殿厅内。

白玉雕“太平有象”（图 086）：童子与象嬉戏或给象洗澡是清代多年来最受欢迎的玉器题材之一，寓意“太平有象”“喜象升平”。此题材的受欢迎程度也彰显于漆器和景泰蓝等其他艺术品中。白玉圆雕立象，身披璎珞，纹饰细腻精彩，肌体憨态可掬。另一件青玉“太平有象”摆件（图 087）以一种较为含蓄巧妙的方式雕制而成。摆件能小巧地上手把玩，且玉石的粗犷与自然质地也被保留下来，整件玉雕的构图和雕刻都非常地讨喜、精美。

白玉鹅型盖盒（一对）（图 107）：这对鹅型白玉盖盒充分地展示了十八世纪的清朝皇室对玉器制作的审美观和工艺制作标准。巧合的是它与天津博物馆的一只宋代圆雕灰玉鹅型盖盒如出一辙，是难得一见的乾隆宫廷慕古佳作。圆雕精细琢磨，鹅的眼睛和脚部带有该时期玉雕的典型风格。洁白温润的白玉更因擦上了与原皮相配的琥珀色斑沁而增添了不少风采。

白玉梅花绶带鸟纹笔筒（图 149）：这只笔筒再次印证了当时最优秀的玉雕工匠们的巧妙构思和精湛技艺。此笔筒造型让我们想起了传统的中式花鸟画卷构图和其他材料的笔筒，如竹质笔筒等，它们都在十七、十八世纪大受欢迎。青玉雕松随形洗（图 158）：这是一个极具魅力的水洗，同时也说明了很多在竹雕中受欢迎的纹饰与风格，也会同样呈现于同时期的玉器作品中。

最后，我想以白玉雕“福寿万年”如意（图 223）来结束我短暂的欣赏之旅。白玉如意，整料雕琢，饰寿桃与蝙蝠纹。玉如意是十八世纪最受中国宫廷重视的玉器并被视为重要的赏赐礼物，正如本文开头所说到的一样。在此借着本书中收录的美玉的吉祥寓意，祝愿大家：诸事顺遂，喜乐安康。

这本集合了如此多重要玉器艺术品的画册，为人们提供了一个绝佳的契机，让人们更多的关注与思考玉器——这个大自然的馈赠与人类智慧的完美结合体。

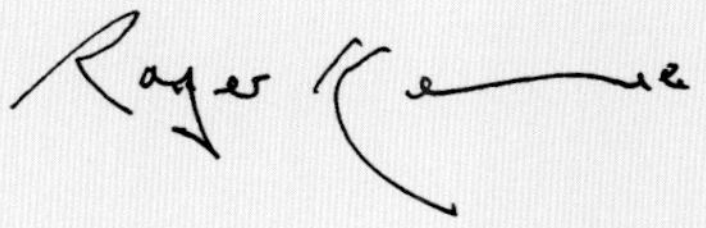

前英国古董商协会主席

前伦敦亚洲艺术主席

世界著名中国玉器专家

2023 年 6 月

Preface Ⅲ

In September 2021, the twenty-one-year-old Summer Palace Wenchang Gallery has been renamed the Summer Palace Museum. This is in response to China's call on making Beijing a "City of Museums". As the head of the new Summer Palace Museum, my first task would be to organize an exhibition to make full use of the magnificent collections and unique facilities of the Summer Palace Museum and to enhance and exemplify the museum's quality and vision. More importantly, this would be in response to the call for the great rejuvenation of the profound Chinese culture in early 2022.

The use of Jade has been one of the unique branches of traditional Chinese culture enduring through a long history with unending zest and energy. The culture of jade reflects the unique Chinese aesthetic taste and philosophy. The Summer Palace has one of the greatest Ming and Qing period jade collections in China with over 1600 ancient jade artefacts, many of which are of profound importance. In 2018, we collaborated with the Renmin University's Institute of Qing History (RUIQH) to host "The Treasure of Imperial Jade – The Collection of the Qing Court Special Exhibition". A total of 93 Ming and Qing imperial jade items were on public display in that exhibition with very enthusiastic response. After that exhibition, I expressed my idea to Professor Liu Wenpeng, vice dean of the RUIQH, together with his student Dr. Li Ruifeng, to have in the near future, another collaboration in hosting a bigger and more comprehensive ancient jade exhibition encompassing a wider range of jade items.

My idea of collaborating another larger and more comprehensive ancient jade exhibition was immediately met with favorable response from Professor Liu and Dr. Li. The subject of ancient jade items with animal themes were on the top of our agenda then as we found that jade with animal themes were revered in the Chinese jade culture over thousands of years.

Together with my colleagues from the Summer Palace Museum, we went through our selection process to identify the potential jade with animal themes for the coming exhibition. Professor Liu and Dr. Li also respectively did their part of the selection at the RUIQH. Very soon, the two teams both discovered and perplexed by the same predicament. We discovered that although jade with animal themes are in abundance, they are however also accompanied by plant or floral themes. It was difficult to choose the animal without the accompanying plant/floral themes. Why not host an exhibition for ancient jade with animal and plant themes instead of only the animal themes? Professor Liu and Dr. Li both agreed. A new idea thus came into agreement between the two sides. The new exhibition would be extended to also include jades with plant/floral themes.

With the agreement of a new exhibition of both animal and plant themes, the two teams from SPM and RUIQH first selected some 300 jade items for the exhibition. To help with furtherance of the quality of exhibition, we have also invited Zhang Guangwen, researcher at the Palace Museum, Wu Junling and Zhang Caijuan, researchers from the Capital Museum, to participate in the selection and verification process. Eventually a total of 225 jade items from the Shang to the Qing and Republic of China periods were selected for the coming exhibition.

The selected 225 jade items also include a very small proportion of lazurite, turquoise, coral and jadeite items to reflect the Chinese traditional idea of "beautiful stones". We endeavor this exhibition to be more artistically popular and the selection only includes 2 items from the Shang to Qin periods, the rests are 39 items of Song to Ming periods, 183 items of Qing jade and 1 item of jade from the recent Republic of China period, making a total of 225 items. To compensate for the insufficiency of the Song to Ming items, I suggested to Wang Dan, the head of the Beijing Art Museum, to collaborate in the coming exhibition and received her overwhelming support. We then selected 5 items of small jade carvings from the Liao-Jin and Yuan periods from her Beijing Art Museum list. This additional 5 items then made a total of 230 items, achieving the scale for a medium-size cultural relic exhibition.

From the original Animal and Plant Sections, we later categorized the 230 items into five sections. They are:

Section 1: Dragons and Phoenix

Section 2: Auspicious Beasts and Birds

Section 3: Domestic and Wild Animals

Section 4: Plants and Flowers

Section 5: Vegetables and Fruits

We named this exhibition "Ancient Chinese Jades Exhibition of Animals and Plants". The exhibition was opened on January 28, 2022 and was received with enthusiastic acclaim to the press and public. The exhibition lasted 72 days with around seventy thousand attendants.

In order to record the accomplishment of this exhibition, a catalogue book of the exhibition is published. This is the great effort from Dr. Li Ruifeng, a protégé of Roger Kerverne, the British Asian art dealer and jade scholar of great renown. Dr. Li's contribution to this exhibition book is invaluable.

Jade carvings with animal and plant themes are an important part of the Chinese jade culture for thousands of years. It emanates the Chinese people's love of nature, virtue and life. As this is the beginning of the second century to realize the great rejuvenation of the Chinese nation, we hereby dedicate this book to all who love and revere our jade culture.

Qin Lei

The Summer Palace Museum

December 2022

序三

2022年初，在全国人民迎接即将召开的党的二十大的喜庆氛围里，颐和园博物馆也迎来了挂牌后的第一个年头。2021年9月28日，已经建成开放21年的颐和园文昌院挂牌更名颐和园博物馆，这是北京市公园管理中心和颐和园管理处贯彻落实习近平总书记“让文物活起来”思想的有力举措，以及对国家级“三山五园文物保护利用示范区”建设和北京市“博物馆之城”建设的积极响应。作为新挂牌的颐和园博物馆的馆长，我首先面临着的一个紧要工作就是策划一个什么样的年度首展，既能体现发挥自身馆藏文物优势和特色，体现颐和园博物馆的品质和视野，更重要的是，还要展现出颐和园文化遗产守护者对党的二十大胜利召开的热烈企盼和美好祝愿，反映新时代实现中华民族伟大复兴的深厚历史文化底蕴。尽管从开始谋划到年初开展只剩有三个月的时间，有的同事不免面有难色，我坚持认为，只有达到这些目标，才是一个合乎“天时、地利、人和”的年度首展。

其实，有一个想法已经萦绕脑际，只是还欠打磨。古代玉器，是中国传统文化中历史最为悠久独特和生生不息的文化载体和文化符号，深刻反映了中华民族的哲学思想、道德观念、民族性格、审美眼光和工艺特色等；颐和园藏古代玉器有1600余件，是国内收藏明清宫廷玉器重镇之一，品类丰富，工艺精湛，其中不乏巨制重器；颐和园举办玉器专题展也有一定的经验，特别是2018年与中国人民大学清史研究所合作举办了“御宝璆琳——清宫旧藏玉器展”，共展出明清宫廷玉器精品93件，在文博界产生了良好的反响。在那时，我与展览的共同策划人——清史研究所副所长刘文鹏教授及其学生李瑞丰博士，就有一个意犹未尽的想法和约定，将来再合作举办一个古代玉器的专题展览。对于展览的范围和内容，通过对明清宫廷玉器乃至古代玉器的梳理，我们也有一些初步的共识，我们感到动物题材在中国古代玉器中或许是一个历史最为悠久、最为普遍常见、艺术表现力最强的一个类型，集中和生动反映了几千年来古代中国人对自然动物从敬畏到驯服的如影随形过程，以及尊重自然、热爱生命、天人合一的思想观念。我想，以颐和园和人大清史所的力量及以往合作的经验和模式，具备办好这样一个展览的基础。

我就办展设想与刘文鹏教授及李瑞丰博士沟通，二人一拍即合，相约分头推进，我带领颐和园博物馆与颐和园文物管理科的同事，先对颐和园的动物题材玉器藏品进行全面梳理，挑选展品；文鹏教授与瑞丰博士亦如是。很快，双方的动物题材藏品目录和照片初步整理出来，动物题材的玉器非常丰富，但是我们也发现了一个有意思的现象和划分标准的困惑，那就是很多动物题材玉器都组合有各种植物的纹饰，甚至植物纹饰成为构图主体，动物纹饰成为植物的配角和点缀，这一类是选还是不选？不选，确实有动物形象；选了，似乎又有些跑题儿！这一发现倒让我眼前一亮，豁然开朗：何不扩大范围，做一个动物与植物题材的古代玉器展呢？一是解决了部分藏品动、植物混一问题；二是扩大了展览规模；更重要的是，主题更加完整和深化，既然动物与植物构成了人类生存的主要外部世界与环境，动植物题材的玉器不正是反映了古代人对自然界“鸟兽草木之迹”的观念与态度吗？文鹏教授和瑞丰博士对此十分赞同，于是，原来设想的动物题材玉器展扩大成为动植物题材玉器展。

主题的确定，为挑选展品明确了方向和范围，颐和园博物馆与清史研究所按照这一主题分头工作，共初选出三百多件从文化期至清后期的动植物题材玉雕作品。为了确保展品断代精确和展览的学术、艺术质量，我邀请了故宫博物院的张广文研究员、首都博物馆原保管部主任武俊玲研究员和张彩娟研究员三位专家来馆共同对初选展品一一上手过目，鉴定评判，最后从中选出225件作为上展展品。三位资深玉器专家的现场把关，为展览的学术和艺术水准提供了重要保障。

从展品的数量、材质和时代性上看，所选225件玉器上至商代，下迄清末民初。从展品的玉器材质看，反映了中国传统的“美玉”范畴，所选展品所取玉材，除了白玉、青玉、碧玉、青白玉、黄玉，还有青金石、绿松石、珊瑚、翡翠等，体现了古人玉乃“石之美者”的观念。考虑到颐和园博物馆藏玉器的特点和优势，也为了更好地体现展览的艺术性与通俗性，对于学术性较强的上古和三代玉器没有多予拣选，而是选取了两件商周秦汉玉器作为代表，以下宋辽金元明时期玉器39件，清代玉器183件，以乾隆时期为主，民国时期玉器1件，总体以明清宫廷玉器为主体，既基本贯穿了商代以后中国三千多年的玉器发展史，又突显了展品的宫廷品质。为了弥补中古玉器的不足，我向北京艺术博物馆王丹馆长提出提供展品联合举办该展的建议，得到了王馆长的大力支持，很快提供了供挑选的文物清单，从中挑选了5件有特色的辽金元时期的小件玉雕，充实了中古部分的表现力，也使得展览的文物数量增加到230件（套），达到一个中型文物展览的规模。

展品反映了非常丰富的古代玉雕中的动植物形象，具有一定的系统性和代表性。在动物题材玉器中，有龙17件、螭龙9件、凤凰11件、螭凤1件、龙凤3件、虎2件、鹿5件、獾2件、貘1件、仙鹤6件、獬豸3件、（龙）马3件、饕餮8件、狮子5件、鹰熊3件、鳌鱼2件、蟾蜍5件、象4件、狻猊1件、鹦鹉3件、麒麟3件、羊8件、骆驼2件、鹅4件、凫鸟2件、鸠鸟1件、喜鹊2件、鸳鸯5件、鹭鸶1件、犬4件、猴7件、公鸡1件、牛7件、鱼8件、绶带2件、猫1件、猫戏蝶1件、蝴蝶1件、螳螂1件、天鹅1件、鹌鹑1件，共计有41种动物形象。自原始文化时期至明清以来，动物题材玉器在中国玉文化中一直占据长盛不衰的重要地位，并随着历史文化的演进而具有不同的特点，如史前时期的神秘深邃，商周时期的抽象凝重，两汉时期的灵动大气。此时的玉雕动物尚以沟通天人的神玉、礼玉、葬玉功能为主，艺术风格充满了写意与夸张的雄奇之风。唐宋以后，动物玉雕全面走向写实性风格，能够攫取最能表现动物生动细节特征的部分，达到了生动传神的艺术境界。至明清两代，动物题材在玉器的写实手段更加逼真和繁复，玉材质量和打磨工艺更趋极致，把玩性与观赏性达到了中国玉雕工艺的顶峰。如此丰富的古代动物题材玉雕文物集中展出，在文博界还是不多见的。

在植物花卉题材中，有松1件、松梅1件、松竹梅1件、莲荷8件、西番莲1件、菊1件、兰1件、梅1件、灵芝1件、玉兰4件、牡丹2件、莲蓬5件、豆荚2件、佛手4件、蘑菇2件、木瓜

3件、葫芦3件、灵芝4件、石榴2件、柿子3件、桃12件、三多（佛手、桃、石榴）4件、菱角1件、白菜1件，共有24种植物和植物果实形象，大小不同、神态各异、组合变化，各尽其美，琳琅满目。中国古代植物花卉题材玉器的真正形成自隋唐开始，比起动物题材玉器起初就少了“神灵气”，是玉文化世俗化的产物，并在不同的历史时期形成了鲜明的时代、地域、民族等艺术特色，如隋唐之簪花梳篦、辽金元之春水秋山等。至明代特别是清代，玉器的观赏性与实用性进一步融合，植物题材的杯盘瓶盒等文房器和插屏、山子等陈设器推陈出新。植物题材玉器吸收了中国古代雕塑与绘画的艺术营养，能够巧妙处理空间、结构、虚实等关系，采用浮雕、圆雕、镂空、线刻等多种形式，以炉火纯青的工艺技巧和图必吉祥的文化寓意为中国玉文化宝库增添了新颖别致的表现形式。

文物展品基本选定后所显现出的丰富性和系统性，也增强了我对展览品质的信心，但一个展览的品质并不可能只是通过精美丰富的展品自然显现出来，而是必须对展品进行深入的研究、分析、挖掘、梳理展品内在的规律和特点，系统性呈现和释读其深藏的文化内涵，因此，提炼大纲文字、展览单元和展览主题的工作尤为重要。我统筹颐和园博物馆常务副馆长周尚云、副馆长卢侃带领两位新入职的文博硕士研究生段润宇、杨川组成小组进行大纲文字的撰写，最后由我总其稿。在小组多次研讨和前期工作的基础上，我将原来的展览结构由动物篇和植物篇两个单元细分为五个单元，第一单元名为“龙飞凤舞”，表现龙和凤这两种中国传统文化中被“神化”至最高等级的动物形象；第二单元为“瑞兽灵禽”，表现中国传统文化中龙凤之外其他大量被赋予“神性”“和“祥瑞”的各种走兽飞禽；第三单元为“家豢天养”，表现的是大自然中与古人和谐共生的各种鸟兽虫鱼等；第四单元为“贞木美卉”，反映的是自然界中被人们赋予了各种美好寓意的乔灌花木；第五单元为“时蔬佳果”，汇集的是各种亦具有美好寓意和寄托的各种植物果实等。结合动植物题材玉器的独特文化内涵，我将展览的主题定名为——“玉”见生机：中国古代动植物题材玉器展。“玉”为“遇”之谐音，“玉”见生机，不仅是赞叹欣赏中国古代工匠将动植物的生机活力倾注入坚硬的玉石材料中的非凡工艺和美好寄托，向绵延数千年的中国古代玉文化致敬，同时也是向我们所处的这个文明传续复兴和文化繁荣发展的伟大时代致敬，向即将召开的党的二十大献上一份颐和园文物工作者及首都文物和文史工作者的礼物。

展览的举办得到了各级领导、同行的热情支持和广大观众的充分肯定。2022年1月28日上午，展览对游客开放，中国博物馆学会理事长刘曙光、北京市文物局二级巡视员刘洪昌、北京市公园管理中心副主任张亚红、北京市博物馆学会会长刘超英、中国人民大学历史人文学院院长朱浒、中国人民大学清史研究所副所长刘文鹏、北京市艺术博物馆馆长王丹、北京艺术博物馆副馆长张巍、北京市公园管理中心服务处处长缪祥流，颐和园管理处党委书记、园长杨华共同见证了展览的开幕。来宾们用“炫富”“豪华”来形容展览的规模和品质。展览展期共72天，接待观众7万余人，新华社、中新社、北京电视台、北京日报、北京晚报等12家媒体进行了报道，各类报刊转载报道2736条，电视报道316条，网络传播超过20万次，取得了良好的社会反响。

这个展览也有相当的学术研究价值，通过欣赏按照时代和题材分类排列的丰富展品，我们可以比较几千年来不同时代各种动植物形象流变的特征规律，可以发现古代玉器使用功能类型的时

展览开幕式嘉宾合影

代变化，可以感受不同时代的审美情趣和工艺特点。在展览初期展品分类的过程中我就有一个有趣的切身感受，就是动植物题材玉器在汉唐之前是很好划分的，基本动物就是独立的动物形象，如龙是龙，凤是凤，羊是羊；宋元以后特别是明清时期，动植物题材玉器越来越难以划分，动物雕塑也越来越多加入了植物形象，植物纹饰也会加入动物形象，如凤口常衔桃，羊嘴叼灵芝，鹭鸶要卧莲，莲叶负青蛙，寿桃配蝙蝠等等，呈现出“你中有我，我中有你我”的特点，特别是一些新的玉雕品种如山子、插屏、笔筒文房等，更是将动植物、山水、楼台、人物等汇集一身，这显示出随着时代的演进，中国古代玉器越来越褪去了“神性”的色彩，呈现出艺术化、世俗化、图案化的特点。当然，也并非没有缺点和不足，由于时间、场地等条件制约，这个展览总体上偏重于明清宫廷玉器，特别是高古动植物玉器一带而过，中古方面也还稍显薄弱，如果高中古方面再丰富充实一些，中国古代动植物题材玉器的产生、变迁的演变过程就会呈现得更加完整和清晰，这个展览的厚重性和学术价值也将大大提高，我们愿意将此作为下一步努力的方向。

为了将这一展览的成果记录下来，并提供给广大的玉器文物爱好者、研究者作为观赏和进一步研究的素材，在各参展方的共同努力特别是李瑞丰博士的辛勤付出下，我们编辑出版了这本展览图录。李瑞丰博士师从英国的亚洲古代艺术品专家 Roger Keverne 先生，多年从事中国古代艺术品相关研究工作，对中国古代玉器的研究和收藏情有独钟，造诣颇深。他不仅积极支持展览的合作举办，对于这本图录更是积极奔走、协调各方、筹集经费、统筹文字，付出了巨大心力。从李瑞丰博士以及参与这次展览的颐和园管理处、北京艺术博物馆等文博机构的年轻人身上，我们也能够深深感受到那种蓬勃不息的文物保护传承的青年力量。

在展览的结尾，我写下这样一段结语：动植物题材玉器，是中国数千年玉文化的重要组成部分和精彩内容，反映了中华民族绵延不断的热爱自然、敬畏生命、尊崇美德、追求幸福的人生观和价值观，精益求精、坚忍不拔的精神品格，以及丰沛卓越的艺术想象力与创造力。时值实现中华民族伟大复兴的第二个百年奋斗目标的开局之年，及具有历史性意义的中国共产党二十大的召开之年，以此展致敬与赓续“君子比德于玉”和“艰难困苦，玉汝于成”的伟大民族精神。

是为序。

颐和园党委副书记

颐和园博物馆馆长

2022 年 12 月

"Ancient Chinese Jades Exhibition of Animals and Plants" A First View

Zhang Guangwen

The Summer Palace is a Qing-period imperial garden of world renown and exquisite landscape. Other than the majestic royal buildings and landscaping, it is also a repository of many great cultural relics.

The Ancient Chinese Jades Exhibition of Animals and Plants organized by the Beijing Summer Palace Administration Office in collaboration with the Institute of Qing History is a major exhibition in recent years for ancient Chinese jades.

1. The Development of Ancient Jade Artefacts of Animal and Plant Themes

The Chinese use of jade began in the neolithic period and has almost ten thousand years of history.

Jade artefacts of animal and plant themes had appeared in abundance during the neolithic period distributed over the Hongshan culture in the North-East of China about 5500 years ago. Jade artefacts excavated include jade dragons, turtles and birds. The Shijiahe culture in the middle of the Yangtze River about 4000 years ago also produced jade items such as birds, cicadas and jade animal faces. The Lingjiatan culture of Anhui province had excavated jade objects of leaf shapes. These neolithic period jades of animal and plant themes are mainly carved with straight lines, circles and other geometrical shapes. Other embellishments are rare.

The Xia, Shang and Zhou periods also produced many jade objects with animal themes including dragon and phoenix; bear, tiger, elephant; horned beasts, domesticated animals, insects and birds. The current exhibition includes Shang period jade tiger carved in the round and embellished with long and curved lines showing the typical style of the period. Although there is only few example of Shang and Zhou jade in this exhibition, every object the vogue of the era.

The Eastern Zhou, Qin and Han is yet another period of Jade development when the carving of jade became more complicated with patterns and embellishments more compact and plentiful. Jade carvings of dragon, chi-dragon, and other auspicious beasts and birds like phoenix began to appear in large numbers. Patterns and decorations symbolizing plant themes like the "grain patterns" and "hexagonal net decorations" also appeared during this period.

Realistic Jade carvings began to appear after the Tang and Song periods with an abundance of animal and plant theme jade works. Such themes could be divided into two categories: the mythical beasts and the ordinary wild or domestic animals and birds. Some of the mythical beasts had their origins in ordinary animals.

These mythical beasts are usually centered around the dragon with its many derivative forms such as the cloud dragon, kui-dragon, chi-dragon. Other auspicious beasts include the bixie, xiezhi, suanni, qilin and lions. The current exhibition also includes traditionally loved animal themes such as the elephants, three rams, monkeys on horses, lotus with fish. Traditional animals symbolizing a peaceful life such as the dogs, buffalos, double badgers, roosters, mandarin ducks, bats, phoenix, geese, also appear in the current exhibition.

Those Qing court jades in this exhibition, especially the fanggu jades (imitating the ancient objects) are usually embellished with the beast-face patterns, one of the earliest jade designs. Many jade artefacts from the neolithic period have quite standardized beast-face patterns. After the Song to Ming period, the beast-face patterns on jade items could be classified into three categories: the free style form of beast-face; those imitating the Han style beast-face; and those large beast-face patterns appearing on jade censers and jade vases.

2. The Qing Imperial Jade of Animal and Plant Themes in the Summer Palace Collection Exbihition

The Qing period jade is the pinnacle of ancient Chinese jade while the jade from the imperial collection is the cream of Qing period jade. The Qing imperial jades are mainly housed in the Beijing Palace Museum and the Taipei National Museum respectively. There are also some other institutions, notably the Summer Palace, with such high-quality collections. The Summer Palace is a large imperial garden and building establishment with a large Qing imperial jade collection detailed below:

The imperial palace large dragon vats.

Before the Qing period, there are few large jade artefacts. A notable exception is the Dushan large jade vat of the Yuan period. There are practically no large jade carving items in the Ming period until the Yongzheng reign in the Qing dynasty. Large jade carvings practically only came after the 24th Year of Qianlong (1759) after the emperor squashed the rebellion in Xinjiang where large volume of jade materials could come inland to Beijing.

After 1759, many large jade items were made in the Qing imperial palace. The large jade boulders, screens and vats being those large items. However, the large jars and vats required jade material of very large sizes and the carvings were quite intricate. As such, only very few such jade vats or jars were made and extant items are even fewer. These large jars and vats were mainly used for the storage of water for the prevention of fire in the palace.

The Qing Palace Fanggu Yi and Ding

There are many fanggu (imitation of the ancient) jade ding and yi in the Summer Palace collection. Examples are the celadon jade dragon pattern square censer (figure 011), the white jade vase with beast head loose rings (figure 012), and various others. These ding and yi are quite standard display items in the Qing palaces. They are many of these items of various categories in the Qing palace with very intricate carvings and requiring high quality jade materials. They are usually used as display objects on tables but seldom found as floor furnishings.

Other Animal and Plant Theme Jade Artefacts

A large amount of other Qing period jade items with animal and plant themes are exhibited in this exhibition. These include various objects like jade washers, dishes, and ewers. Many scholar's table objects such as the scepters, brush pots, brush washers are also on display. The current exhibition also provides many Qing period jade pendants, ornaments with various chicken-heart shaped, beast-face, chi-dragon, and cloud patterns.

Precious Stone Items such as Lazurites, Rock Crystals, Jadeite and Corals

These precious stone carving items with animal and plant themes are usually used as display objects or jewelry adornments. Rock crystal items were popular in the Qing period and many are in the imperial collections. The Qing period rock crystal gu in the current exhibition is of a very high quality made according to strict imperial requirements seldom found in other Qing imperial collections.

The current exhibition includes a rare blue lazurite boulder (shanzi)(figure 163) with engraving of a royal poem of Emperor Qianlong. This blue stone boulder is carved with an exceptional quality lazurite with intricate carving of rockeries and pine landscape. It is indeed a rare piece of artwork. Other rare items like the large green table screen, censer, and the coral flower receptacle are also very notable exquisite items.

“玉见生机——中国古代动植物题材玉器展”展品概览

张广文
故宫博物院

颐和园是清代皇家园林，享誉世界，最著名的是优美的山湖景色、雄伟奇巧的宫廷建筑，还有珍藏的奇珍异宝。

北京市颐和园管理处与中国人民大学清史研究所在颐和园共同举办了《玉见生机》中国古代动植物题材玉器展，展出了部分中国古代玉器。这是一个很好的展览，其中的很多作品是一般玉器展览中不可多见的艺术珍品，是能够代表时代玉器特征的典型佳作。展览从一个侧面表现出中国古代玉文化的特点及发展脉络，具有普遍性、系统性和展品的珍稀性，可供观赏、研究。

一、古代动植物题材玉器的发展过程

中国玉器产生于新石器时期，有一万年以上的发展历史，黑龙江饶河小南山新石器时代遗址，遗存有一万年前制造的玉器，这些玉器的造型、工艺非常成熟，可以看出，此前玉器已经经历了很长的发展时期。

动植物题材玉器在新石器时代大量出现。分布于中国东北地区的红山文化，距今5500年左右，遗址中出土有玉龙、玉龟、玉鸟等多种玉雕动物；分布于长江中游的石家河文化，距今约有4000年，遗址中出土有玉鸟、玉蝉、玉兽面等玉器；安徽含山凌家滩新石器文化遗址出土有叶形器，其上叶脉纹均匀细长，是植物题材玉器的代表性作品。新石器时期的动植物题材玉器，边线直、圆，多呈几何形，器表面少纹饰。

夏、商、周玉器中有大量的玉雕动物，龙凤、熊虎象、有角兽、家畜、虫、蛹、候鸟等各种飞禽。片状作品较多，表面少起伏，多有长线条的华丽装饰，如此次展览中的商代玉虎，立体圆雕，形象威猛，虎身饰长线折线纹装饰，是动物型玉器的典型作品。此期玉器中虽然商周玉器较少，但都时代特征明显。

东周、秦、汉是中国玉器发展的又一阶段，此时的玉器装饰复杂，纹饰满而密，动物类玉器作品充满想象，出现了大量玉雕龙、螭、鸠、雀、瑞兽、凤凰，同时在众多平面玉器上装饰有象征植物的“蒲纹”“谷纹”。

唐宋以后，玉器中出现了大量现实主义作品，动植物题材大量出现，作品强调造型的写实性和生动性。

一般动物题材作品可分为两种类型：带有神话色彩的想象中的动物和与人们生活密切相关的家畜、飞禽等动物。但即便动物形象中的神异类作品，也多是由现实动物改造而来。

带有神话色彩的动物题材主要以龙为中心，龙有多种派生，如云龙、夔龙、螭龙。神话色彩的动物题材还有辟邪、獬豸、麒麟等瑞兽，以及狻猊、狮子等猛兽形象。此次展览中还有大量人们喜闻乐见的动物题材作品，有表示吉祥祥瑞的太平有象、三阳开泰、马上封侯、金玉满堂、连年有余，有表示生活安逸的卧犬、牧牛、双獾、雄鸡、鸳鸯、蜻蜓，也有表示福寿绵长的蝙蝠及凤凰、绶带、鹅、鸭、雀、鸠等多种鸟类。

此外，此次展出的清代宫廷玉器皿，尤其是仿古玉器，大量装饰兽面纹。兽面图案为玉器中最古老的图案。新石器时代龙山文化、良渚文化、石家河文化玉器中都有较为统一的兽面图案样式，周、秦、汉、唐玉器中也有较为固定的兽面纹样式。宋、明以后，玉器中兽面纹多为三类：一为样式较自由的兽面纹，如四川广汉窖藏宋代兽面；一为仿汉代样式的兽面纹；一为炉、瓶玉器皿主体装饰的大兽面纹。

二、颐和园珍藏及展示的清代动植物题材宫廷玉器

清代玉器是中国古代玉器发展的顶峰，宫廷玉器又是清代玉器的精华所在。清代宫廷玉器主要收藏在故宫博物院和台北故宫博物院，此外还有一些收藏单位。颐和园是清代皇家园林及建筑群，藏有大量清代宫廷文物，其中的宫廷玉器收藏规模大、品种多、质量高。动植物题材玉器包括了宫廷玉器的方方面面。许多都是宫廷玉器中的典型作品，具有独一性和珍贵性，是研究、欣赏、了解中国古代玉器不可缺少的，也是到访参观颐和园所必看之宝。颐和园收藏的最具代表性的宫廷玉器有如下几种：

（一）宫廷大型陈设龙纹玉瓮

清代之前，很少有大型玉器。元代渎山大玉海是数得着的作品，明代大型作品几近于无，清代雍正以前大型玉器也很难见到。清代大型玉器的制作几乎都在乾隆二十四年（1759 年）以后，其中原因之一是清政府平定了新疆地区的叛乱，新疆玉料得以大量进入内地。

乾隆二十四年（1759 年）后，宫廷造办处组织制造了多种大件玉陈设。目前，尚存于世的大件玉陈设主要有大玉屏、玉插屏、玉山、玉瓮、玉鼎彝器、玉动物。其中，玉山、玉瓮体积大，制造复杂，数量很少。尤其玉瓮存世仅数件。故宫院内多有储水大缸，室内则用瓮，既是陈设又可养殖，玉瓮是清代宫廷室内重要陈设玉器，较其他作品更为珍贵。

（二）宫廷仿古动物纹玉鼎彝、玉器皿

颐和园收藏有较多的典型宫廷仿古彝，如：碧玉雕龙双环方炉（图 011），白玉龙纹活环扁壶（图

012)，碧玉螭纹觥（图 019），白玉仿古蟠螭纹兽耳瓶（图 020），白玉兽面纹双环瓶（图 067）等。此次展出的白玉双凤六环尊（图 030），雕双凤相背，身下海水，凤背驮宝瓶，如意纹盖，玉质上乘，工艺精湛，属清代宫廷珍品。

鼎彝类玉陈设是最具代表性的宫廷玉陈设，数量多、品类多、加工精制且难度大、对玉材要求极高、流传广泛。玉鼎彝以器皿为主，一直是宫廷玉器制造的代表性作品。式样有一定的要求，称为御廷恭造样式。作品大小不一，使用时多置于条案、几座上，几乎不见墩座于地的，因而无特大型作品。作品除了形体外，还注重盖、钮、耳、足的样式。

乾隆时期是清代宫廷玉彝制造的高峰，乾隆对此有较高的要求，很多作品的制造都要亲自过问。一些经典的样式或乾隆偏爱的样式，还要重复制造。颐和园收藏的青玉"大清乾隆仿古"款兽面纹方鼎（图 068），是在《西清古鑑》周代金银错召夫鼎的样式上加以设计的，制造多件，此件高 27.8 厘米，较故宫博物院收藏的略高，是清代宫廷玉器精品。

（三）其它动物植物题材玉器

此次展出清代动植物题材玉器较多。除仿古彝器外，还有多件玉洗、玉盘、玉壶。其中白玉龙柄莲瓣纹壶（图 173），玉质优良，工艺精细，瓜棱上有西番莲叶图案，亦属精品。展品中还有如意、盖盒、笔筒、水洗，反映出人们生活方方面面所使用的玉器。

颐和园展出的还有典型的清代动物题材玉佩、坠，如碧玉仿汉鸡心佩（图 023）、水晶兽面纹觚（图 066）、螭纹、勾云纹玉饰。

（四）珍贵的青金石、水晶、翡翠、珊瑚类作品

高质量的青金石、水晶、翡翠、珊瑚、玛瑙等属珍贵材料，多用于加工装饰品、首饰，体积较小。也有用于表现动植物题材作品，因造型多变化，需较大的材料。但一般较大的料，多材质平平。

水晶在我国有几千年的使用历史，清代广为流行，优秀作品多为宫廷用品。此次展出的清代水晶兽面纹觚（图 066）材质优良，造型端庄，典型宫廷恭造样式，在清代宫廷器物中少有重复。

清代宫廷往往将孔雀石及青金石称为崔生石。好的青金石呈深蓝色，带有极少的白色方解石和黄铁矿斑，很珍稀。此次展出的青金石御题翠云岩山景（图 163），材料属上等青金石，雕层峰茂林，刻乾隆御制诗，属难得的艺术珍品。

展出中的翡翠雕"玉堂富贵"仿乾隆御题插屏（图 181）色泽翠绿，材质细润，透明度好，如此宽大、质地优质的材料非常难得，且图案雕琢精彩诱人，经得起细细欣赏。翠炉及珊瑚花插、珊瑚摆件，材料大，材质优良，加工工艺亦属精美。

Dragon amid Peonies and Chi-dragon with Lingzhi in Mouth

The Characteristics and Artistic Styles of the Yuan Period Jade Objects in the Beijing Art Museum

Gao Shuang

1. Overview

In 1206, Genghis Khan united the various Mongolian tribes to form the Mongol Khanate. It later conquered Xixia, Jin and the Southern Song and changed its name to Yuan. After 162 years, in 1368, the Yuan was defeated and succeeded by the Ming. Before the rise to power, the Mongols were grassland nomads and hunters. With the forming of a nation-state, a large-scale military expansion with the plundering of various peoples, the Great Mongol Nation (Da Mengguguo) became more established to have an early modest scale handicraft industry. The aristocracies had already been in the habit of using jade ware and jade objects. The green jade figurine belt ornament excavated from the tomb of Damaoqi Mingshui in Baotou Inner Mongolia, was identified to be made at the period of the Great Mongol Nation. It belongs to the Wanggu Tribe living in the area of Daqingshan. The style and design of this jade ornament is quite different from those in the traditional Zhongyuan (China proper) area. Into the Yuan period, Kublai Khan encouraged a centralized government placing importance on agriculture. The handicraft industry also became highly developed under a well-developed transportation and trade systems within the country. The use and the making of jade objects had to rely on a high level of development in the handicraft industry. The Yuan period jade culture was influenced by the Han ethnic culture and also the culture from the Jin dynasty. Incorporating this with its own robust and unconstrained Mongol culture, the unique Yuan period jade artistic style was established. Eminent Yuan jade objects such as the jade seal bestowed by the emperor upon the highest monk Basiba (Drogön Chogyal Phagpa) in the Tibet Museum, also the national jade seal from Kublai Khan to the imperial preceptor Basiba with inscription of "the First Year of Zhongtong" (1260) had always been kept at the Potala Palace in Tibet. This is the earliest extant standard Yuan jade object with well-recorded provenance. In addition, the huge *Dushan dayuhai* (Dushan Jade Vat) in front of the Chengguangdian in Beijing's Beihai Park was also a standard example of Yuan jade art. There are 47 important archeological sites for Yuan period jade excavations. They include 36 burial tombs, 3 Buddhist pagodas, and 8 historical sites. Of these, the Fan Wenhu tomb in Anhui Anqing; the Xianyu Shu tomb in Hangzhou; the Qian Yu tomb in Wuxi; the Zhang Shicheng parental tomb in Suzhou; the Wang Shixian tomb in Zhangxian Gansu; and the Ren Ming tomb in Qingpu, Shanghai; were excavated with clear and definite burial dates. These excavated jade objects include curtain-weights, vases, belt hooks, jade fish, peach-shaped washers, belts, finial ornaments, figurines, and sword ornaments. These are all standard jade objects providing reliable measure and comparison in dating purposes for other extant Yuan jade objects.

2. The Four Yuan Period Jade Objects in the Beijing Art Museum

There are 12 Yuan period jade objects in the Beijing Art Museum (BAM). These include categories like jade finial ornaments, belt ornaments, pendants, and jade in the style of ancient objects. The four Yuan period jade objects discussed in this article were transferred to the newly established BAM in 1987 from the Beijing Municipal Bureau of Cultural Heritage. From the designs and functions, they are: 2 jade finial ornaments and 2 jade belt ornaments. The 2 jade finial ornaments were judged to be from the Ming period when they were first transferred to the BAM. In the subsequent few decades, more archeological excavations were made together with new archeological papers on those extant jade objects published by the various museums. The awareness and understanding of Yuan period jade objects became more precise. In 2020, the topic of "Research on the Art of Jade Objects in the Beijing Art Museum" has revised and reset the date of these two finial ornaments to the Yuan period. According to the classification by patterns and decorations, these four jade objects are separated into the categories of "dragon amid peonies" and "chi-dragon with lingzhi in mouth". They are typical and representative design themes in Yuan period jade objects and are considered to be the finest of the Yuan period jade in the BAM.

The Theme of Dragon Amid Peonies

This theme of dragon amid peonies was popular in the Yuan and the Ming periods. The BAM has two jade objects of this theme, one is a belt ornament (figure 1) while the other is a finial ornament (figure 2). Both are typical standard Yuan period jade objects.

The main subject of the "dragon amid peonies theme" is invariably the dragon. The dragon is a very important theme and decorative pattern in the Chinese culture. The dragon pattern is a common decorative pattern in Yuan period jade objects. The Dushan Large Jade Vat in Beijing's Beihai Park is a good example. One side of the vat is carved with dragon and a combination of sea wave patterns. The Dushan large jade vat was completed in the second year of Zhiyuan (1265 CE) with its decorative patterns emanating the style of the early Yuan period. Other excavated Yuan period jade objects are: the Canglong Jiaozi (Green Dragon Teaching Son) belt hook with the carving of a dragon head from Xiaozhai Nanxiang in Xi'an Shaanxi, is a typical Yuan period dragon head carved in the round; the Yuan period "double dragon pursuing pearl" stone casket (figure 3) excavated from the Fahua Pagoda underground palace in Jiading Shanghai, could be regarded as a standard Yuan period dragon design pattern. Many Yuan period porcelains were decorated with the dragon patterns, these could be used as references for the late Yuan period dragon pattern characteristics. A good example is the Yuan blue and white dragon pattern meiping (figure 4) excavated in Baoding, Hebei province. The main characteristics of the Yuan dragon patterns are: the placement of the dragon had been extended from the normal clouds in the past to the rivers and the sea, or amongst cluster of flowers. The head of the dragon is comparatively smaller while its manes are thicker and longer. The neck is thinner while the body is stocky. The body is wrapped with streamer or cloud-ribbons and covered with scales. Sometimes flame patterns could be seen around the body. Other than the three-clawed dragons, others such as the four-clawed or five-clawed could also be found. The BAM has a "white jade openwork carving of dragon amid peonies" belt ornament with the dragon head looking sideways with open mouth and upward pointing nose. The brows are long with staring eyes, the two horns slanting backwards. The manes are side-parting, thin neck, while the shoulder and loin are muscular. It has a straddling gait with one front limb lifting up while the other limb supports the body. The two back limbs bended and preparing to lunge. The claws had been made to be five-clawed and the four limbs had grid-net patterns forming the scales. Its tail points upwards. The jade finial ornament has a hunkered dragon carved in the round with a large part of its body immersing in the peonies. However, the head and the claws still emanate the characteristic style of the Yuan period.

As the supplementary pattern in the "dragon amid peonies" theme, the peony also possesses its distinctive characteristic style of the period. Jade objects with peony patterns first appeared in the Tang dynasty. The Song and

Yuan period peonies could be a stand-alone pattern or in a combination with dragons, phoenix and other auspicious beasts or birds. The flower-shaped jade petals are almost carved in the round with three-dimensional clear layers. The peony patterns appeared extensively in the extant and excavated jade objects of this period many of which are now in the National Museum of China and the Beijing Palace Museum. A good example of the excavated object is the "double phoenix with peony stone casket" (figure 5). The peony stamens are carved in plaid line patterns with the petals unfolding outward. Compared to the Song period, the Yuan period flower jade objects would have more flowers and less leaves. The leaves and twigs are only playing a supporting role.

The peony of the belt ornament in the BAM is at the top right corner in response to the head of the dragon. The petals are very distinctive and the carvings are robust. The peony on the jade finial object appears in half-section with stack layers of long and short petals. The edges of the leaves are serrated. The petals and leaves are engraved in intaglio making this a distinctive characteristic of the Yuan period jade carvings.

The jade themes of "dragon amid peonies" or "cloud dragons" were also quite popular in the early Ming period. Similar theme jade objects were excavated from some Ming period tombs or historical sites. However, judging from the characteristics of these jade objects, some were actually the products of the Yuan period while the rest were from the Ming period. "The dragon pattern openwork cloud dragon jade plaque ornament" unearthed from the Ming tomb in Lehuafengling, Xinjian County, Jiangxi province (figure 6); the "white jade dragon pattern belt ornament" excavated from the Wang Xing ancestral tomb in Nanjing, Jiangsu; both belong to the style of the late Yuan to early Ming period. Also, the exquisite jade belt ornament and dragon jade finial ornament were excavated from the Liangzhuangwang tomb in Zhongxiang, Hubei province. Zhu Zhanji was the ninth son of the Ming emperor Renzong and was conferred the title of Liangzhuangwang (Prince of Liangzhuang) in the twenty second year of Yongle (1424). He died in the Sixth Year of Zhengtong (1441). The jade artifacts excavated from the Liangzhuangwang tomb spanned a period of the Jin and Yuan and then to the Ming. Of the two jade finial ornaments excavated, one was of the theme of "dragon amid peonies" (figure 7) while the other was the "cloud dragon" theme. The two jade objects had quite similar shapes, both belonging to the Yuan period. The "dragon amid peonies" object was closely similar to the jade finial object in the BAM. It can be seen that the designs and patterns of these jade finials had become standardized. During the late Ming period, embedded precious stones with gold holders showing the lavish living style of the *fanwang* (prince). Similar Ming period jade objects of themes could also be seen in the "dragon amid peonies jade belt ornament" (figure 8) excavated from the Xilin Pagoda underground palace in Shanghai. The manes of the dragon were fluttering upwards while the peony flower, leaves and twigs, made distinctive upper and lower layers emanating a very clear typical style of the jade carvings of the Ming period. However, the composition and presentation of the dragon and flower forms still showing some leftover implications of the Yuan. This clearly showed the continuation of similar jade themes from the Yuan period.

On the question of whether the dragon pattern jade objects were made exclusively for royal use, opinions were divided among scholars. According to the system set on the first year of Yanyou (1314) in the Yuan period, the Mongolian aristocrats were not allowed to use the dress or costumes with the dragon or phoenix ornaments. Other officials' use of these patterns in their costumes are also limited. Also there are opinions that the dragon patterns were not being exclusively used by the imperial family in the Yuan period but being used as a common auspicious design pattern. With respect to current opinions, there were very few Yuan period dragon pattern objects excavated from tombs. (The tombs with excavated jade objects were not of a high social class.) The tombs of early Ming *fanwang* (princes) and high-ranking officials did unearth such jade artifacts. Maybe this did reflect from a different view that the Yuan period dragon pattern jade objects portrayed a certain status hierarchy or rank.

The Theme of Chi-dragon With Lingzhi in Mouth

There are two "chi-dragon with Lingzhi in mouth" jade objects in the BAM. One is an embedding ornament (figure 9) while the other is a finial ornament (figure 10), (both were exhibited in the "Ancient Chinese Jades Exhibition of Animals and Plants"). They display the typical style and characteristics of the Yuan period chi-dragon pattern jade objects.

The chi-dragon pattern was a representative pattern of the Han period jade objects. However, this pattern rapidly vanished after the Han period. Only when the *fanggu* (imitating ancient) jade objects were in vogue in later periods, the chi-dragon, as a *fanggu* pattern, was again becoming popular. The chi-dragon pattern jade objects of the Song period mainly appeared in jade *bi*, sword ornaments, and *she*-shaped ornaments. Those of the double chi-dragon combination patterns usually would have the chi-dragon mouth-holding each other by the tail. However, the double chi-dragon with lingzhi in mouth pattern was more popular in the Yuan dynasty. Comparatively more Yuan period chi-dragon pattern jade objects were excavated. Examples are the two chi-dragons round plaques unearthed from the Hejia Village in Nanjiao, Xi'an; the chi-dragon with lingzhi in mouth *huan* from the Nanjiao Yuan period tomb in Lishui, Nanjing; the *zimu* (double-combination) chi-dragon belt hook from the tomb of Wang Shixian, Xujiabang, Zhang County in Gansu province; the chi-dragon belt hook from the tomb of Liu Kui in Gaoxinqu, Xi'an, Shaanxi province; the chi-dragon ornament (figure 11) from the Xilin Pagoda underground palace in Songjiang, Shanghai; the chi-dragon with lingzhi finial from the Suojianglou pagoda in Jiujiang, Jiangxi province; the *fanggu* chi-dragon pattern sword ornament from the tomb of Xianyu Shu in Hangzhou; the chi-dragon pattern on the lid of the jade *zun* from the tomb of Fan Wenhu in Anhui province; and others. All these could be used as standards to determine the Yuan period chi-dragon characteristics. One can see the Yuan period chi-dragon pattern inherited some of the characteristics of the Song period but later also developed its new traits such as: the body became slander and curved; the five sense organs shifted to the front occupying about a quarter of the head; the manes fluttered backwards, the body has a long engraved line; the long tail was forked and curved; the front limb and elbow with spiral patterns, the four legs are slender with front legs bending and the strong back legs in lunging positions. Since fine round awl drills and cutting discs were used in the Yuan period jade carvings, powerful cutting and drill marks could be seen at the neck and the bottom of the limb area, almost near to being severed. The paper rubbings of these jade objects would show almost like the necks and heads were cut off. The green jade chi-dragon patterned embedding ornament in the BAM has two chi-dragons, one large and the other small, with the two heads gazing at each other at recumbent positions. The bodies and the forked tails are curved to an oval configuration suiting the shape of an embedding ornament. The larger chi-dragon's mane is parted in two with fine intaglio lines and short fine lines for the brows. The smaller chi-dragon has a bald head and single intaglio lines as brows. Both the chi-dragons have one of the legs pressing the tail giving an elegant yet forceful pose. The backs have intaglio carvings on the two sides forming double diagonal lines. This style is a common design for Yuan period chi-dragon patterns. The "double chi-dragon with lingzhi in mouth jade finial ornament" also emanated the typical Yuan characteristics. The size, shape and design are almost identical to that of the Yuan "chi-dragon with lingzhi finial" unearthed from the Suojianglou pagoda in Jiujiang, Jiangxi province (figure 12).

The lingzhi mushroom had always been regarded by the ancient Chinese as a very auspicious plant. Zhang Heng (of the Han dynasty) in his poem called the lingzhi "sacred wood". Cao Zhi, in his article *Lingzhipian*, also praised the lingzhi very highly. The lingzhi held in the mouth of the Yuan period double chi-dragon had shapes and design very similar to the ruyi-shaped cloud pattern. The outer fringes are wavy, bulging and extending outward forming wavy layers. For actual excavated objects, we could refer to the Yuan "white jade *shancai* boy ornament" unearthed from the Xilin Pagoda underground palace in Songjiang, Shanghai (figure 13). In addition to the "chi-dragon with lingzhi in mouth", other combination jade objects with rich designs and patterns like "chi-dragon with flowers", "chi-dragon with dragons" were also in vogue during the Song and Yuan periods.

3. The Multilayered Openwork Artistic Style

It could easily be seen that similar themes of jade carvings in the Yuan period are converging to form standard models and types. However, in jade objects with different functions, the patterns still emanate various manifestations. The four jade objects from the BAM discussed in this article correspond to two types of jade carving themes showing the difference in their artistic functions.

Yuan period jade carvings inherited many of the Song multilayered openwork engraving styles. Merging with the ethnic customs of the nomads, some new jade carving styles and themes were established. The multilayered reticulated carving, according to Mr. Fu Zhongmo, was actually the "deep layered three-dimensional reticulated pierced carving" first appeared in the Northern Song period. Mr. Yang Boda pointed out that the advanced level of Song painting actually led the way for the development of jade carving towards the art of painting. [1]First appeared were the full view three-dimensional jade carvings. It specifically incorporated the tri-viewpoint method of traditional Chinese landscape painting into the multilayered reticulated openwork jade carvings. This made the full view style of jade carving during the period emanating a multi-layer viewing effect, producing a very strong three-dimensional feel. The Yuan period jade carving inherited this special trait. The detailed carvings were not polished or burnished as finely as those of the Song period often leaving traces of cutting and drilling marks. Although not as fine and detailed, the Yuan period jade showed an abundance of rich themes. Combining with the multilayered reticulated openwork method, it however created a great period of brilliance in the history of Chinese jade carving. Whether it be the *chunshui qiushan* jade (jade carving showing the nomadic Spring and Autumn hunting scenes); or the dragon, phoenix and chi-dragon subjects absorbed from the traditional culture of the Chinese central plains, could all be given lively and vigorous new scenes through multilayered openwork carvings.

The jade finial ornament popular in the Song and Yuan periods was the highest embodiment of the multilayered openwork jade carving style. The Yuan jade finial ornament has the look of a Chinese steam bun. Similar to their Song counterparts, they presented a small but full scene. The Yuan popular jade finial ornaments were abounded with rich themes. The "dragon amid peonies", the "chi-dragon with lingzhi in mouth" were common Yuan finial ornament subjects. In addition, the "lotus with egret", "mandarin duck with lotus in mouth", "deer with Chinese oak" were also popular. Current archeological excavations of jade finial ornaments mainly came from the Xilin Pagoda underground palace in Shanghai (11), Zhangye City in Gansu province (4), Liminggang in Chengdu (3). The Yuan Dadu Ruins, and the Ren Ming tomb of Qingpu, Shanghai, also produced some excavations of these. The tombs with specific burial date came mainly from the late Yuan period.

The function of the Yuan period jade finial ornaments was propounded by Shen Defu in his book *Wanli Yehuobian* of the Ming dynasty. When the early Ming emperors forbid the use of jade hat finial, many Yuan period hat finials were being modified as censer finials and were popularized in the Ming upper class. Scholars had been skeptical whether there were actually Yuan period jade hat finials. They surmised that the pearl on top of the hat during the Yuan period were not the currently seen reticulated multilayer jade finials in the shape of a Chinese bun. [2]The dominant view is that the larger size jade finials are actually censer finials. The smaller size reticulated pearl shape objects might be the hat finials. This would require further analysis on a case-by-case basis. From those currently designated jade objects, the jade finials capable of creating a viewing scene are quite large in size. The two jade finial ornaments in the BAM should be termed censer finials, to be more appropriate.

The "ring supported high relief carving" was another type of multilayer openwork carving style. Jade carvings of this artistic type were first seen in the Jin period such as the "falcon hunting swan jade scarf ring"[3] from the tomb

1 Yang Boda: *Lun Zhongguo Gudai Yuqi Yishu (A Discussion of the Ancient Chinese Jade Art)*, Palace Museum Journal, 1995 Issue 01, page 160

2 Wang Shuzheng: *Luding, Maoding Bianshi (Differentiating Between the Censer Finial and the Hat Finial) Symposium on Chinese Jade from Sui and Tang to Qing Dynasties*, Shanghai Classics Publishing House, 2002, page 287

3 Gu Fang et al. editors: *Chutu Yuqi Quanji 2 (Complete Excavated Jade Objects Volume 2 Inner Mongolia, Liaoning, Jilin, Heilongjiang)*, The Science Press, 2005, pages 192,193

of Wanyan Xiyin in Xiaochenzi, Shulan county, Jilin province. The Yuan period "ring supported high relief" jade carvings were common. Another is the oval shaped jade braid ring [4]in the set of belt ornaments excavated from the tomb of Qian Yu in Wuxi, Jiangsu province. These two examples represented the two eminent functions of the "ring supported high relief" jade carvings. There are two main characteristics of this type of jade art. The first is the "support". The whole object has either a round ring, an oval ring or blunt ring shape as support. The carved object is higher than the ring frame as it was supported high by the ring. The second was presented in the carving technics. The "ring supported high relief" jade carving is flatter than the other jade finial ornaments. It made use of the openwork and high relief carving technique to present a three-dimensional effect.

These multilayered, reticulated openwork and "ring supported high relief" carvings declined in popularity after the Yuan period. Although there still were jade finial ornaments in the Ming period, however the layers became simplified placing more importance on the outer surface. The ornaments with just a layer on the surface was common. In the Ming period, jade belts were highly developed. However, the "ring supported high relief" carvings were not found in the jade belt plaques. The belt ornament object was not higher than its supporting frame and the ornament scene became flattened. The rich multilayer high relief slowly transformed to become a top layer with a bottom layer combination of the so called "flower pressing flower" artwork style.

4. Summary

Some scholars suggested that the Yuan period jade decorative style of very fine and detailed flower-and-plant subjects were related to that of their gold and silver wares and colorfully decorated porcelains. They seemed to be influenced by the fine and dense Arabian Patterns from Central Asia and were quite different from the elegant and succinct traditional embellishing patterns. With the addition of the reticulated openwork and high relief method of carving techniques, utilizing the green white jade color as background, it also strengthened the energetic visual effect making the subject more dynamic. This had become the most important of the Yuan period jade carving characteristics. The Yuan period jade carvings were in fact an amalgamation of the cultural and artistic elements from the various different ethnicities.

Judging from the many archeological excavations and extant jade collections from museums, the "dragon amid peonies" and the "chi-dragon with lingzhi in mouth" jade objects from the BAM first appeared in the middle Yuan and were popular in the Yuan and Ming periods. These two jade themes had their origins from the Chinese central plains showing that the Yuan jades were actually an inheritance of the traditional jade cultures, especially from that of the Southern Song period. The multilayer reticulated openwork carving of jades were very popular in the Yuan period. It combined the different functions and themes to manifest a huge variety of jade artistic styles. Similar themes when appearing in different objects such as finial ornaments, belt embellishments and scarf ornaments emanated different three-dimensional effects showing its distinguished artistic appeals.

---

4 Gu Fang et al. editors: *Chutu Yuqi Quanji 7 (Complete Excavated Jade Objects Volume 7 Jiangsu, Shanghai)*, The Science Press, 2005, page 187

龙穿牡丹与螭衔灵芝

北京艺术博物馆藏元代玉器的时代特征与艺术风格

高瑛

北京艺术博物馆

一、概述

1206 年成吉思汗统一了蒙古各部落，建立蒙古汗国。此后相继灭西夏、金、南宋，改国号为元，至 1368 年元为明所灭，共存在 162 年。蒙古族兴起前夕，经济主要以草原游牧和森林狩猎为主。随着国家的建立，经过大规模的军事扩张和对工匠的掠夺，大蒙古国时期形成了门类齐全、初具规模的手工业。上层贵族已经有了使用玉器的先例。出土于内蒙古包头达茂旗明水墓的青玉人物带饰是目前被判断为大蒙古国时期制作的玉器，属于生活在大青山一带的汪古部。[1] 其风格与中原传统玉器有较大区别。入元后，忽必烈倡行重农统政，手工业在交通发达、国内贸易活跃的促进下得到极大发展。而玉器的使用和制作，特别依赖于手工业的发展水平。元代玉文化受到汉文化和金代文化影响，并结合本民族粗犷豪放的艺术风格，形成了元代玉器艺术特色。著名的元代玉器如藏于西藏博物馆的皇帝赐予八思巴等高僧的玉印，其中中统元年的国师之印为忽必烈授予八思巴的玉印，一直收藏于布达拉宫，传承有序，是已知有明确记载的最早的元代传世玉器实物。此外，藏于北京市北海公园团城承光殿前的渎山大玉海也是元代玉器艺术的典型标准器。全国考古出土的元代玉器据统计共有重要遗址 47 处，包括墓葬 36 处、佛塔 3 处、遗址 8 处[2]。其中安徽安庆范文虎墓、浙江杭州鲜于枢墓、江苏无锡钱裕墓、江苏苏州张士诚父母墓、甘肃漳县汪世显墓、上海青浦任明墓等墓葬有明确纪年，出土的玉押、玉瓶、玉带钩、玉鱼、桃形玉洗、玉带、玉纽饰、玉人、玉剑饰等作为元代标准器物群，为传世元代玉器提供了断代的标准。

二、北京艺术博物馆藏四件元代玉器

北京艺术博物馆藏（以下简称艺博藏）元代玉器共计 12 件，包括了玉纽饰、带饰镶件、佩饰、

1 于宝东：《辽金元玉器》，内蒙古大学出版社 2007 年出版，171~172 页

2 张宏明、吴沫、于宝东、张彤著：《玉器通史 · 宋辽金元卷》，海天出版社 2013 年出版，551 页

图 1　白玉镂雕龙纹带饰
北京艺术博物馆藏

图 2　白玉镂雕龙纹纽饰
北京艺术博物馆拍摄

仿古器等种类。本文介绍的四件元代玉器均为 1987 年北京艺术博物馆建馆之初，由北京市文物局调拨至我馆的传世玉器。从器型与功能上划分，分别为两件玉纽饰和两件玉带饰。其中两件玉纽饰入馆时原定明代，在此后的几十年时间里，随着各地考古资料的丰富，以及各博物馆藏传世玉器的发表，使得人们对元代玉器的时代特征有了更准确的认识。在 2020 年《北京艺术博物馆藏玉器艺术研究》课题进行的过程中，将这两件玉纽饰改定元代。从题材纹饰上划分，四件玉器分别为龙穿牡丹和螭衔灵芝两类题材，这是元代玉器的常见题材，具有代表性，同时，这些玉器也可以说是艺博藏元代玉器中的精品。

1. 龙穿牡丹题材

龙穿牡丹题材的玉器，流行于元代、明代，艺博藏的两件龙穿牡丹题材的玉饰一为带饰（**图1**）一为纽饰（**图2**），两件玉器都属于较为典型的元代玉器类型。

龙穿牡丹题材的主体纹饰是龙，龙纹是中国文化中重要的传统纹饰之一。元代龙纹玉器较多，如北海公园收藏的渎山大玉海上的一面以琢刻龙与海浪组合纹，渎山大玉海制作于至元二年（1265年），纹饰特点体现元代早期风格。出土的元代玉石雕刻见于：陕西西安小寨南乡出土的苍龙教子带钩上琢龙首[3]，是元代圆雕龙首的标准造型；上海嘉定区法华塔地宫出土元代双龙戏珠石函（**图3**）[4]可作元代龙纹饰的标准。元代瓷器上也出现大量龙纹饰可作元代晚期龙纹特征的参考，如河北保定窖藏元青花龙纹梅瓶（**图4**）。元代的龙纹大体特点为：龙所处环境由以往的多在云中增加为在江河海水、花丛中；龙的头较小、头发较浓长、颈细身粗，身披飘带（或称云带）、鳞片覆身，有似火焰形饰，除了三爪龙也出现了四爪、五爪的样式。艺博藏白玉镂雕龙穿牡丹纹带饰上的龙纹，

3　杨伯达编：《中国玉器全集》（中卷），河北美术出版社 1994 年出版，476 页

4　上海市文物管理委员会编：《上海出土唐宋元明清玉器》，上海人民出版社 2001 年出版，20 页

龙首侧视，张口翘鼻，长眉瞪目，双角后伸，长发分作两股，颈部细，肩、臀颇富肌肉感。其姿态呈行走状，一前肢抬起，另一前肢撑起身体，两后肢呈弓字步；龙爪为桯钻四孔分出五爪造型，四肢饰网格纹阴刻线鳞片；尾巴上翘。玉纽饰上的龙呈圆雕蹲坐姿态，其身体的大部分掩于牡丹花中，但头部、爪部仍能看出类似的时代特点。

牡丹作为龙穿牡丹题材的辅助纹饰，同样具有鲜明的时代特点。牡丹纹饰的玉器，始于唐代[5]，宋元时期牡丹花或单独作主纹饰或与龙、凤等灵禽瑞兽组合出现，花形玉片近似圆雕，图案立体、层次分明，这一时期传世与出土玉器上都可见到牡丹花纹饰，传世玉器鉴藏于中国国家博物馆和故宫博物院。出土器可参考上海嘉定区法华塔地宫出土的双凤牡丹石函（**图5**），牡丹花蕊以阴线琢菱格纹，花瓣舒展，琢竖向的阴线。相较宋代，元代花卉题材玉雕“多见花朵、少见花叶，枝叶仅起衬托作用”[6]。艺博藏带饰上的牡丹花出现在右上角的位置上与龙首相呼应，花瓣片片分明，雕琢粗犷；玉纽饰上的牡丹花如半剖式，花瓣长短层层分明，叶片上有锯齿状缺口，花瓣、叶片上均

图3　元代双龙戏珠石函
上海嘉定区法华塔地宫出土
引自上海市文物管理委员会编《上海出土唐宋元明清玉器》上海人民出版社 2001 年出版

图4　元青花龙纹梅瓶
河北保定窖藏
引自曹凯等编《中国出土瓷器全集 3 · 河北卷》科学出版社 2008 年出版

图5　双凤牡丹石函
上海嘉定区法华塔地宫出土
引自上海市文物管理委员会编《上海出土唐宋元明清玉器》上海人民出版社 2001 年出版

5　黄英：《“富贵吉祥”任雕琢——故宫博物院藏牡丹纹玉器》，《紫禁城》2016 年 06 期，38 页

6　殷志强：《元代玉器鉴定探微》，《故宫文物月刊》1999 年 01 月，195 页

图 6　镂雕云龙纹牌饰
江西省新建县乐化枫岭玥墓出土
引自北京艺术博物馆等编《气度与风范：明代江西藩王墓出土玉器》北京出版集团北京美术摄影出版社 2014 年出版

图 7　龙穿牡丹
梁庄王墓出土
引自湖北省博物馆编《梁庄王墓》文物出版社 2007 年出版

图 8　龙穿牡丹玉带饰
上海西林塔地宫出土

饰以阴刻线，视为元代玉雕的特点。

明代早期也十分流行龙穿牡丹或云龙这一题材的玉器，一些明代墓葬、遗址中的出土了类似样式的玉器，根据器物本身的特点判断有些是元代遗留，有些则是明代本朝制作。如江西省新建县乐化枫岭明墓出土镂雕云龙纹牌饰（**图 6**）、江苏南京汪兴祖墓出土白玉龙纹带饰[7]等应属元末明初风格。此外，湖北钟祥梁庄王墓出土了精美的玉带饰与龙纹玉纽饰。梁庄王朱瞻垍为明仁宗第九子，永乐二十二年（公元 1424 年）封梁庄王，正统六年（公元 1441 年）去世。梁庄王墓出土的玉器时代跨度由金至元，再到明本朝制作均有所见，其中出土的两件玉纽饰一件为龙穿牡丹题材（**图 7**）、一件为云龙题材，两件玉饰造型相近，都属元代制作[8]，龙穿牡丹的一件更是与艺博藏玉纽饰如出一辙，可见这类造型的玉纽已形成了定式，明代后加配嵌宝石金托，显示藩王级别用度奢华。明代同类题材的典型器物可参考上海西林塔地宫出土的龙穿牡丹玉带饰（**图 8**），龙的须发上飘，牡丹花、叶与枝条粗细形成了较为明显的上下两层，主次纹饰分明，显现出明代琢玉的典型风格，

7　嵇若昕：《元代玉帽顶》，《中国隋唐至清代玉器学术研讨会论文集》，上海古籍出版社 2002 年出版，273 页
8　袁伟：《元代出土玉器研究》，《宋辽金元玉器研究学术研讨会论文集》，科学出版社 2018 年出版，166 页

图 9　青玉双螭衔灵芝纹饰件
北京艺术博物馆藏

图 10　青白玉螭衔灵芝纹玉纽
北京艺术博物馆藏

但构图、龙与花卉的表现形式还存有一些元代意蕴，应是对元代同类题材的风格延续之作。

对于龙纹玉器是否为元代皇家专用，学术界存在争论。元延祐元年（公元 1314 年）制定的舆服制度规定：即使蒙古贵族都不得使用龙凤纹的服饰器用，职官衣饰也仅限用龙凤纹。[9] 也有人认为元代龙纹的使用并未被皇室垄断，而是一种普遍的吉祥纹饰。[10] 就目前情况看，元代墓葬少见龙纹玉器（出土玉器的墓葬等级不高），明代早期藩王、重臣级墓葬中确可见到，或许也从侧面反映出元代龙纹玉器具有一定的身份等级象征。

2. 螭衔灵芝题材

艺博藏两件螭衔灵芝纹玉饰，一件为嵌饰（**图 9**）一件为纽饰（**图 10**），均为《玉见生机——中国古代动植物题材玉展》展览中的展品，展现了元代螭纹玉器的典型特征。

螭纹是汉代玉器的代表性纹饰，但在汉以后迅速消逝，直至仿古玉兴起，螭纹作为一种仿古纹饰再度流行。宋代螭纹玉器多见于玉璧、剑饰、韘形佩等，宋代玉器上的双螭组合纹饰多作首尾相衔造型，与之相比，元代更为流行双螭衔灵芝的题材。元代螭纹出土玉器较多，如西安市南郊何家村出土圆形螭纹牌 2 件、南京溧水县南郊元墓出土口衔灵芝螭纹环、甘肃省漳县徐家坪汪世显墓出土子母螭带钩、陕西西安高新区刘逵墓出土螭纹带钩、上海松江西林塔地宫出土螭纹佩（**图 11**）、江西九江锁江楼塔出土螭纹灵芝纹纽、杭州鲜于枢墓出土仿古螭纹剑饰、安徽范文虎墓出土的玉尊盖上也有螭纹 [11] 等等，这些可作为判断元代螭纹特点的标准。元代螭纹对宋代螭纹有一定继承，也发展出新的特点：身体细长弯曲，头上五官集中在前部，占四分之一位置，长发后披，身脊有一道长阴线，长尾分叉卷曲，肘与臂有螺旋纹，四脚细瘦，前肢弯曲，后肢有力常作蹬地状。

9　同上
10　王书正：《"炉顶"、"帽顶"辨识》，《中国隋唐至清代玉器学术研讨会论文集》，上海古籍出版社 2002 年出版，287 页
11　袁伟：《元代出土玉器研究》，《宋辽金元玉器研究学术研讨会论文集》，科学出版社 2018 年出版，153 页

图11　螭纹佩
上海松江西林塔地宫出土
引自上海市文物管理委员会编《上海出土唐宋元明清玉器》上海人民出版社 2001 年出版

图12　元代螭纹灵芝纹纽
江西九江锁江楼塔出土

图13　元白玉灵芝善财童子饰件
上海松江区西林塔地宫出土
引自上海市文物管理委员会编《上海出土唐宋元明清玉器》上海人民出版社 2001 年出版

由于元代琢刻时使用砣和圆头细桯钻，在纹饰颈部、腿根部可以看到用“刀”有力，似乎刻断的情况，这使得纹饰在拓片上看如同颈断头掉一般。[12] 艺博藏青玉螭纹嵌饰中的双螭一大一小，头部相对，呈伏卧状，身体和分叉的卷尾婉转环绕成椭圆形，勾勒出嵌饰的形状。大螭发分两股，上饰细密阴线，以短细阴线刻粗眉；小螭头上光素，以单阴线饰眉。两螭后肢均有一条腿压住卷尾，姿态优美而不失力量，背部阴刻脊线并于两侧各饰成组双横线，为元代螭纹常见装饰手法。另一件双螭衔灵芝的玉纽饰，螭纹同样具有元代典型特征，其体量、造型与江西九江锁江楼塔出土元代螭纹灵芝纹纽（图12）几乎完全一致。

灵芝被古人视为具有灵气之物。张衡《西京赋》中称其为“神木”，曹植的《灵芝篇》中描述：“灵芝生天地，朱草被洛滨；荣华相晃耀，光采焕若神。”元代双螭所衔的灵芝瑞草，造型与同时代的如意形云纹十分相似，外沿周边多波折，由中心向外兜转起凸，并形成波浪状层面。出土实物可参考上海松江区西林塔地宫出土元白玉灵芝善财童子饰件（图13）。除螭衔灵芝，宋元时期还流行螭与花卉、螭与龙等组合纹饰的玉器，题材丰富、造型多样。

三、多层镂雕艺术风格

从前述中不难看出，元代同一类型题材的玉雕已出现了趋同的现象，具有一定模式化的样本。但在应用于不同功能的玉器上，仍有较为丰富的表现形式。本文介绍的艺博藏 4 件玉器，分别代表了两类题材在元代琢玉艺术之中展现出的不同功能之间的差异。

元代的玉雕艺术继承了宋以来多层镂雕艺术风格，并与游牧民族的生活习俗相融合，形成了一些典型的玉雕题材。所谓多层镂雕，傅忠谟先生称之为“深层立体透雕”，出现于北宋。杨伯达

12　高曼：《西安郊区出土元代玉器的艺术特征》，《出土玉器鉴定与研究》，紫禁城出版社 2001 年出版，256 页

先生指出宋代发达的绘画艺术引导玉器沿绘画艺术途径发展，首现立体全景式玉雕。[13] 具体表现为传统山水画中的三远式布局与多层镂雕技法相结合，使得这一时期的场景式玉雕营造出多重景致错落分布的视觉效果，具有强烈的立体感。元代玉雕艺术继承了这一特点，在细部表现上不及宋代打磨规整，常留下钻痕砣痕。虽不及宋玉琢磨细腻，但元代玉雕所呈现出的丰富题材，加之多层镂雕手法相结合，创造了古代玉器艺术史上的辉煌一笔。无论是反映北方游牧民族四时捺钵的春水秋山玉，还是汲取于中原传统文化之中的龙、凤、螭等元素为主题的玉雕，皆可以通过多层镂雕的手法，表现一副生机盎然的场景。

兴起于宋元时代的玉纽饰是玉器多层镂雕艺术风格的极致体现。元代玉纽饰，外廓为馒头状，与宋代玉纽饰一样，多为营造一个小场景。元代流行的玉纽饰题材丰富，龙穿牡丹、螭衔灵芝都是元代玉纽饰的常见题材，除此之外，莲荷鹭鸶、鸳鸯衔莲、鹿与柞木等也比较常见。目前考古出土玉纽饰主要集中于上海西林塔地宫（11 件）、甘肃张掖市（4 件）、成都利民巷（3 件），以及北京元大都遗址、上海青浦区任明墓等地也有出土，其中有明确纪年的墓葬都集中在元代晚期。关于元代玉纽饰的功能，根据（明）沈德符《万历野获编》的说法，明初皇帝下令禁止使用玉帽顶后，很多元代制作的帽顶此时被改制为炉顶流传于明代上层社会之中。学术界曾对元代是否有玉质帽顶产生质疑，认为元代帽子上的顶珠并非今日常见的馒头状多层镂雕玉纽。[14] 主流观点认为，体量较大的玉纽饰为炉顶，而一些体量略小而状似“顶珠”的镂雕玉饰，不排除为帽顶的可能，需要具体问题具体分析。从目前的定名看，营造场景的玉纽体量都不小，艺博藏两件玉纽饰定为炉顶似乎更恰当。

环托高浮雕是多层镂雕艺术风格的另一种表现形式，这种艺术风格的玉雕始见于金，如吉林舒兰县小城子乡完颜希尹墓出土一对鹘攫天鹅玉巾环 [15]；元代环托高浮雕玉饰更为常见，著名的如江苏无锡钱裕墓出土的一套带饰中的椭圆玉绦环 [16]。这两例也代表了环托高浮雕艺术风格玉器的两大类功能。所谓环托高浮雕，其艺术特点主要有两点：其一体现为“托”，玉饰件整体形状为圆环、椭圆环或倭角方环，所琢景物高出边框，犹如被下面的环高高托起的状态。其二体现为雕刻技法，环托高浮雕玉饰比玉纽饰图案扁平，通过镂雕、高浮雕的手法来体现图案的立体感。

多层镂雕、环托高浮雕的艺术风格，在元以后逐渐衰落。明代虽然也能见到玉纽饰，但层次简化，重外表轻内部，纹饰留于表面一层的情况明显。明代的玉带制度发达，但玉带板已不见环托高浮雕的样式，带饰的图案不再高出边框，景物也逐渐扁平化，层次丰富的高浮雕逐渐转变为上层主纹饰与下层地纹饰相结合的“花上压花”艺术风格。

13　杨伯达：《论中国古代玉器艺术》，《故宫博物院院刊》1995 年 01 期，160 页

14　王书正：《“炉顶”、“帽顶”辨识》，《中国隋唐至清代玉器学术研讨会论文集》，上海古籍出版社 2002 年出版，287 页

15　古方等编：《出土玉器全集 2 · 内蒙古、辽宁、吉林、黑龙江》，科学出版社 2005 年出版，192、193 页

16　古方等编：《出土玉器全集 7 · 江苏、上海》，科学出版社 2005 年出版，187 页

四、小结

有学者提出，元代玉器的装饰风格多以细密、饱满的花草为主题，与同时代的金银器、彩绘瓷器等的装饰技法一脉相承。由于受来自中亚的细密琐碎的“阿拉伯纹样”影响，使其与或雍容洗练、或简洁清秀的传统装饰方法不同。加以使用镂雕、高浮雕的琢玉雕技法表现，再以玉材特有的青白色调映衬，强化了动感，使得表现主题更加富有力量，成为元代玉雕的重要时代风格。实际上元代玉器是吸收了多民族不同文化艺术因素，加以融合形成的。

本文介绍的艺博藏龙穿牡丹、螭衔灵芝两种题材的元代玉器，依据诸多考古出土与各博物馆传世玉器的收藏情况看，见于元代中晚期，流行于元明之际。两个题材的文化内涵，源自中原传统文化，体现了元代玉器对以南宋玉器为代表的传统玉文化的继承。在琢刻手法上，多层镂雕技法在元代依然十分流行，与玉器的功能、题材相结合，表现出多样的艺术风格，同一题材在组饰、带饰、巾冠饰等不同立体效果的玉器上都可展现自身艺术魅力。

Jade is a beautiful stone revered and treasured by the Chinese since antiquity. It has acquired its very unique cultural and spiritual value. For thousands of years, the Chinese utilized their careful observations from nature and daily lives of plants and animals to blend in their cultural values and trendy interests. Through the very rare natural material of jade, they created myriads of lively and interesting carvings of unending variations. These jade carvings had created strong vitality and inspirational life force of their own. The current exhibition has carefully amassed more than 230 items of plant and animal carvings of jade from the Shang period to the early years of the Republic of China era to present the high levels of carving skills and unique aesthetic standards of the Chinese people.

玉石之美者，自古以来即为中华民族所珍重，并赋予其独特的文化品格与精神价值。千百年来，中国人将对自然界和生活中之鸟兽草木的细致观察与认识，融入文化意义与时代趣味，通过玉这种珍罕的天然材质，千磨万琢，运思幻化，创造出种类繁多、栩栩如生、意趣盎然的动植物题材玉器，为玉石材料注入了温暖灵动的生命活力。本展览精选商代至民国初年历代动植物题材玉器 230 余件，展现了中华民族对自然万物独特的审美观念和高超卓绝的玉雕工艺。

List of Plates

Flying Dragon and Dancing Phoenix

Auspicious Mystical Beasts and Birds

Domestic and Wild Animals

Woods and Flowers

Vegetables and Fruits

图版目录

龙飞凤舞

瑞兽灵禽

家豢天养

嘉木良卉

时蔬佳果

龙飞凤舞

Flying Dragon and Dancing Phoenix

The dragon and the phoenix are mythical animals deeply rooted in the Chinese culture. Since time immemorial, they have been used by the rulers to signify the highest authority with uncanny mythical powers. They are however also seen as the emanation of the various auspicious and moral excellence and virtue. Through the understanding of jade's cultural development, we would also comprehend the cultural status of the dragon and phoenix and discern their historical progress over the various periods.

龙与凤，是中国传统文化中最深入人心的神化动物，自古以来即被视为统治者最高权力和神秘力量的代表，也被看作预示着各种美德和祥瑞降临的化身。通过玉器文化发展史，我们不仅可以了解龙凤形象的文化地位，也可以窥见不同历史时期龙凤形象的演进特点。

001 A white jade carving of seal with "Hongchan Fozong"

Ming Dynasty, Yongle Period (1403-1424)
Length 5.9cm, Width 5.9cm, Height 4.5cm
Provided by The Institute of Qing History Renmin University of China

The top of the seal has a recumbent dragon in a lunging pose carved in the round. It was bestowed during the early Ming period by the emperor to the Buddhist monk of high rank in Tibet. The original string-ribbon is still intactly attached to this seal.

『弘阐佛宗』玉印

明永乐（1403—1424 年）
长 5.9 厘米，宽 5.9 厘米，高 4.5 厘米
中国人民大学清史研究所提供

此方玺印质地细腻，色泽温润，由整块籽料雕成。印钮雕工精美，圆雕卧龙于印台之上，双目圆突，鼻扁平上翘，体弓而颈细，前爪微收，紧扣印边，呈欲动之势，为典型的元末明初玉质玺印之佳例。

印文以九叠篆砣刻『弘阐佛宗』。九叠篆始创于宋代，多用于宋元至明初官印之上，其特点是笔画折叠堆曲，讲究均匀对称。

这枚玉印为明初永乐宫廷赐予藏地高僧大德之玺印，与罗布林卡藏同时期玺印相类，尤为难得的是宫廷制式的原绶带依然保留完好，具有极高的历史、政治和艺术价值。

"Hongchan Fozong" and the Yuan and Ming Period Imperial Bestowed Seals

By Sun Weizu

Most of the Yuan and Ming period imperial jade seals bestowed upon the various regional religious heads are now in the collection of Norbulingka Palace (a short distance to the Southwest of the Potala Palace) in Tibet. These jade seals are of the most importance in the research and understanding of the Tang to Qing Imperial seals.

Extant jade seals from the Sui and Tang Emperors to the regional heads or religious leaders have yet to be found. The earliest of such extant seals are the Yuan period "Tongling Shijiao Dayuan Guoshi" Seal (Figure 1) by the Yuan emperor to the Buddhist Sector head of Tibet; The "Tianyan Hengpai" of the Ming period and some other such imperial seals of later periods.

The Yuan period *Guoshi* (the Nation's Buddhist Head) commands the highest respect and position. Kublai Khan had bestowed the title of *Guoshi* and many other high titles to Basiba (Phags Pa), leader of the Tibetan Buddhism together with the jade seal of the highest rank. The jade seal bestowed upon Basiba was a seal with a dragon knob, similar in rank to those of the empress, regional secular kings, and princesses.

The Ming emperors also followed the Yuan tradition of bestowing great honors and titles to Tibetan religious leaders. The Fourth Year of Yongle's bestowing titles such as the "Rulai Dabao Fawang" and the Eleventh Year of Yongle's "Zhengjue Dacheng Fawang". All these titles came with their accompanying dragon knob jade seals (Figure 2).

The Ming jade dragon knob seals inherited those of the Yuan style in carving and style of inscriptions on the seals. However, there are slight variations in the Qing period seals but these are inevitable due to the change in the Qing period carving styles and techniques.

From the above, we could see that the "Hongchan Fozong" jade seal (Figure 10) which was lost abroad in the early years is a typical example of the early Ming period style, in terms of its dragon-knob shape and inscriptions.

The Chinese characters engraved on this "Hongchan Fozong" jade seal are the very skilled and masterful *jiudie zhuanshu* (nine-folded seal script). It shows the typical characteristics of the early Ming dynasty. More openwork carving was used on the arch-shaped dragon knob of this seal which also exhibit its Yuan period legacy. This style is quite dissimilar to the later period dragon knob with a more corpulent body.

The four Chinese characters of "Hongchan Fozong" could be translated as "Propagate the Principles of Buddhism". The Yuan and Ming emperors' bestowing such titles with the accompanying dragon knob jade seals was a way to extol and appease these regional religious leaders. The Qing period Celadon Jade seal "Dachan Fozong with chi-dragon knob" (Figure 4) now at the Norbulingka Palace is a good reference example of such jades bestowed by emperors.

It could be seen that this "*Hongchan Fozong*" jade seal was in fact a bestowed seal from the Ming central government to the high-ranking Tibetan Buddhist leaders. When did this seal came to be lost overseas is now difficult to determine. Fortunately, with the appearance of this seal, many of its details conform to the Yuan Ming and Qing period bestowed jade seals now in the Norbulingka Palace collection. This is of vital importance in enhancing the understanding of the history of Chinese seals and the relationship between the central government with the Tibetan regional and religious sectors.

Note: Ou Chaogui, Qi Mei: *Xizang Lidai Changyin (Seals of the Various Periods in Tibet)*, Tibet People's Publishing House, Dec 1991

“弘阐佛宗”与元明朝廷赐印

孙慰祖
上海博物馆

现存元明时代朝廷封赐地方僧俗首领的玉印，以保存于西藏罗布林卡的最为集中。这部分玉印，代表了目前存世的元明两代最高等级的玉印形制体系，是唐至清代玺宝体制演化史研究中连接中间环节的不可或缺的佐证资料。

中原王朝由唐代变革印制，皇帝的玺宝目前没有实物发现。但是，印面增大并形成蹲龙式的印钮，可以由五代后蜀皇帝王建的谥宝上获得推证（图 1）。王建是禁军将领而为唐僖宗封为蜀王，后又自立为帝的，因而他的谥宝本于唐代帝后玺宝的规制是顺理成章的。谥宝印面纵 11.7 厘米、横 10.7 厘米，印钮形态为拱起的蹲龙造型，与代表秦汉帝后玺形态的如“皇后之玺”那样完全盘踞于印台的所谓螭钮已完全不同（图 2）。如此就形成了由唐而下，由上海博物馆藏北宋玉押（图 3）、罗布林卡藏元代“统领释教大元国师”（图 4）、故宫博物院藏明代“天潢演派”（图 5）以及罗布林卡藏明代“如来大宝法王之印”（图 6）和故宫博物院藏清代“天子之宝”（图 7）串联起来的形制演化谱系，钮式由高耸而渐向低伏的变化轨迹是连贯的。

元代的国师，后亦称帝师，地位极为尊崇，忽必烈曾赐国师八思巴号曰“皇天之下，一人之上，开教宣文辅治大圣至德普觉真智佑国如意大宝法王”“西天佛子”“大元帝师”。故元代国师、灌顶国师、大元国师等得赐给最高层级的印材——玉印，钮式亦从帝后、宗王、公主同等的规制，采用龙钮。这一体制是元代最上层崇尚佛教的意识使然，同时也体现了以此加强对吐蕃地区控制的政治方略。此外，元在尊封八思巴为帝师的同时，又封有世俗王位，如泰定间封琐南藏卜为白兰王，赐给金印，位号十分尊贵。(《元史释老传》)

这一体制在明代仍然基本因循。《明太祖实录》载：洪武六年，封故元摄帝师喃加巴藏卜为炽盛佛宝国师，赐玉印。另据史载，有明一代对宗教和地方首领先后封有如来大宝法王、正觉大乘法王至善大慈法王和阐化王、阐教王、护教王、赞善王、辅教王等，又封有国师、大国师、禅师、喇嘛、都、宗教领袖的政策，但采用多封众建的方略，使西藏地方首领和各宗教领袖直接受命于朝廷，

图1　后蜀王建谥宝

图2　皇后之玺

图3　北宋　玉押

图4　元　统领释教大元国师

有利于中央集权政权的巩固。在赐封位号的同时，颁给印章，这是中原印章制度延伸到西藏僧俗社会的重要的历史阶段，也是古代玺印的政治功用的又一拓展。

现存明代赐封藏传佛教领袖人物的印章，自太祖洪武始，代有颁赐，这在《明实录》中多见记载。其中成祖永乐时期制作的玉印尤为精整而具时代特征，如永乐四年封“如来大宝法王”，永乐十一年封“正觉大乘法王”等，皆赐龙钮玉印，与“弘阐佛宗”（图10）相类。现在所见的象牙龙钮“灌顶国师阐化王印”虽为明代制作，但风格与永乐年间记载所赐为“螭钮玉印”不同，应是《明世宗实录》所载嘉靖年间帕莫竹巴第悉劄思巴箚失坚参受封为阐化王时赐印。

明代朝廷制作的各级正式官号印，体格严谨，多以采用九叠篆文为规制（图9）。从罗布林卡所藏的元明玉印来看，其琢治印文的工艺亦力求取得与铜印同样的风格。宽边细文，笔画方折竣拔，文字空腔深凹，乃沿袭元代工艺。至清代中期玉质玺宝文字多已略见转折浑脱。此种工艺上的细微差异，乃时代书风演变与制作人技法传承更替所形成，是难以逆转的。

由上述文字、形制细部演化脉胳的回顾，我们可以看到早年流失海外的“弘阐佛宗”，文字及钮式属于典型的明代工艺风格，可以确定为当时朝廷赐封地方某宗教领袖之物。

图 5　明　天潢演派

图 6　明　如来大宝法王之印
长 12.8 厘米，宽 12.8 厘米，高 8.7 厘米

图 7　二十五宝 - 青玉“天子之宝”

图 8　元　统领释教大元国师
边长 11 厘米，高 11.4 厘米

图 9　明　灵山卫中千户所百户印

图 10　明　弘阐佛宗

此印印文四字，九叠篆笔形方峻端严，字腔深入，琢制精整，应该说年代标志是鲜明的。玉印的钮式造型中间略为隆起，形体更多缕空雕刻，明显地保留元代的风格元素，与后期趋向丰满敦厚的龙钮形态则存在较大差异，故将此印定位于明代前期，可以说是无庸置疑的。

“弘阐佛宗”意谓弘大开显佛法之宗旨。《尔雅·释诂》谓“弘”：大也。疏：弘者，含容之大也。《易·坤·象》：含弘光大。《论语》曰：人能弘道。佛教有“弘教”术语，义为弘扬教法。又，《易·丰卦·象》孔颖达正义：“阐者，弘广之言，凡物之大，其有二种，一者自然之大，一者由人之阐弘使大。”元明颁给地方佛教领袖的封号，多有称颂嘉美之义。罗布林卡藏清代螭钮青玉印“大阐佛宗”，其义可与“弘阐佛宗”相为参证。

我由此进一步推断，这件玉印应为明代中央政府赐予藏传佛教上层人物的封号印。至于何以失群、流散，则与包括帝后玺宝在内的元、明两代高等级宫廷玉印在动荡变迁之中不知所终一样，已经无从考究。所幸的是，此印的保存与公开发表，得以与西藏罗布林卡所藏元明清三朝赐印资料汇合，互为印证，获得比较明确的断代结论，这不啻为天作之合，对于中国印史以及中原王朝与西藏地区政治、宗教关系的研究，都具有重要的价值。

002 A celadon and white jade dragon finial

Yuan/Ming Dynasty (1271–1644)
Length 8.3cm, Width 4.7cm, Height 12cm
Provided by The Institute of Qing History Renmin University of China

This is a pale celadon jade censer finial with some light russet markings and high relief carving of a dragon pursuing a pearl amid the clouds together with sea wave patterns at the bottom. The skill of carving of this large censer finial was exquisite.

青白玉龙纹钮

元至明（1271—1644年）
长8.3厘米，宽4.7厘米，高12厘米
中国人民大学清史研究所提供

云龙纹玉炉钮玉质青白，莹润带沁色。高浮雕海水江崖纹于底部，通体雕祥云纹，苍龙盘旋其中，四爪腾于云中，口吐祥瑞，逐龙珠于祥云之间。炉钮通常指香炉盖上的装饰，随着元代以后香炉地位的不断提高，工匠们在制作香炉时结合了更多的装饰与镶嵌工艺。此龙纹钮不仅尺寸硕大，且雕工与造型均为同一时期不可多见之佳作。

003 An archaistic white jade *gui* with dragon shaped handles with "Zi Gang" seal and mark

Ming Dynasty (1368-1644)
Length 12cm, Width 7cm, Height 7cm
The collection of the Summer Palace

The shape imitates the ancient bronze gui with two flanking dragon handles and the "Zi Gang" inscription at the foot. Zi Gang was an eminent Suzhou jade carving artist active during the Jiajing to Wanli period in the Ming dynasty.

白玉『子冈』款兽面纹龙耳簋

明（1368—1644年）
长12厘米，宽7厘米，高7厘米
颐和园藏

白玉质，有绺。仿青铜器簋造型，深膛，圆撇口，圈足。饰龙耳一对，器身雕仿古兽面纹饰。足底阴刻篆书『子冈』款。子冈，是明嘉靖、万历年间活跃于苏州一带的玉雕名家。

004 A celadon jade carving of cup with handles

Ming Dynasty (1368-1644)
Length 12cm, Width 7.5cm, Height 4cm
The collection of the Summer Palace

This round cup has some cracks and an encircling line of grain patterns in its outer body with two flanking dragon handles. The inner center has a "Shou" (longevity) character carved within a circle.

青玉『寿』字谷纹龙耳杯

明（1368—1644年）
长12厘米，宽7.5厘米，高4厘米
颐和园藏

青玉质，有绺裂。玉杯圆形，内侧掏膛后打磨光滑。外壁环绕谷纹一周，正中一圆圈内雕刻『寿』字。两侧透雕龙耳一对，单角卷尾，用于持拿。圈足矮小，形似玉璧。

005 An imperial pale celadon jade "ziqiang buxi" seal

Qing Dynasty, Qianlong Period (1736-1795)
Length 4.9cm, Width 4.9cm, Height 6.5cm
Provided by The Institute of Qing History Renmin University of China

This large square imperial seal was one of the seals made to celebrate Emperor Qianlong's eightieth birthday. With the inscription of "Ziqiang Buxi" (striving constantly to be stronger), this was one of the seals in a three-seal set.

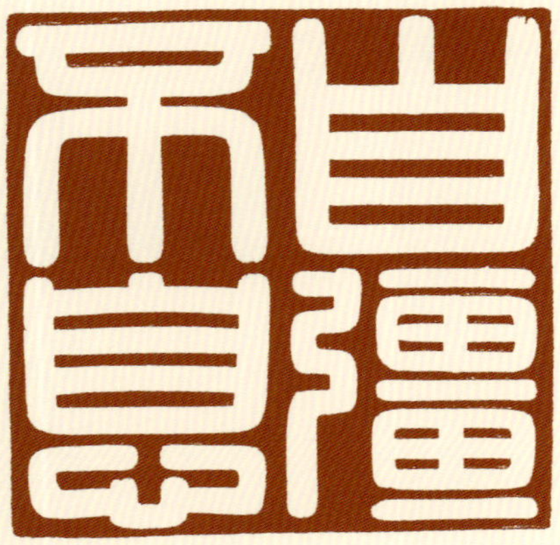

"乾隆宝薮"局部

青白玉『自强不息』玺

清乾隆（1736—1795年）
长4.9厘米，宽4.9厘米，高6.5厘米
中国人民大学清史研究所提供

青白玉质。玉质莹润密实，印钮以镂雕仿宋龙钮式样，阴刻篆书『自强不息』四字。

此方玉玺正是乾隆皇帝为庆贺自己八十大寿而特地定制的一众宝玺之一，是主宝『八徵耄念之宝』的副宝。常见将主宝『八徵耄念之宝』、副宝『自强不息』与另一枚引首宝相配，成为三方一套的组玺，其中较为集中使用过的是『嚮用五福』为引首宝印文。『八徵耄念』『嚮用五福』『自强不息』的固定搭配所体现的正是乾隆皇帝年高德劭之际，得意而又自我鞭策的心境。

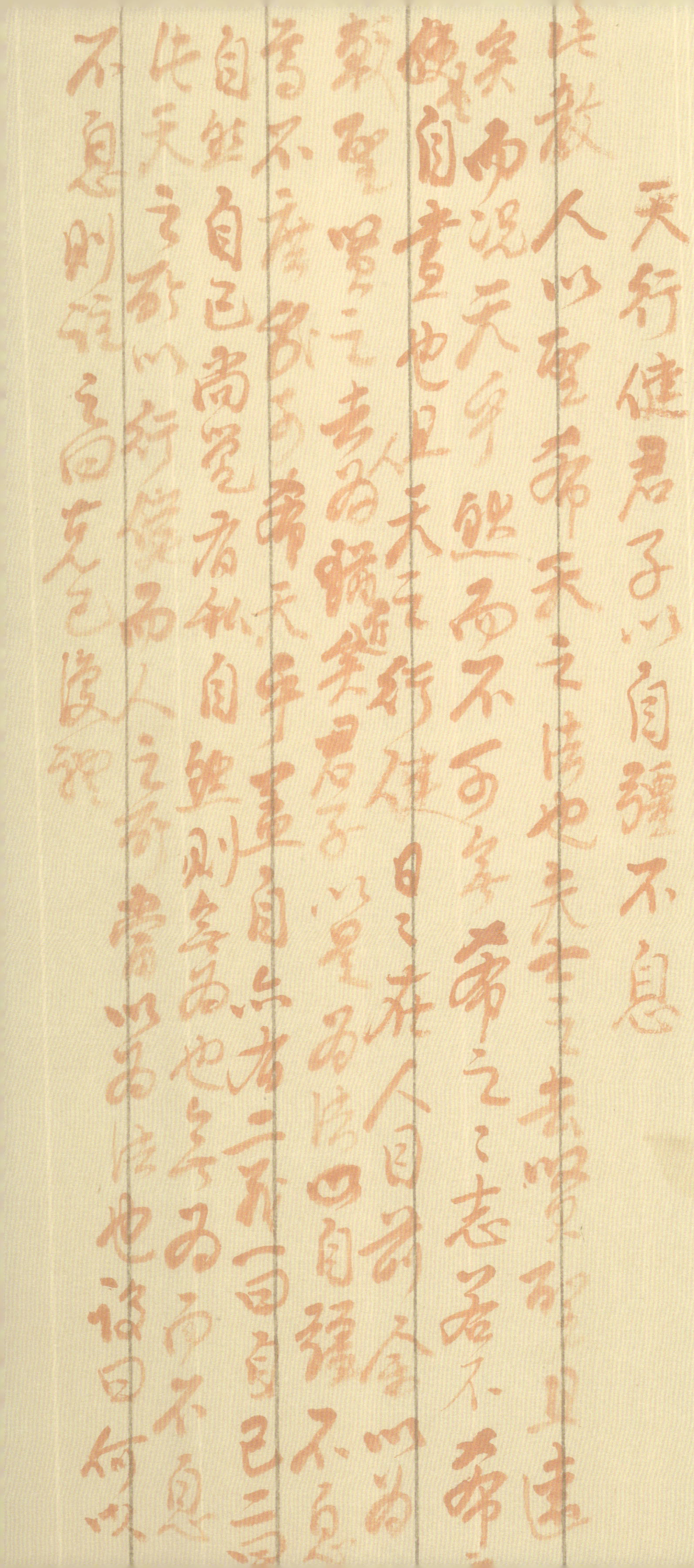

自强不息

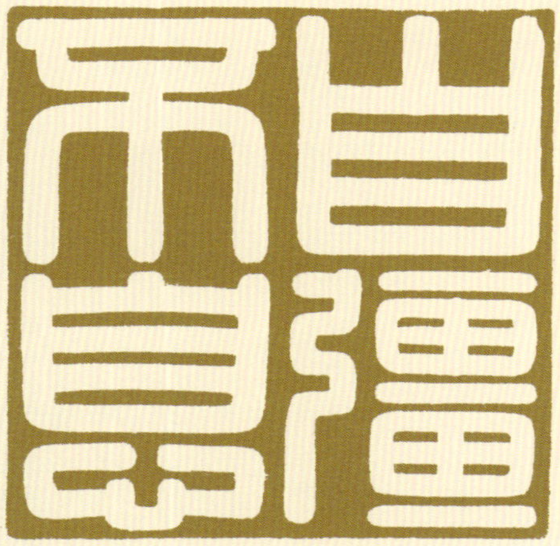

06 A celadon jade caving of double dragons seal

Qing Dynasty, Qianlong Period (1736-1795)
Length 12.8cm, Width 12.8cm, Height 10.7cm
The collection of the Summer Palace

There are speckles on this celadon jade square seal. Two opposite crawling dragons are carved in the round at the top. The seal surface is smooth but inscriptions are absent.

青玉交龙纽玺

清乾隆（1736—1795年）
长12.8厘米，宽12.8厘米，高10.7厘米
颐和园藏

青玉质，青绿色中夹有斑点。玺纽以圆雕、浮雕、浅刻等技法雕刻两条爬伏状龙，龙首方向相背，双脊同身，龙睛圆睁，嘴微张，鬓须飘逸，神态威严。玺印呈正方形，光素润洁，印面无铭文。

007 An important celadon jade carving of vat with dragon and clouds

Qing Dynasty, Qianlong Period (1736–1795)
Length 55cm, Width 41cm, Height 25cm
The collection of the Summer Palace

This large vat with light russet markings was made from a single piece of jade material. The outer body was carved with sea waves and cloud dragon in relief. The inner bottom of the vat was engraved with a poem of Emperor Qianlong together with the seal mark of "Qianlong Chenhan"

青玉乾隆御题云龙纹瓮

清乾隆（1736—1795年）
长55厘米，宽41厘米，高25厘米
颐和园藏

青玉质，局部有浅褐色玉皮。器形硕大，为一整块玉料制成，挖海棠形深腹，外壁浮雕海水云龙，扬爪腾身，出没于惊涛骇浪之中。内底琢刻隶书乾隆御制诗文：『云宛流兮龙见行，品诚称美制尤精。轻浮叆叇容将布，动出之而态若生。本以无形思蕴石，忽成有象拟连城。六清醴齐奚堪置，祇和尧年宝露盛。乾隆丁酉春，御题。』阴刻方形篆书『乾隆宸翰』印章。

雲宛流
芳龍見行品
誠稱美製尤精
輕浮靉靆容將斧動出
之而態若生本以無形
思蘊石忽成有象擬連
城六清醴齊奚堪置祗
合恭承寶露盛
乾隆丁酉春
御題

乾隆宸翰

008 A white jade carving of brush washer with dragon and clouds

Qing Dynasty, Qianlong Period (1736–1795)
Diameter 13.5cm, Height 7cm
The collection of the Summer Palace

This white jade washer has a deep belly for the storage of water. The outer belly has cloud dragon carved in the round. The bottom has scrolling clouds in relief.

白玉云龙纹洗

清乾隆（1736—1795 年）
直径 13.5 厘米，高 7 厘米
颐和园藏

白玉质。椭圆形唇口，深腹，内空可贮水。腹外环绕采用圆雕技法雕刻云龙纹饰，底部浮雕卷云纹。

009 A pale green jade "dragon and young" group

Qing Dynasty, Qianlong Period (1736–1795)
Length 14.5cm, Width 4.5cm, Height 13cm
Provided by The Institute of Qing History Renmin University of China

This display object is carved with a dragon wriggling on sea waves and underneath auspicious clouds. A young dragon popping up on the sea waves gazing at the larger dragon. This theme was common in the Qianlong period alluding the fatherly love of "dragon teaching his son".

青白玉苍龙教子摆件

清乾隆（1736—1795年）
长14.5厘米，宽4.5厘米，高13厘米
中国人民大学清史研究所提供

玉质白中闪青，圆雕苍龙翻腾于海水江崖之上，盘旋于祥云之间，下方一条幼龙微探于海浪之上，大龙俯视小龙，威严肃穆，小龙昂首凝视大龙，将苍龙教子的场景表现得淋漓尽致。苍龙教子是乾隆时期较为常见的题材，寓意父爱如山，望子成龙。

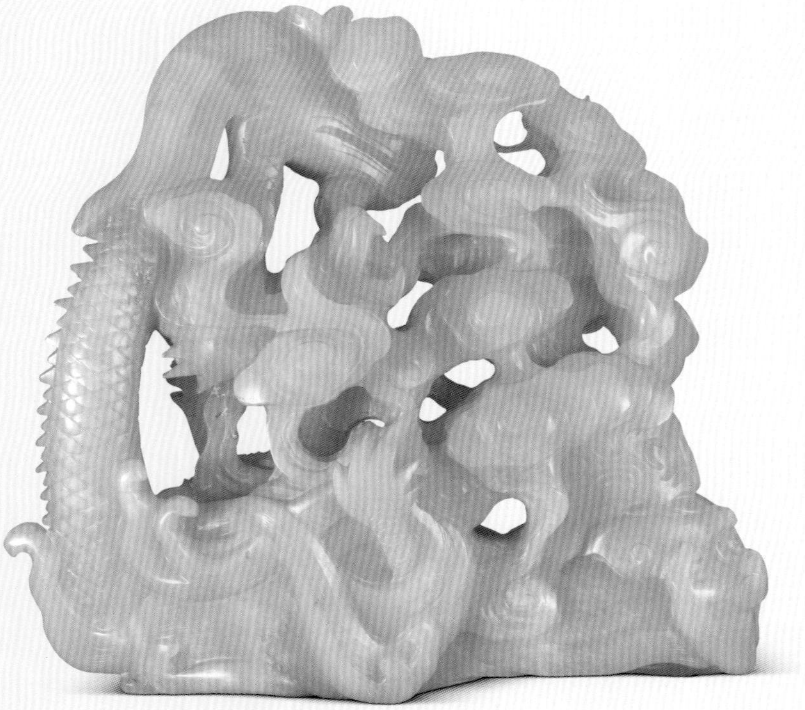

010 A pale celadon jade "lingzhi" libation cup

Qing Dynasty, Qianlong Period (1736-1795)
Height 19cm, Mouth diameter 16.5cm
Provided by The Institute of Qing History Renmin University of China

The whole jade gong was carved with the high relief technique representing the archetype style of the Qing court workshop. The foot was carved with lingzhi in the round. The rim has a large dragon with two smaller dragons underneath alluding the "dragon teaching his on" concept conforming to the Confucianist ideals much practiced by the Qing imperial family.

青白玉灵芝龙纹觥

清乾隆（1736—1795 年）
高 19 厘米，口径 16.5 厘米
中国人民大学清史研究所提供

青白玉质。整件器物均使用高浮雕手法，属于典型的清代宫廷风格，杯足高浮雕灵芝数朵，杯身饰两小螭龙，另有蝙蝠振翅。整体上宽下窄，随料雕大如意型，口沿盘踞戏珠苍龙，大龙威严，两小龙在其下，有苍龙教子之意，体现了清代皇家秉奉『君臣父子』的儒家治国思想。底部八枚灵芝，杯体自成一枚灵芝，九灵芝寓意『九如』，为祝寿之词。此器形似犀角杯亦有祝寿之意。

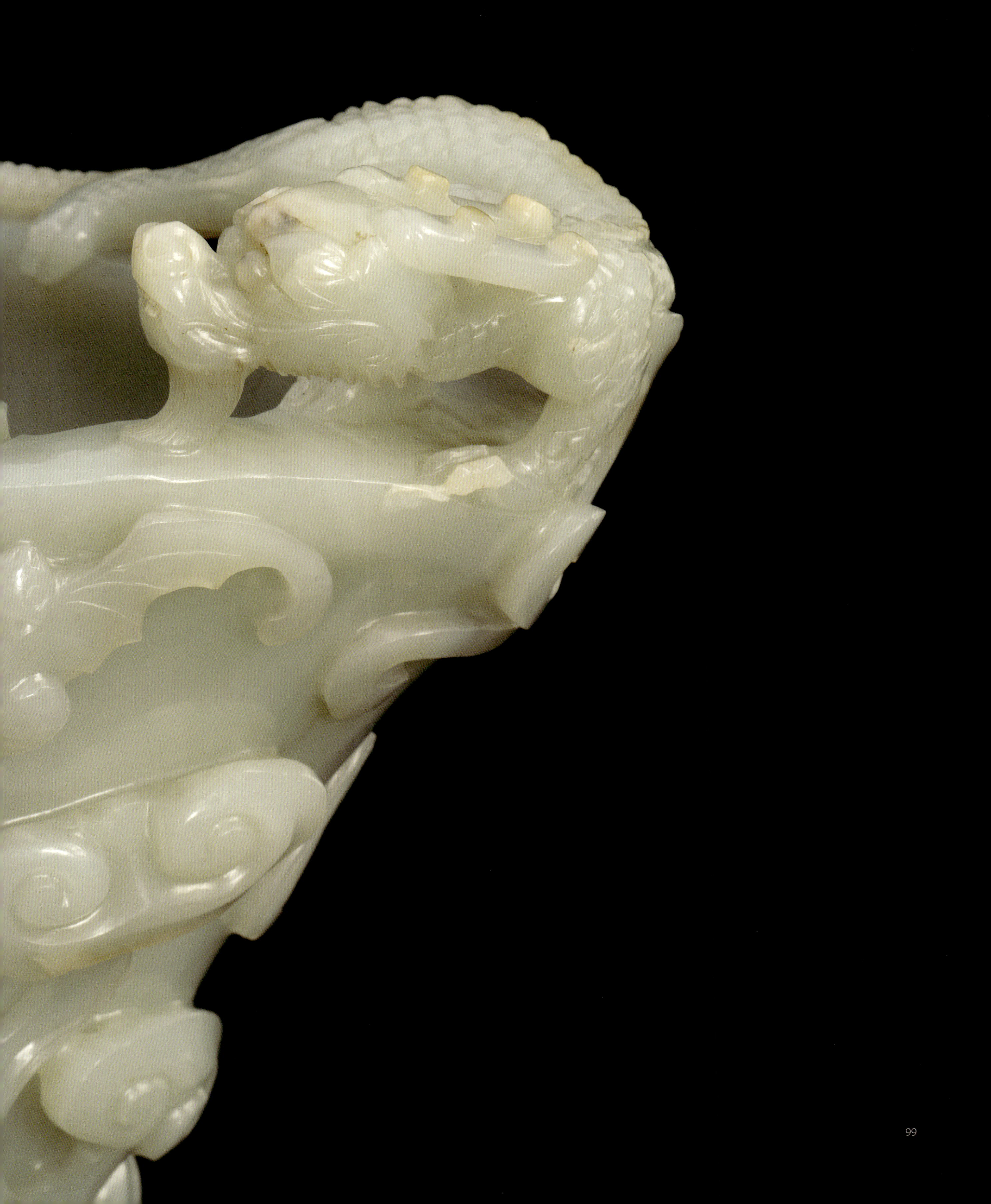

A spinach jade carving of dragon censer

Qing Dynasty, Qianlong Period (1736–1795)
Length 16.8cm, Width 9.6cm, Height 15cm
The collection of the Summer Palace

This spinach jade censer is four-footed and squarish in shape. The lid and the feet are carved with chi-dragons. The body also has two flanking chi-dragon head handles each attached with a loose ring.

碧玉雕龙双环方炉

清乾隆（1736—1795年）
长16.8厘米，宽9.6厘米，高15厘米
颐和园藏

碧玉质，局部有黑色斑点。该器呈方形，盖上镂雕趴伏状螭龙，脚下雕螭龙，两侧雕有二螭首耳，耳衔活环。炉体为四柱形，底足收敛。器身雕螭龙、番莲、团寿纹。此器为焚香道具。

012 A white jade carving of vase with cover and handles

Qing Dynasty, Qianlong Period (1736-1795)
Length 11.7cm, Width 4.2cm, Height 29cm
The collection of the Summer Palace

This oblate lidded vase was flanked with two handles each attached with a loose ring and a square foot. The belly was carved with dragon patterns while the underbelly with lotus-petals.

肩，深腹，方圈足。盖饰云雷纹，盖纽为短提手状，左右各饰活环；平口，束颈，饰蕉叶纹，颈侧饰环形兽耳，耳配活环，腹中饰龙纹，腹下部饰莲瓣纹。

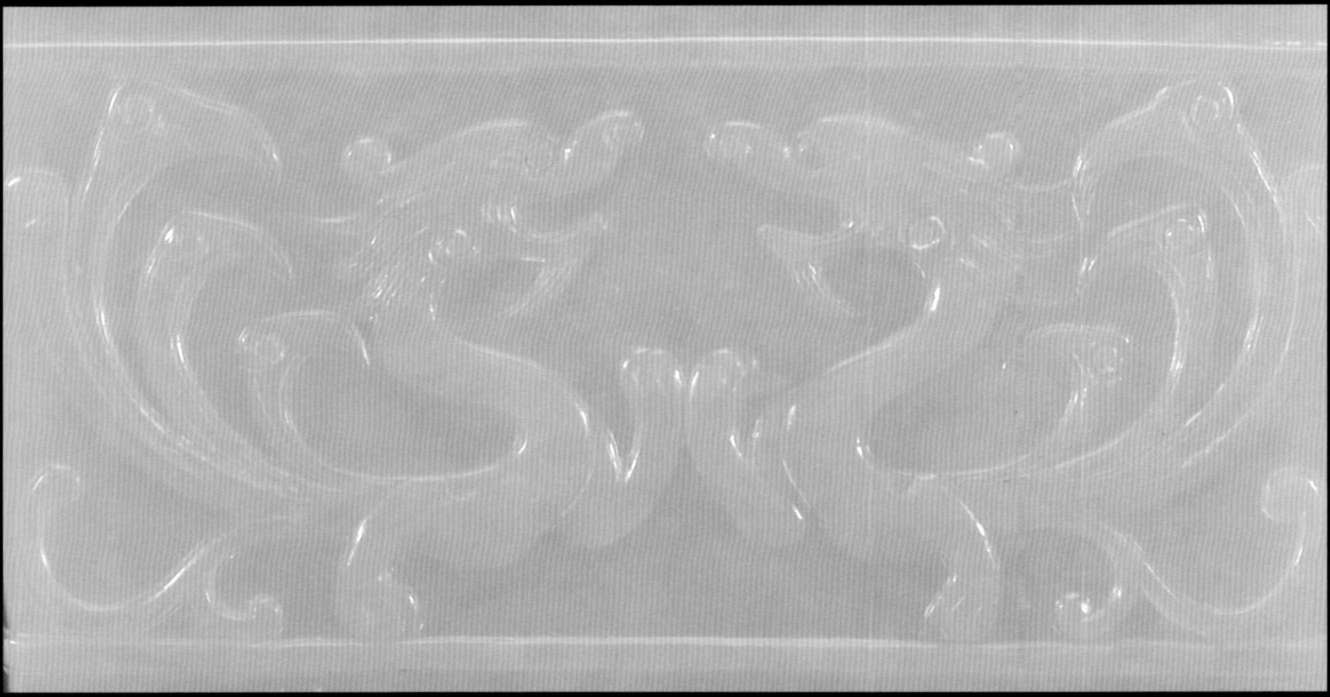

013 A white jade carving plaque with dragon and phoenix

Qing Dynasty, Qianlong Period (1736–1795)
Length 16cm, Width 9cm, Height 33cm
The collection of the Summer Palace

This is a plaque ornament with blunt corners and nine winding chi-dragons carved in the pierced openwork technique. The plaque ornament is equipped with a hard wood screen stand.

白玉雕龙纹佩

清乾隆（1736—1795年）
长16厘米，宽9厘米，高33厘米
颐和园藏

白玉质。此器呈片状倭角椭圆形佩，以减地阳起镂空的技法雕琢九条玲珑剔透、盘曲缠绕的螭龙，线条疏朗，生动逼真。屏芯下配有硬木屏架。

014 A white jade table screen with landscape and figures

Qing Dynasty, Qianlong Period (1736–1795)
Length 8.5cm, Width 0.3cm, Height 11.5cm
The collection of the Summer Palace

This table screen is rectangular in shape with landscape and a scholar carving and a royal poem on one side and sea waves and cloud dragon on the other side. The jade screen is accompanied by a hard wood stand.

白玉刻御制诗山水龙纹插屏

清乾隆（1736—1795年）
长8.5厘米，宽0.3厘米，高11.5厘米
颐和园藏

白玉质。屏芯呈长方形，正面阴刻山水楼阁，一书生于书斋内欣赏美景。屏芯右上侧雕刻御制诗：『江南山色四时青，只有群芳别性灵。底识春归花坞里，锦烟轻喷麝檀馨。御制诗，臣王杰敬书。』刻『臣』『杰』二字章。屏芯背面阴刻海水云龙。该器雕工洗练，寥寥数笔，刻画出山间恬静之美，意境深远。玉屏下配有硬木屏架。

江南山色四時青衹
有羣芳别性靈處識
者歸苍隖裡錦煙輕
噴麝檀馨
御製詩
臣王杰敬書

015 A white jade carving of flower receptacle with dragon and boy

Qing Dynasty, Qianlong Period (1736–1795)
Length 10cm, Width 4cm, Height 12cm
The collection of the Summer Palace

This is an oblate shaped flower receptacle with the outer wall carved with a boy holding ruyi in one hand and pearls on the other. A cloud dragon is carved at the side with a chi-dragon popping its head out of the sea.

白玉仙童戏龙花插

清乾隆（1736—1795 年）
长 10 厘米，宽 4 厘米，高 12 厘米
颐和园藏

白玉质。整料雕琢扁圆形笔筒，唇口，筒外壁雕一仙童，一手持如意，一手持灵珠，向外高举；一侧镂雕龙纹，腾云驾雾，龙首朝向灵珠；下方雕一螭龙，头部从海浪中探出。

016 White jade belt buckle with openwork carving of dragon

Yuan Dynasty (1206–1368)
Length 5.8cm, Width 4.7cm, Height 1.5cm
The collection of Beijing Art Museum

The belt buckle with some russet markings is rectangular in shape with blunt corners. It has a multilayered openwork carving of dragon amid peonies. There are a pair of perforated holes in each of the four corners. This belt buckle ornament is a standard design of dragon amid peonies pattern of the Yuan period.

白玉镂雕龙纹带饰

元（1206—1368年）
长5.8厘米，宽4.7厘米，厚1.5厘米
北京艺术博物馆藏

青白玉质，局部略带土黄色沁。带饰整体作委角长方形，正面略弧凸，多层镂雕龙穿牡丹纹，背面内凹，四角各有一对穿孔。龙侧视，口大张，长眉瞪目，双角后伸，长发分作两股，细颈，肩、臀颇富肌肉感；一前肢抬起，另一前肢撑起身体；两后肢呈弓字步，尾上翘。龙身周围花朵和叶枝环绕。

在玉雕中，龙与花卉纹饰相结合，始于宋元时期，明代也比较多见。元代玉龙颈细身粗，琢刻粗放有力，图案具有立体感。龙的姿态常表现为穿行于花木之中的行龙和蹲龙，此带饰为典型的元代龙穿牡丹样式。

017 Rhyton with five dragons libation cup

Song/Yuan Dynasty (960–1368)
Length 11cm, Width 8cm, Height 21cm
Provided by The Institute of Qing History Renmin University of China

The rhyton was originated from West Asia and came during the Han to Tang periods. The shape is quite similar to the gong bronze libation cup of the Shang dynasty. The body of this rhyton was carved with the taotie pattern and five chi-dragons in high relief. This vessel was made in the Song to Yuan period although the inner body was later carved with a Qing imperial inscription of "Daoguang Xinmao Yuci Tingchengyan".

青灰玉饕餮纹螭龙觥

宋至元（960—1368年）
长11厘米，宽8厘米，高21厘米
中国人民大学清史研究所提供

灰白玉质，选料大而完整。器型由汉唐时期西亚来通杯（又称角杯，Rhyton）演变而来，工艺造型与商代觥杯相类，整体风格与汉代玉质觥杯一脉相承，与广州南越王墓出土的玉觥相类，通体满雕蟠虺纹，有饕餮纹隐于其中，高浮雕五条螭龙，攀于杯口与杯身，底部雕一龙首收口，呈瞠目张口状。内膛砣刻隶书『道光辛卯御赐廷臣宴』。为宋元时期的仿古佳作，刻文可推断为清宫旧藏。

018 A spinach jade rhyton *gong*

Qing Dynasty, Qianlong Period (1736–1795)
Diameter 10.2cm, Length 16.5cm
Provided by The Institute of Qing History Renmin University of China

This rhyton imitates the shape of the Shang period elephant-head gong with the elephant head as the base and the ivory tusks and trunk forming a tripod base support. The outer wall was carved with three chi-dragons in high relief. The bottom of this vessel has a gold gilded inscription of "Qianlong Nian Zhi" (made in the reign of Qianlong).

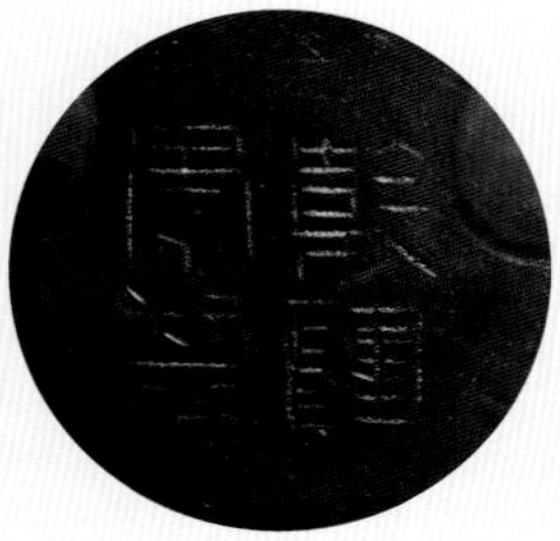

碧玉仿古螭龙纹觥

清乾隆（1736—1795年）
直径10.2厘米，高16.5厘米
中国人民大学清史研究所提供

碧玉质，有黑色碳斑。整料雕琢，以商周时期青铜象首觥为蓝本，象首作杯底，象牙与象鼻呈三足鼎立状，面向下，象耳呈如意状置于两侧，期间阴刻双目，象鼻自然蜷于一侧，鼻上镂空雕仿古瑞象呈手柄状。杯壁四周高浮雕三条螭龙，左右各一条，另有一条攀探于杯口。杯身饰汉式仿古勾云纹，杯底部砣刻鎏金『乾隆年制』四字篆书款。觥原指古代用兽角做的酒器，后为流行于商代晚期至西周早期的青铜器。汉人用『觥筹交错』来形容宫廷酒会之盛况，此玉觥为乾隆时期以碧玉仿商周青铜器的慕古佳作。

A spinach jade rhyton *gong*

Qing Dynasty, Qianlong Period (1736–1795)
Length 7.5cm, Width 6.2cm, Height 11.7cm
The collection of the Summer Palace

This vessel imitates the shape of the ancient rhinoceros-cup. The upper body was carved with openwork panchi (ancient mythical beasts) and the lower body with a dragon head.

碧玉螭纹觥

清乾隆（1736—1795年）
长7.5厘米，宽6.2厘米，高11.7厘米
颐和园藏

碧玉质。整料雕琢，仿古犀角杯造形。器呈上宽下窄的不规则柱形，中空，上部镂空雕蟠螭纹。下部凸雕龙头，龙发上披于器另一侧，龙角构成器足。

020 An archaistic pale celadon and russet jade vase and cover

Qing Dynasty, Qianlong Period (1736–1795)
Length 10.5cm, Width 8cm, Height 27.5cm
Provided by The Institute of Qing History Renmin University of China

The pale celadon vase has some russet markings and two opposite beast-head handles with loose rings. The belly was fully carved with panhui (coiled serpent) patterns. The vase imitates the shape of the Spring and Autumn period bronze vase.

白玉仿古蟠螭纹兽耳瓶

清乾隆（1736—1795年）
长10.5厘米，宽8厘米，高27.5厘米
中国人民大学清史研究所提供

白玉质，留红皮。籽玉圆雕整挖，掏膛均匀，颈部高浮雕饕餮纹饰，两侧兽首耳带活环，腹部浮雕蟠螭纹，盖顶圆雕蟠螭纹。造型纹饰取法春秋时期蟠龙纹青铜方壶，巧用籽料红皮仿作青铜斑驳，惟妙惟肖，是不可多得的乾隆时期宫廷仿古佳作。

021 A white jade *gui disk* with chilong

Qing Dynasty, Qianlong Period (1736–1795)
Length 14.5cm, Width11cm, Height 0.5cm
The collection of the Summer Palace

The body of this disk was carved with chi-dragons. The Guibi (gui disk) was used by the ancient emperors as a ritual object.

白玉螭龙纹圭璧

清乾隆（1736—1795年）
长14.5厘米，宽11厘米，高0.5厘米
颐和园藏

白玉质，上雕螭龙纹。圭璧是古代帝王、诸侯祭祀或朝聘时所用的一种礼器。

022 A rare large pale green and russet jade "lingzhi and chilong" libation cup

Yuan/ Ming Dynasty (1271–1644)
Length 16.5cm, Width 9.6cm, Height 8.6cm
Provided by The Institute of Qing History Renmin University of China

The Yi libation cup was scattered with yellowish gold markings and carved with the relief and openwork techniques. The body was adorned with ruyi and lingzhi patterns while two chi-dragons were carved encircling the mouth of the cup with another three chi-dragons swirling amid lingzhi.

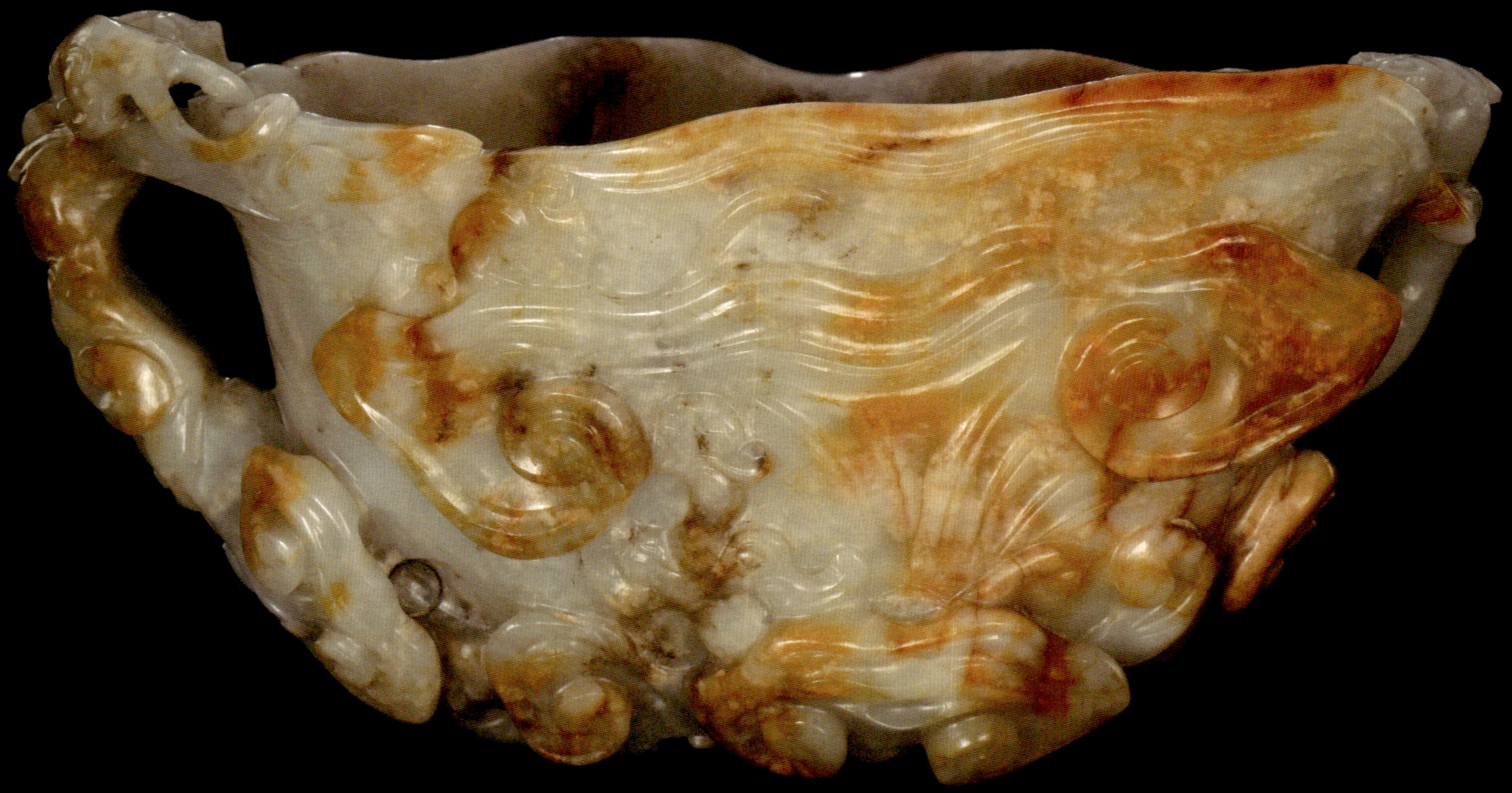

青白玉俏色螭龙纹玉匜

元至明（1271—1644年）
长16.5厘米，宽9.6厘米，高8.6厘米
中国人民大学清史研究所提供

玉质青灰，通体棕金色皮。整料雕琢，采用浮雕与镂空雕刻相结合的手法，杯体以如意灵芝装饰，其中一枝巧雕为手柄，两条螭龙盘于杯口，手柄上方与对面杯口各一条，另有三条螭龙蜿蜒穿梭于灵芝之间。传说螭龙为龙子之一好酒贪杯，常饰于各式宫廷酒器杯具之上以添饮用之趣。整件玉杯寓意吉祥添寿，为慕古佳作。

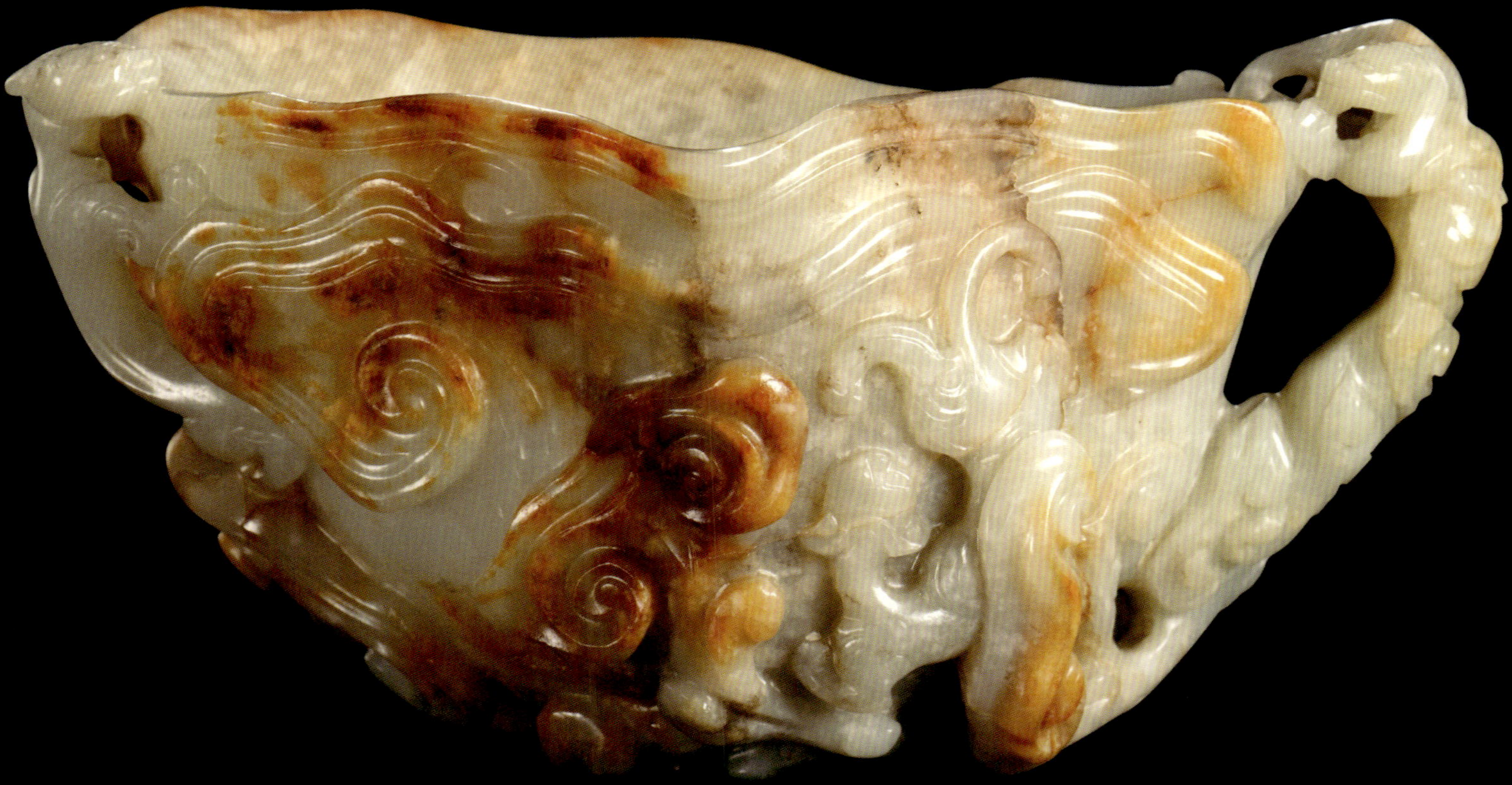

023 A superb archaistic spinach-green jade pendant

Qing Dynasty, Qianlong Period (1736-1795)
Length 7.3cm, Width 5.2cm, Height 0.5cm
Provided by The Institute of Qing History Renmin University of China

The spinach green jade has some blackish mineral markings with carvings of five auspicious beasts: a kui-dragon, three chi-dragons and an aolong. The chicken-heart shaped pendant first appeared in the Shang and flourished in the two Han periods.

碧玉仿汉鸡心佩

清乾隆（1736—1795年）
长7.3厘米，宽5.2厘米，高0.5厘米
中国人民大学清史研究所提供

碧玉质，内含黑色斑。鸡心佩又名韘型佩，起于商周盛于两汉，上端出尖，椭圆形玉佩中穿圆孔，与鸡心相类。五只神兽交错蟠绕于圆孔四周。上方雕一夔龙一螭龙，右侧一只小螭龙，圆孔正下方雕一螯龙，玉佩底部雕另一螭龙。五只龙形态各异，首尾相交，背部阴刻仿汉云纹。传说龙凤韘形佩是西楚霸王项羽与虞姬的定情信物，此韘形佩为乾隆宫廷仿汉之佳作。

024 A celadon jade carving of double chilong and lingzhi

Yuan Dynasty (1206–1368)
Length 8.2cm, Width 6cm, Height 1.4cm
The collection of Beijing Art Museum

The surface of this oval shaped ornament has some greyish-white markings and some crackles. Two recumbent chi-dragons, one large and one small, were carved using the high relief and openwork technique. The chi-dragon pattern flourished in the Han period but dwindled in popularity in later periods. It later came back in vogue with the popularity of the fanggu (imitating antiquity) wares and the "double chi-dragon holding lingzhi in mouth" became a popular design pattern in the Yuan period.

青玉双螭衔灵芝纹饰件

元（1206—1368年）
长8.2厘米，宽6厘米，厚1.4厘米
北京艺术博物馆藏

玉色青绿，表面有灰白色沁和绺纹。器整体作椭圆形，正面略弧凸，以浮雕镂雕手法饰口衔灵芝的大小两螭。背面平，中部原有一孔，现已被物填实。双螭呈伏卧状，肩宽身细，背部阴刻脊线并于两侧各饰成组双横线，后肢一足在前一足在后，歧尾，一股长一股短，自一后腿下穿过并回卷，四爪尖利。大螭发分两股，上饰细密阴线，以短细阴线刻粗眉；小螭头上光素，以单阴线饰眉。

螭纹是汉代玉器的代表性纹饰，但在汉以后迅速消逝，直至仿古玉兴起，螭纹作为一种仿古纹饰再度流行。元代螭纹特点为身体细长弯曲，头上五官集中在前部，占四分之一位置，长发后披，肘与臂有螺旋纹等。双螭衔灵芝为元代流行的纹饰。元代雕刻延续了宋金时期分层为景的特点，主体纹饰琢刻蜿蜒交错，主次分明，立体感强。

025 A celadon and white jade chilong and lingzhi finial

Yuan Dynasty (1206–1368)
Length 3.6cm, Width 2.2cm, Height 3.7cm
The collection of Beijing Art Museum

The ornament has the shape of a Chinese mantou (bun) with some crackles and brown markings. It came with a wooden stand. The two chi-dragons of almost similar sizes were carved in the three-dimensional openwork technique.

青白玉螭衔灵芝纹玉纽

元（1206—1368年）
长3.6厘米，宽2.2厘米，厚3.7厘米
北京艺术博物馆藏

青玉质，有绺裂及褐色斑点。器呈馒头形，带木托，以立体镂雕加饰阴刻线的技法琢双螭衔灵芝纹。双螭造型基本相同：立耳，发后披，扭身，歧尾，嘴叼灵芝根，灵芝如卷云状，大而肥。

双螭衔灵芝为元代流行的纹饰，既有平面纹饰，也有如此器一样的圆雕立体样式。玉器纽流行于元明之际，清代亦有少量制作。玉器纽饰在元代是否作为帽顶装饰曾引起过学术界的讨论，明清时期，玉器纽常见嵌于木托上，装饰于香炉等文房陈设器之上。

026 A white jade carving of phoenix pendant

Song/Ming Dynasty (960-1644)
Length 5.2cm, Width 7.7cm, Height 2.1cm
Provided by The Institute of Qing History Renmin University of China

The pendant ornament has some very pale red markings with a phoenix carved in the round. The phoenix (Fenghuang) was an auspicious bird normally presented in pairs. The male bird was called Feng while the female was Huang. In the Ming and Qing periods, the phoenix was always depicted together with the dragon and were popular in the imperial wares signifying the harmonious union within the Royal family and the imperial court.

白玉凤纹带饰

宋至明（960—1644年）
长5.2厘米，宽7.7厘米，高2.1厘米
中国人民大学清史研究所提供

白玉质，边缘略带红沁。圆雕凤凰，曲颈回首，圆目核眼，双翅回扣，头颈部翅端均饰有仿汉谷纹，凤冠绶带垂于颈部一侧，尾部回蜷于右侧翼下。双足卧于胸口，整件玉佩线条优美流畅，凤凰体态雍容，翎羽分明，阴刻羽翼层次丰富多变。凤凰，为雌雄相伴的一对神鸟，雄为『凤』，雌为『凰』。明清两代，多与龙纹相伴，为皇廷恭制器皿之常见纹样，寓意皇家内廷合和之意。

027 A white jade caving of phoenix water pot

Ming Dynasty (1368–1644)
Length 10cm, Width 6cm, Height 4cm
Provided by The Institute of Qing History Renmin University of China

This waterpot has some russet markings and a phoenix carved in the round. The encircling phoenix holds a lingzhi in the mouth. This pattern signifies peace and happiness together with good fortune. The phoenix was recognized as having a noble and elevated quality. As an object used in the studio or study, the scholar is also alluded to having a noble and dignified character.

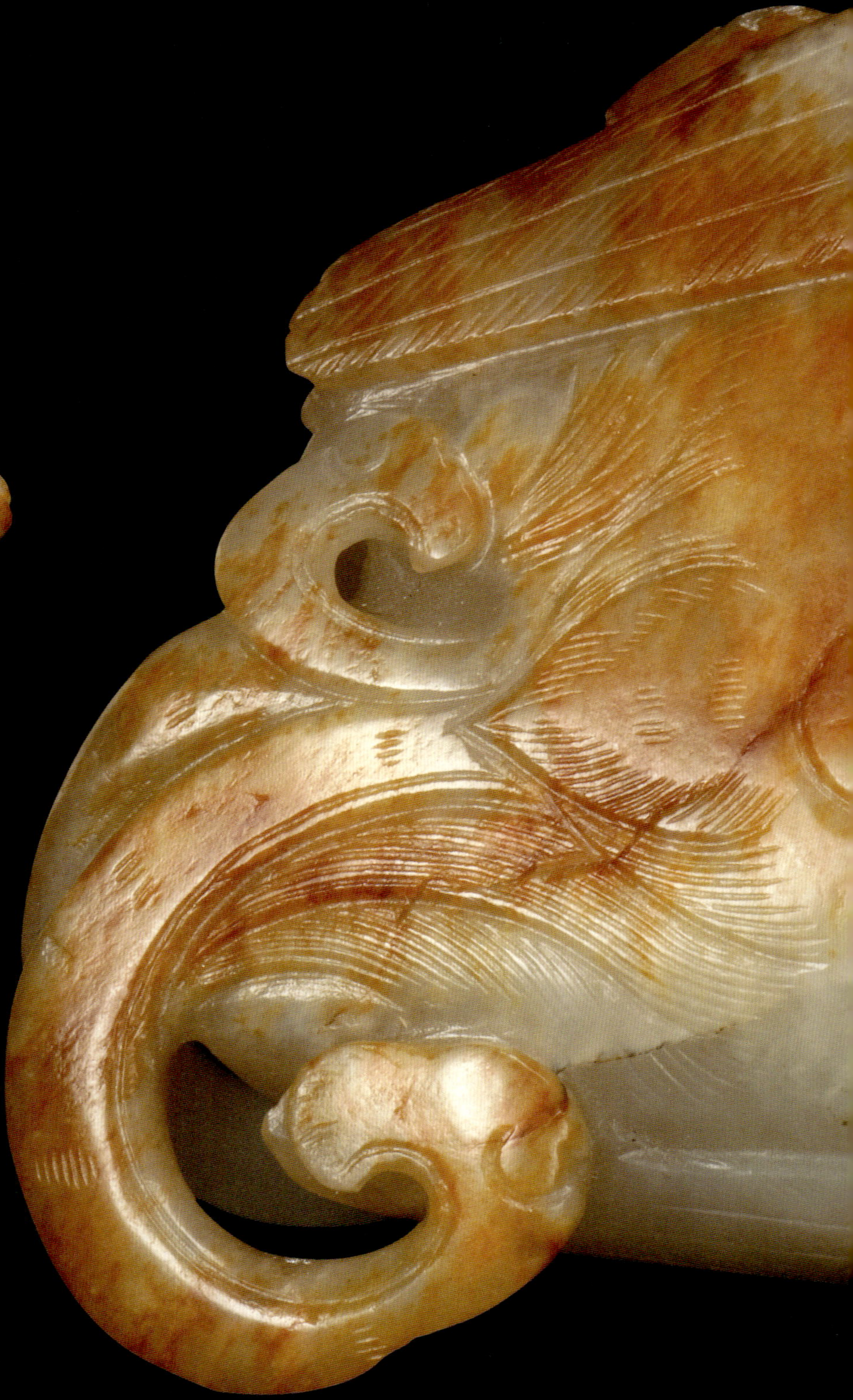

白玉凤凰水盂

明（1368—1644年）

长10厘米，宽6厘米，高4厘米

中国人民大学清史研究所提供

白玉质，籽料留红皮，圆孔居中，掏膛匀称，皮壳厚重。随形圆雕一凤凰，内胆掏空呈一水盂，口有唇沿，打磨光滑细腻。凤凰呈蜷卧状首尾相照，衔灵芝一束，头戴红冠，双爪紧扣赤竹一簇。整体线条流畅优美，翎羽雕刻细腻生动，纹饰变化丰富自然，抛光细致，巧色留皮恰到好处，有平安如意，鸿运当头之意。竹有高洁中空，不畏寒霜，『刚柔忠义』之德。『非竹实不食』代表了凤凰崇高尚洁的品质，将此寓意至于文房佳器之中，更加暗喻了古代文人对高尚品格的自勉与向往。

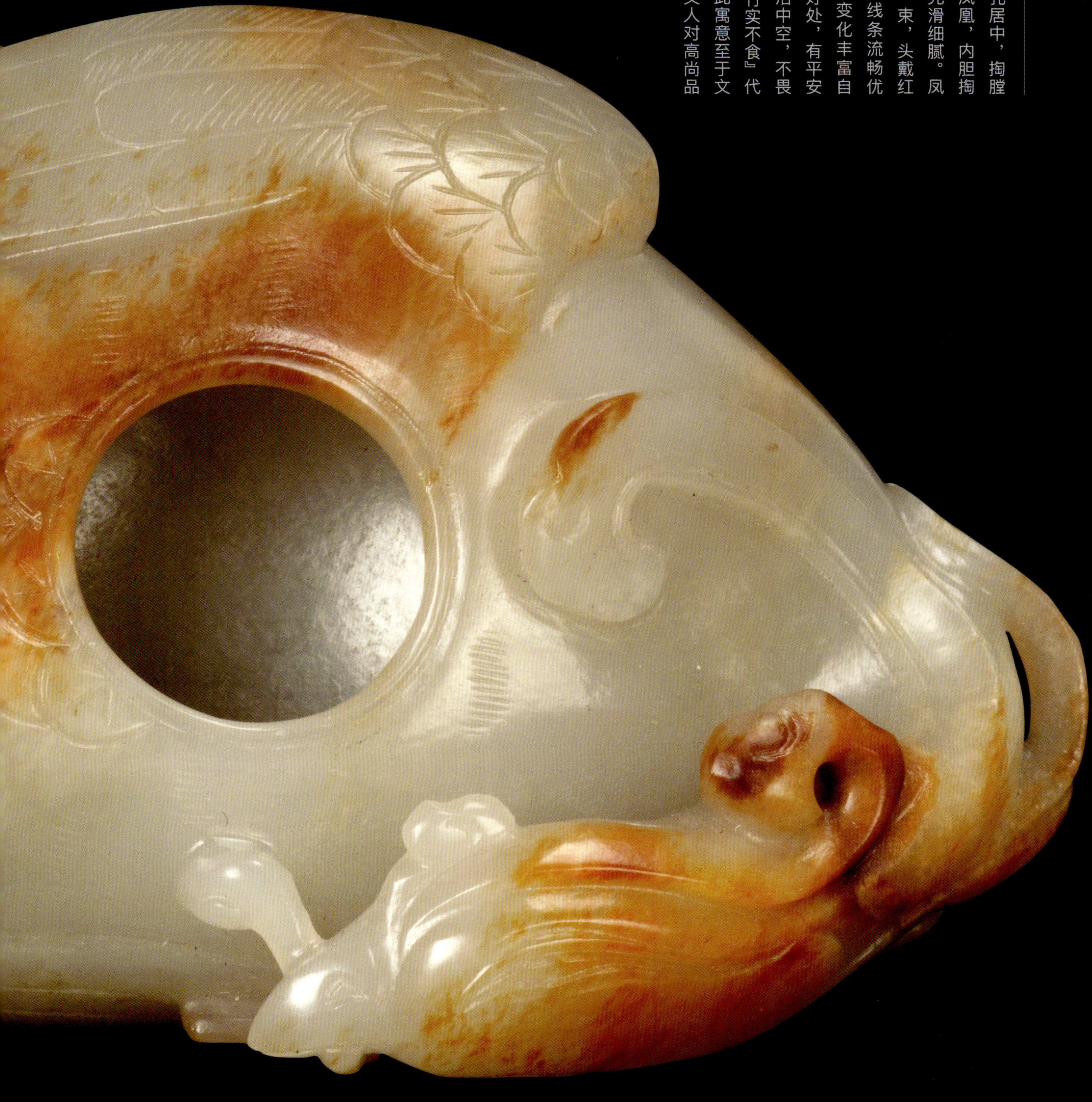

028 A xiuyan jade carving of phoenix and bamboo

Qing Dynasty (1616–1911)
Length 14cm, Width 5cm, Height 25cm
The collection of the Summer Palace

This is a xiuyan jade shanzi (small boulder) with phoenix, bamboo and auspicious cloud patterns. The phoenix was seen as the king of the birds in ancient Chinese folklore with its status only next to the dragon. It also signified a time of peace and prosperity.

岫玉雕「凤鸣岐山」山子

清（1616—1911年）
长14厘米，宽5厘米，高25厘米
颐和园藏

岫玉质。器身正面略鼓，背面稍平，图案由凤凰，山竹，祥云组成。凤凰是中国古代传说的百鸟之王，在中国文化中的地位仅次于龙。古人认为时逢太平盛世时，便有凤凰来飞。

A celadon jade carving of a chilong phoenix vase

Early Qing Dynasty (1636–1795)
Length 7.5cm, Width 3cm, Height 14cm
Provided by The Institute of Qing History Renmin University of China

The vase was made of white jade with some amber markings. A chi-dragon was carved in high relief climbing onto the neck of the vase while a smaller winged chi-dragon below was gazing upwards. The rest of the body was carved with cloud patterns in low relief.

青白玉夔凤螭龙纹瓶

清早期（1636—1795 年）
长 7.5 厘米，宽 3 厘米，高 14 厘米
中国人民大学清史研究所提供

青白玉质，擦琥珀皮色。籽玉整挖，圆雕呈纸槌形。瓶颈细长，口微收，有高浮雕螭龙攀于颈上，向下俯视；其下雕螭龙，抬头仰望。长幼双螭姿态优雅，线条流畅，栩栩如生。瓶身多处浮雕饰以云纹。

030 A white jade *zun* with double phoenix

Qing Dynasty, Qianlong Period (1736–1795)
Length 20cm, Width 10cm, Height 19cm
The collection of the Summer Palace

白玉双凤六环尊

清乾隆（1736—1795 年）
长 20 厘米，宽 10 厘米，高 19 厘米
颐和园藏

白玉质。该尊由盖和身组成，纽顶雕四只蝙蝠，盖雕饰蕉叶纹和四个如意式系，系垂活环；尊身雕琢双凤和磬纹；凤首下坠活环。此尊采用圆雕、镂雕、透雕、线刻等技法。

The zun has a lid and with a finial calved with four bats. There are four ruyi type string with loose rings attached. The body was carved with two phoenixes with each phoenix head attached with a loose ring.

031 A white jade carving of a phoenix

Qing Dynasty, Qianlong Period (1736–1795)
Length 15.5cm, Width 2.7cm, Height 12.5cm
Provided by The Institute of Qing History Renmin University of China

The display object with a standing phoenix with the beak holding a lingzhi carved in high relief openwork. The "phoenix holding lingzhi in beak" signifies the coming of good luck and all things going according to one's wishes.

白玉有凤来仪摆件

清乾隆（1736—1795 年）

长 15.5 厘米，宽 2.7 厘米，高 12.5 厘米

中国人民大学清史研究所提供

白玉质。籽玉整料雕琢，采用镂雕与高浮雕结合的手法，雕立凤一只。凤头微垂，顶部戴冠，喙中衔一株灵芝仙草，羽翼微张，腿部弯曲，尾羽舒展，曲于身体右侧蜿蜒卷曲。通体翎羽细腻，间刻仿汉纹饰。凤凰衔灵芝，寓意有凤来仪，祥瑞降临。

032　A white jade carving of phoenix plaque

Qing Dynasty, Qianlong Period (1736–1795)
Length 16cm, Width 9cm, Height 33cm
The collection of the Summer Palace

The plaque has four blunt corners with nine kui-phoenix carved in the reticulated openwork technique. It has an accompanying hard wood stand.

白玉雕凤纹佩

清乾隆（1736—1795 年）
长 16 厘米，宽 9 厘米，高 33 厘米
颐和园藏

白玉质。此器呈片状倭角椭圆佩状，以减地阳起镂空的技法雕琢九条玲珑剔透、盘曲缠绕的夔凤，线条疏朗，生动逼真。屏芯下配有硬木屏架。

033 A jadeite and *zitan* carved *ruyi* with dragon and phoenix

Qing Dynasty, Guangxu Period (1875–1908)
Length 53cm, Width 14cm, Height 10cm
The collection of the Summer Palace

The handle of this ruyi scepter was made of zitan wood. Three inlays of Jadeite each with carvings of "dragon pursuing pearl" at the top part while the middle and lower parts are with carvings of phoenix. This connotes the auspicious meaning of "Longfeng Chengxiang" (dragon and phoenix bringing blissfulness and good fortune).

紫檀嵌银丝三镶翡翠『龙凤呈祥』如意

清光绪（1875—1908年）
长53厘米，宽14厘米，高10厘米
颐和园藏

翡翠质，紫檀木柄。云头形首，海棠形腹和尾部，皆嵌有翡翠饰片。首部雕『祥龙戏珠』，龙身体弯曲，似从海中跃出，口吐仙气，将悬于空中的灵珠包裹其中。中腹及尾部雕饰为凤纹，与首部纹饰呼应，取『龙凤呈祥』之意。尾有象鼻孔，系黄穗子。紫檀柄刻多字，内嵌银丝。

034 A white jade phoenix group

Qing Dynasty, Qianlong Period (1736–1795)
Length 8.9cm, Width 5.7cm, Height 14cm
Provided by The Institute of Qing History Renmin University of China

This display object has carving of a phoenix standing on a rock. Its beak holds a spray of peonies. The whole display object was carved in the round combining with the openwork carving technique. The phoenix with peonies also connotes the meaning of prosperity, wealth and good fortune.

白玉凤凰衔牡丹摆件

清乾隆（1736—1795年）
长8.9厘米，宽5.7厘米，高14厘米
中国人民大学清史研究所提供

白玉质，温润带糖色。立体圆雕，凤凰栖息于岩石之上，头顶花冠，回首凝视，衔牡丹一束，双翅贴于两侧，尾羽纤长飘逸。整件玉雕取圆雕与镂雕相结合，线条柔美，气息古拙，既表现了凤凰体态的优美，又彰显了其百鸟之王的雄姿。凤凰牡丹寓意五伦长盛，富贵坚固。

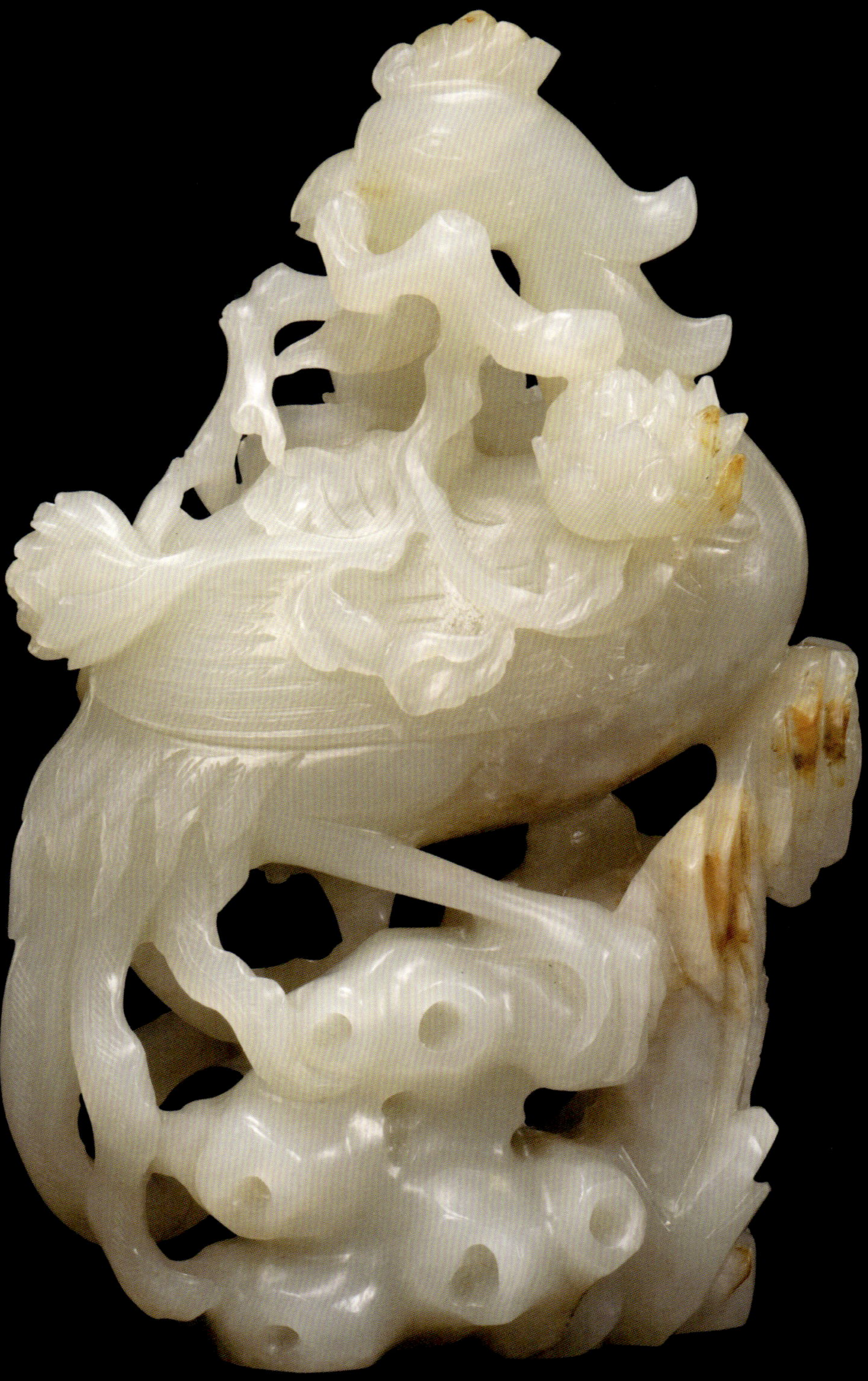

035 A white jade carving of "phoenix and young"

Ming Dynasty (1368–1644)
Length 8.5cm, Width 6cm, Height 3cm
Provided by The Institute of Qing History Renmin University of China

The jade object is oval in shape with carving of the mother phoenix in a resting posture while the fledgling phoenix tucks inside its mother's wing feathers. The mother and child phoenix connotes the meaning of prosperity with many descendants.

白玉子母凤

明（1368—1644年）
长8.5厘米，宽6厘米，高3厘米
中国人民大学清史研究所提供

白玉质，带糖色沁斑。随形圆雕子母凤，母凤呈卧态，脖颈修长，曲颈回望，哺喂幼凤，幼凤藏于羽翼之中。尾羽刻画丝丝入扣，层叠有序，为明末典型的造型风格。母子凤寓意哺喂之恩，更象征吉福延绵，子孙常宜。

036 A celadon and black jade phoenix

Song Dynasty (960-1279)
Length 5.5cm, Width 5.3cm, Height 2.4cm
Provided by The Institute of Qing History Renmin University of China

This celadon jade is full of black tiyou (black dyed patina) with a phoenix in a curled up resting posture carved in the round. The carving skill emanates the archetype Song and Yuan style. Since the Tang and Song periods, the phoenix was regarded as one of the propitious birds and beasts. In the Ming and Qing periods, it was usually being accompanied by the dragon signifying loyalty and faithfulness.

青玉提油凤鸟

宋（960—1279年）
长5.5厘米，宽5.3厘米，高2.4厘米
中国人民大学清史研究所提供

青玉质，通体施黑色提油。圆雕凤鸟蜷卧，昂首凝视一侧，双翅微张收于身体两旁，翅端刻有如意纹。翎羽长尾卷于腹下，双腿收于腹下。工艺特征有典型的南宋风貌。此凤鸟通体黝黑闪青，暗喻上古凤鸟鸑鷟。鸑鷟是古代中国民间传说中的五凤之一，象征着坚贞不屈的品质。唐宋以来，凤凰被誉为传统祥禽瑞兽之一，有品行高洁、忠贞坚毅的象征。

037 A white jade carving of a phoenix with peaches

Qing Dynasty, Qianlong Period (1736-1795)
Length 8cm, Width 5.8cm, Height 3.9cm
Provided by The Institute of Qing History Renmin University of China

The jade was carved with a curled up resting phoenix. Its beak holds a peach branch with three peaches. The "phoenix holding peach" design connotes the idea of auspiciousness and longevity.

白玉俏色凤衔桃枝

清乾隆（1736—1795年）
长8厘米，宽5.8厘米，高3.9厘米
中国人民大学清史研究所提供

白玉质，底部有白瑕，俏琥珀色皮。随形圆雕凤鸟，呈俯卧状，曲颈回首，喙中衔桃枝及三只寿桃，俏红皮于桃上，相得益彰。凤鸟勾嘴长目，头部刻画传神，身体线条流畅，羽毛雕工细密有秩，尾羽卷曲自然，散落于腹下。工匠巧妙利用底部玉皮渲染出尾羽的流光溢彩，更为凤鸟增添一份灵气。凤衔桃有吉祥长寿之寓意。

038 A white jade carving of a small jar of dragon and phoenix

With "Da Qing Qianlong Fanggu"seal and mark
Qing Dynasty, Qianlong Period (1736-1795)
Length 6.5cm, Width 6.5cm, Height 7.1cm
Provided by The Institute of Qing History Renmin University of China

A dragon with phoenix were carved in high relief on the body of this small jar alluding the meaning of "Longfeng Chengxiang" (Dragon and Phoenix Bringing Auspiciousness). The base has an inscription of "Daqing Qianlong Fanggu" (Imitation of Ancient Relics in the Qing Qianlong Period).

白玉仿古龙凤纹瓶

清乾隆（1736—1795 年）
长 6.5 厘米，宽 6.5 厘米，高 7.1 厘米
中国人民大学清史研究所提供

白玉质，籽料留皮。随形圆雕，挖膛中空。仿唐代鎏刻金银器造型，瓶身高浮雕一龙一凤，寓意『龙凤呈祥』。通体线条饱满，敞口短颈，圆足微撇，底刻『大清乾隆仿古』款。虽为清宫造办处常见玉雕款识，但刻于如此精巧文房摆件之上实属罕见。

39 A white jade carving of vase and cover with dragon and phoenix

Qing Dynasty, Qianlong Period (1736-1795)
Length 8cm, Width 4.2cm, Height 17.2cm
Provided by The Institute of Qing History Renmin University of China

The lid of this vase was carved with panchi dragon. One side carved with dragon pursuing pearl while the other side with phoenix amid peonies. The vase was also carved with bamboo, rockery and lingzhi alluding the meaning of "Zhubao Ping'an" (Bamboo Bringing Safeness).

白玉龙凤纹瓶

清乾隆（1736—1795年）
长8厘米，宽4.2厘米，高17.2厘米
中国人民大学清史研究所提供

白玉质。整料圆雕，掏膛匀称，盖顶高浮雕蟠螭纹。玉瓶侧饰苍龙戏珠，宝珠置于玉瓶颈部龙凤之间。另一侧饰凤穿牡丹。玉瓶由底而上饰以竹子、山石、灵芝。题材取『竹报平安』、『龙凤呈祥』、『富贵坚固』之意。

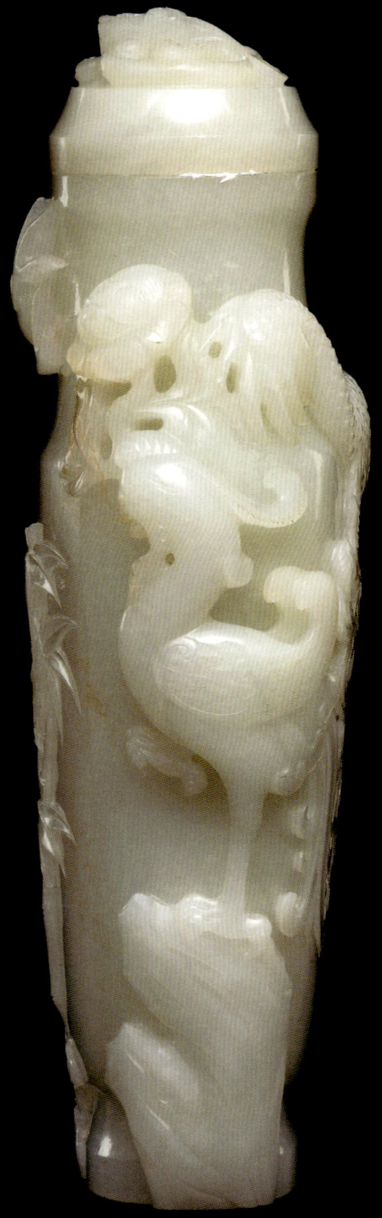

040 A white jade carving of "the dragon fish"

Qing Dynasty, Qianlong Period (1736–1795)
Length 9.4cm, Width 5.5cm, Height 0.5cm
Provided by The Institute of Qing History Renmin University of China

This white jade ornament has an openwork carving of a dragon-fish (beast with the head of a dragon and the body of a fish) in a swirling "S" shaped posture. The dragon-fish conferred the meaning of "success in the imperial examination". It first appeared in the Shang period as jade and bronze patterns.

白玉鱼化龙纹佩

清乾隆（1736—1795年）
长9.4厘米，宽5.5厘米，高0.5厘米
中国人民大学清史研究所提供

白玉质。镂雕鱼化龙纹玉佩，龙首鱼身，龙首霸气威严，身体盘旋，背鳍拱起呈S型，另有夔龙跃于鱼尾，通体饰仿古勾连云纹。鱼化龙常寓意金榜题名，高升昌盛。此造型最早出现于商周时期，多为玉器及青铜纹样，历朝历代沿用并发展至今。

瑞兽灵禽

Auspicious Mystical Beasts and Birds

Beasts and birds are animals most commonly seen in nature. Through the long periods in the natural world, whether living in harmony or in competition and struggle, the Chinese had slowly gave the beasts and birds the concept of morality and meaning. It enabled them to have an implied connotation and supernatural vitality. This slowly became the important content of the Chinese jade culture.

兽与禽，本是自然界中最常见的两类动物，中华民族在长期与自然界和谐相处和拼搏共进的过程中，逐渐赋予了走兽和飞禽文化的寓意和道德的力量，使其拥有了超自然的灵性，成为中国玉文化的重要内容。

041 A chicken bone jade tiger

Shang Dynasty (1600 BCE –1046 BCE)
Length 8.5cm, Width 1.4cm, Height 2.4cm
Provided by The Institute of Qing History Renmin University of China

This jigubai (calcified chicken-bone white) jade is carved with a tiger in the round in a recumbent posture. The tail is pierced with a through hole. In the Shang period, tiger patterns symbolized the prestige of the aristocracy.

鸡骨白玉虎

商（约公元前1600—前1046年）
长8.5厘米，宽1.4厘米，高2.4厘米
中国人民大学清史研究所提供

鸡骨白玉质，局部黄色沁斑有朱砂残留。随形圆雕。虎呈俯卧状，小耳臣目，俯首宣口，脸颊与嘴部以钻孔修饰。身体及四肢饰以阴刻回纹，线条疏朗，肌理自然，尾尖上卷，中间对穿孔，可系挂。造型与殷墟妇好墓出土的玉虎相类，属典型商代琢玉风格，彰显了商代皇家权势的威严。

042 A celadon white jade carving of tiger

Song/Yuan Dynasty (960–1368)
Length 6.2cm, Width 3.9cm, Height 2cm
Provided by The Institute of Qing History Renmin University of China

The tiger is carved in the round in a curled lying down position with its tail tucked to the legs. This emanates the characteristics of a simple and elegant Song period aesthetic taste.

青白玉虎

宋至元（960—1368 年）
长 6.2 厘米，宽 3.9 厘米，高 2 厘米
中国人民大学清史研究所提供

玉质温润，白中闪黄。依料随形圆雕卧虎，身体蜷曲，通体阴刻虎纹，瞠目回首，尾部紧贴于双腿之间。整件玉雕线条简单明快，体现了宋代美学返璞归真，优美简洁的特点。

043 A white jade carving of deer

Song Dynasty (960–1279)
Length 11cm, Width 3cm, Height 5cm
The collection of the Summer Palace

The deer is carved in the round in a recumbent posture with its head turning back. It came with a wood stand.

白玉鹿

宋（960—1279年）
长11厘米，宽3厘米，高5厘米
颐和园藏

白玉质。整料圆雕，卧鹿形，通身光素，臣字形大眼，大耳，短尾，曲颈回首呈卧状带钩形，曲线优美流畅，神态安详自然，体态丰韵。下配木座。

044 A celadon and white jade carving of deer

Ming Dynasty (1368–1644)
Length 7cm, Width 3cm, Height 5.5cm
The collection of the Summer Palace

Two recumbent deer are carved in the round, a mother and her fawn. The deer is seen as an auspicious animal in old Chinese folklore and also regarded by the Daoist as good companions. It also signifies longevity.

青玉双鹿

明（1368—1644年）
长7厘米，宽3厘米，高5.5厘米
颐和园藏

青玉质，带皮，有绺裂。此玉以圆雕和透雕手法，琢一大一小两只卧鹿。大鹿四肢蜷卧，双眼平视，双耳下垂，双角后贴于背，髯垂胸前。小鹿紧伏于大鹿身旁，抬首立耳，一前肢似要站立。鹿自古被视为祥瑞之兽，被道家视为神仙伴侣。鹿在古时有诸多的象征，一象征帝位，《汉书·蒯通传》：『且秦失其鹿，天下共逐之』；一象征长寿；又因与『禄』谐音，也有祝福官运亨通的含义。

045 A white jade carving of deer

Ming Dynasty (1368-1644)
Length 5.3cm, Width 2.3cm, Height 5cm
Provided by The Institute of Qing History Renmin University of China

The deer is carved in the round grasping lingzhi in mouth. Some fine prunus flower patterns are carved on the body. The deer was the mount of the Shouxing (deity of longevity). "Deer with lingzhi in mouth" conveys the message of a healthy and long life.

白玉鹿衔灵芝

明（1368—1644 年）
长 5.3 厘米，宽 2.3 厘米，高 5 厘米
中国人民大学清史研究所提供

白玉质。随形圆雕，包浆厚重。仙鹿昂首阔胸，粗颈肥臀，口衔灵芝，鹿角修长驮于脊背，四肢蜷起呈静卧欲跃之态。鹿身以阴刻线雕梅花若干，细腻入微。

『鹿』谐音『禄』，寓意禄路亨通；『灵芝』寓意『如意』，寓意事事顺意。同时，白鹿是道教文化中南极仙翁之坐骑。故鹿衔灵芝亦有康健长寿之意。

046 A magnificent large pale green jade "stag and young" group

Qing Dynasty, Qianlong Period (1736–1795)
Length 19.5cm, Width 9cm, Height 14cm
Provided by The Institute of Qing History Renmin University of China

This is a large jade with a mother deer and her fawn carved in the round. The doe and fawn share the holding of a bunch of lingzhi in the mouth. Since ancient times, the deer is seen as an auspicious animal bringing good health and long life.

白玉子母鹿衔灵芝

清乾隆（1736—1795 年）
长 19.5 厘米，宽 9 厘米，高 14 厘米
中国人民大学清史研究所提供

白玉质。用料硕大，圆雕子母鹿一对，母鹿回首望向幼鹿，幼鹿伸颈昂首迎向母鹿。母鹿头顶鹿角垂于耳后，神态慈祥。小鹿双耳垂肩，活泼乖巧。双鹿后腿蜷卧，前腿呈腾跃状，动态十足，共衔灵芝一簇。五朵灵芝枝干粗壮，枝头饱满，穿梭于两鹿之间，一动一静相得益彰。自古以来鹿被认为是可与神仙沟通的瑞兽，与『禄』相通，有官运亨通之意，母子鹿常寓意代代食禄，官路昌盛。

047 A white jade carving of deer and young

Qing Dynasty, Qianlong Period (1736–1795)
Length 4.4cm, Width 2cm, Height 5.2cm
The collection of the Summer Palace

The two deer are carved in the round with the mother deer carrying the fawn at her back. The doe's horn touched the fawn's mouth.

白玉子母鹿

清乾隆（1736—1795 年）
长 4.4 厘米，宽 2 厘米，高 5.2 厘米
颐和园藏

白玉质。圆雕双鹿，成鹿头有双角，略微扬起，口衔仙草，似卧非卧；小鹿位于成鹿背部，口部与角相连。

048 A celadon jade carving of a couple of deer

Qing Dynasty, Qianlong Period (1736–1795)
Length 4.9cm, Width 2.9cm, Height 3cm
The collection of the Summer Palace

The two deer both hold lingzhi Ganoderma lucidum in the mouth. The "deer with lingzhi in mouth" is a common theme in Chinese folk-art implying good fortune and longevity.

青玉双鹿

清乾隆（1736—1795 年）
长 4.9 厘米，宽 2.9 厘米，高 3 厘米
颐和园藏

白玉质，双鹿口衔灵芝，鹿为南极仙翁坐骑，灵芝是仙草，珍贵的长生不老药。鹿衔灵芝是中国常见的民俗吉祥图案，寓意祝福长寿。

049 A celadon white jade carving of a couple of badger

Qing Dynasty, Qianlong Period (1736–1795)
Length 7.5cm, Width 3cm, Height 3cm
The collection of the Summer Palace

Two badgers are carved in the round with the openwork technique. The Chinese pronunciation for badger "huan" rhymes with "happiness" and so the two-badger theme also conveys the message of "double-happiness".

青白玉双獾

清乾隆（1736—1795年）
长7.5厘米，宽3厘米，高3厘米
颐和园藏

青白玉质。整料雕琢，采用圆雕、镂雕等技法，雕琢出伏卧双獾造型，身体交错，回头对望，口衔透雕缠枝花叶。『獾』与『欢』谐音，『双獾』即『双欢』，有和睦之意。

050 A white jade carving of a couple of badgers

Qing Dynasty (1616-1911)
Length 7cm, Width 4.1cm, Height 2.3cm
The collection of the Summer Palace

There are some markings and crackles on this white jade. A pair of badgers are carved in the round with mouth holding a sprig of lingzhi. The two-badger theme has the implication of a happy and long-lasting marriage.

白玉双獾

清（1616—1911年）
长7厘米，宽4.1厘米，高2.3厘米
颐和园藏

白玉质，有沁色、绺裂。以圆雕和透雕手法做獾子一对，首尾相连，耳鬓厮磨。美玉一端有沁色，工匠利用其天然颜色巧雕一株灵芝，使双獾口衔灵芝的造型更加生动。獾因成双入对出没，象征夫妻美满、婚姻长久。

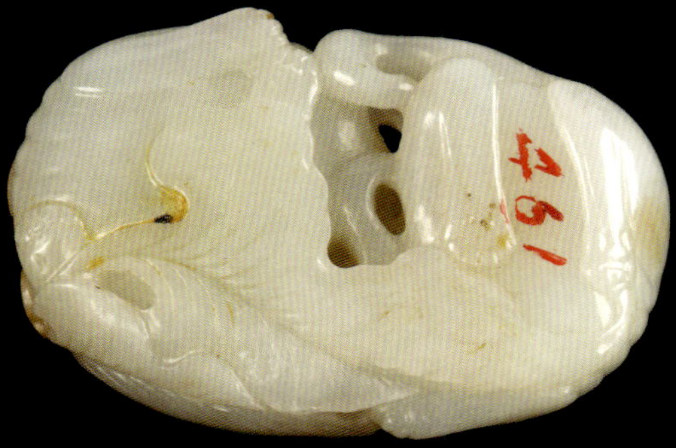

051 A white jade carving of crane with peaches

Qing Dynasty, Qianlong Period (1736-1795)
Length 7.2cm, Width 3cm, Height 5.2cm
Provided by The Institute of Qing History Renmin University of China

The white jade has some brownish red markings. A crane is carved in a resting posture with beak holding a branch with four small peaches. The "crane with peach theme" in Chinese has the same sound of heshou (wishing for a long life) and used for birthday wishes and celebrations.

白玉衔桃仙鹤

清乾隆（1736—1795年）
长7.2厘米，宽3厘米，高5.2厘米
中国人民大学清史研究所提供

白玉质，留红褐色皮。玉质温润，随料圆雕，仙鹤曲颈长喙，体态婀娜，羽翼饱满。坐卧凝视，回首衔桃枝一簇，枝上仙桃错落分布，桃叶蜷曲弯折。仙鹤双足擎竹叶一簇，羽翼层次分明，侧留原皮巧雕灵芝一株。仙鹤和寿桃与『贺寿』谐音，有祝寿祈福之意。

052 A yellow and russet jade carving of a tapir

Song/ Yuan Dynasty (960–1368)
Length 9.5cm, Width 4.6cm, Height 4.6cm
Provided by The Institute of Qing History Renmin University of China

The pale yellow jade bears some red and russet markings with a tapir carved in the round. The tapir was seen as an auspicious animal in ancient Chinese folklore bringing happiness and good luck.

黄玉貘

宋至元（960—1368 年）
长 9.5 厘米，宽 4.6 厘米，高 4.6 厘米
中国人民大学清史研究所提供

黄玉质，留红褐色皮，局部有牛毛状沁。整体圆雕，体态壮硕，作俯卧状，造型敦厚。中国古人认为貘是祥瑞之兽，能食人之梦魇，有驱邪避凶，吉祥如意之意。

053 A white jade carving of red-crowned crane

Qing Dynasty, Qianlong Period (1736-1795)
Length 11cm, Width 4.5cm, Height 6cm
Provided by The Institute of Qing History Renmin University of China

The white jade has some red-russet markings which is skillfully carved as the crown of the crane. The crane is carved in the round with its back carrying two peaches while the beak is holding a peach branch. This display object signifies longevity and good fortune.

白玉雕『鹤寿延年』摆件

清乾隆（1736—1795年）
长11厘米，宽4.5厘米，高6厘米
中国人民大学清史研究所提供

白玉质，留红皮。随形圆雕。仙鹤呈俯卧状，头部轻伏于背上，口衔桃枝，背驮两只寿桃，桃形饱满枝叶丰盈。仙鹤翎羽层次分明，纹饰随部位变化而有所不同。工匠巧妙地留皮于仙鹤头顶、羽毛、寿桃以及桃枝之上。整件摆件寓意鹤寿延年、鸿运当头。

054 A celadon jade carving *ruyi* with cranes and deer

Qing Dynasty, Qianlong Period (1736-1795)
Length 38cm, Width 10cm, Height 5.6cm
The collection of the Summer Palace

青玉雕『鹤鹿同春』如意

清光绪（1875—1908年）
长38厘米，宽10厘米，高5.6厘米
颐和园藏

青玉质。头片雕松鹿鹤、中片雕松鹿、尾片雕松鹤。松，为道教神话中象征长生不死、高洁不群的重要原型。鹤，被道教视为长寿且出世之物。鹿为寿星坐骑，三种仙物结合，寓意祈盼高洁、祈求长寿。

The upper part of this celadon jade ruyi scepter is carved with pine, deer and crane. The middle portion with pine with deer while the bottom part with pine and crane. The pine tree signified eternal life, the crane long life while the deer was the mount of the deity of longevity. The combination of these brings the message of the wish for a very long life.

055 A celadon jade carving of a crane with a pair of peaches

Qing Dynasty, Qianlong Period (1736–1795)
Length 20cm, Width 11cm, Height 10.6cm
Provided by The Institute of Qing History Renmin University of China

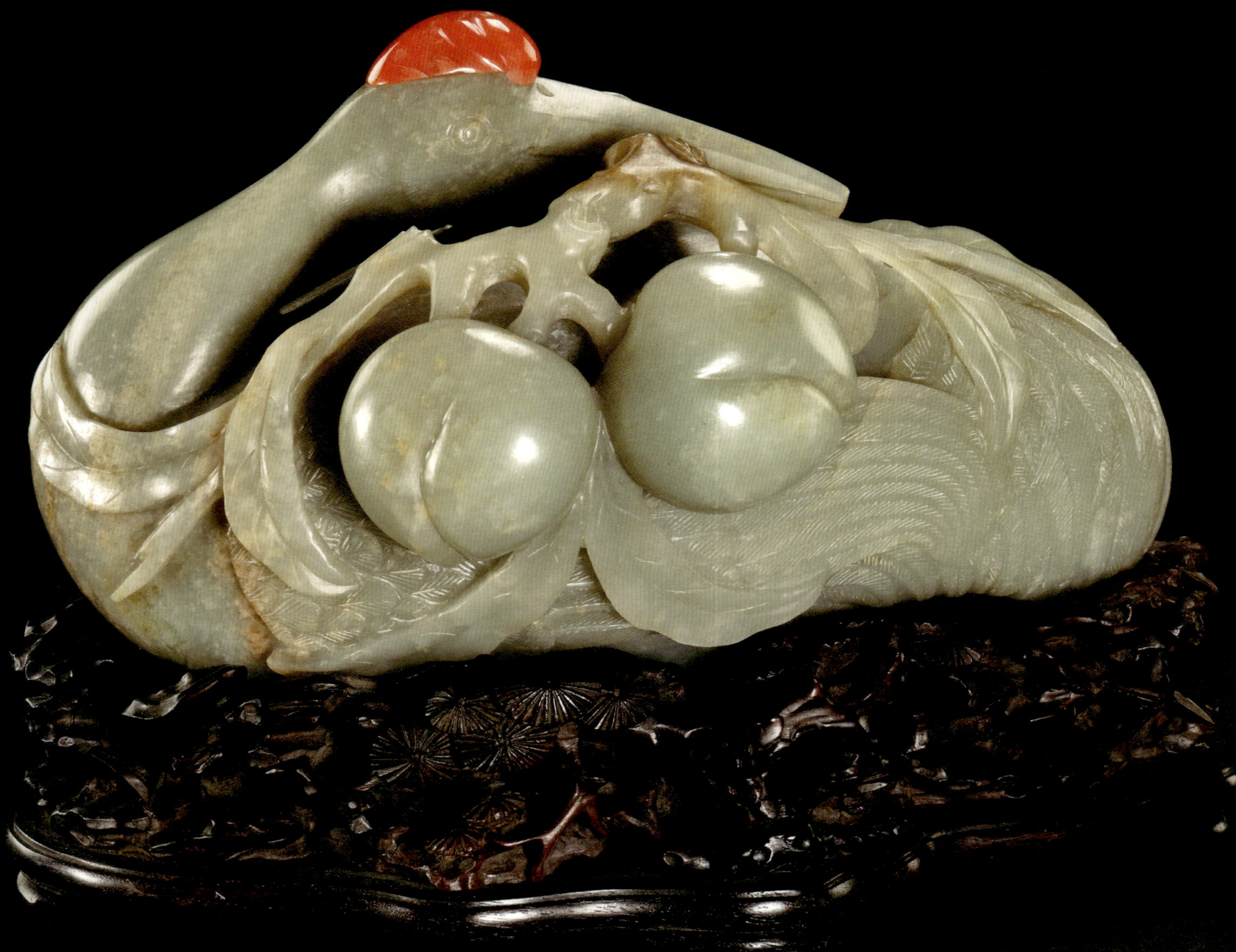

青玉镶南红鹤衔仙桃

清乾隆（1736—1795年）

长20厘米，宽11厘米，高10.6厘米

中国人民大学清史研究所提供

青灰玉质。籽玉圆雕，顶部镶嵌南红玛瑙，用料硕大。随形雕仙鹤回首衔双桃一枝，鹤嘴修长有力，颈部曲线流畅自然，全身肌理丰满健硕。工匠取不同纹饰来表现仙鹤的翎羽。桃枝上寿桃饱满，桃叶徐徐展开，极富动态。鹤顶镶南红玛瑙暗喻鸿运当头。鹤衔桃常寓意『鹤寿』，意同『贺寿』，有福寿延绵之意，是清代宫廷祝寿的常用题材，如此体量巨大的摆件实属罕见。

A crane is carved in the round with its beak holding a branch with two succulent peaches. The top part of the crane's head is inlaid with a nanhong (South red) agate making this crane a red-crowned crane. The theme of crane holding peaches conferred the meaning of "wishing for a long life" most commonly used in the Qing imperial court.

056 A pale celadon and russet jade "crane and peach" group

Qing Dynasty, Qianlong Period (1736-1795)
Length 9cm, Width 3cm, Height 6.5cm
Provided by The Institute of Qing History Renmin University of China

There are some orange-russet markings on the jade. It is carved with a crane in a resting posture with the beak holding a peach sprig full of succulent ripe peaches. The crane is a traditional theme in wishing for a long and fruitful life.

青白玉雕仙鹤衔桃

清乾隆（1736—1795年）
长9厘米，宽3厘米，高6.5厘米
中国人民大学清史研究所提供

青白玉质，玉质温润带红皮，作仙鹤衔桃之状。仙鹤屈腿蜷卧，呈回首状，喙中衔一桃枝，桃叶婉转，桃枝上坠两颗成熟饱满的桃子。仙鹤衔桃是传统的贺寿题材，寓意福寿绵长。

057 A white jade carving of "crane and peach"

Qing Dynasty, Qianlong Period (1736-1795)
Length 12.5cm, Width 2.8cm, Height 5.7cm
Provided by The Institute of Qing History Renmin University of China

Two resting cranes are carved in the round in high relief openwork. The pair of cranes share in their beaks a peach twig with many peaches. The "crane with beak holding peaches" confers the meaning of a long and fruitful life.

白玉雕『双鹤献寿』

清乾隆（1736—1795 年）
长 12.5 厘米，宽 2.8 厘米，高 5.7 厘米
中国人民大学清史研究所提供

白玉质。以圆雕、镂雕、高浮雕等多种工艺琢刻仙鹤一对。双鹤相对而卧，四目相视，共衔桃枝一束，桃枝硕果累累，枝繁叶茂。双鹤衔桃有福寿延绵，贺寿康健之意。

058 A gray jade carving of *xiezhi*

Yuan Dynasty (1206–1368)
Length 4.5cm, Width 2.9cm, Height 6.2cm
Provided by The Institute of Qing History Renmin University of China

The natural gray jade is skillfully carved to fully emanated the majestic characteristics of the xiezhi auspicious beast in a sitting position. Used as a display object on a scholar's table.

灰玉獬豸

元（1206—1368 年）
长 4.5 厘米，宽 2.9 厘米，高 6.2 厘米
中国人民大学清史研究所提供

灰玉质，有褐色提油，包浆厚重。獬豸体态壮硕，双目望天，闭口獠牙，头顶独角，呈站立状。工匠利用其天然的矿石特征呈现了獬豸的古朴凝重。雕工简约，刀法遒劲酣畅。置于案头，有警示公正廉明之意。

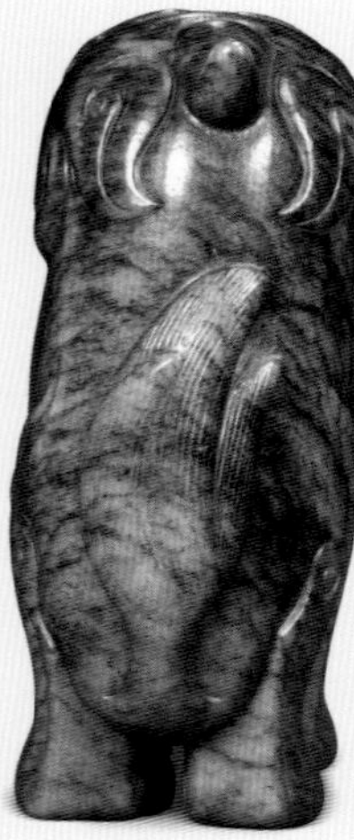

059 A gray jade carving of auspicious beast

Ming Dynasty (1368–1644)
Length 12cm, Width 8cm, Height 4.5cm
Provided by The Institute of Qing History Renmin University of China

This gray jade has a thick patina of dark oily markings. A recumbent xiezhi was carved in the round with its heads looking backwards. The xiezhi was an auspicious beast in ancient mythology believed to be able to talk and understand human behavior. It signified an intrepid, fair and just character.

灰玉獬豸

明（1368—1644）
长12厘米，宽8厘米，高4.5厘米
中国人民大学清史研究所提供

灰玉质，有火烧沁痕，包浆厚重。整料圆雕一獬豸呈静卧状，圆头短颈，毛发环绕，四肢壮硕，眉目威严，闭口獠牙，独角赫然于头顶上方，呈回首状。兽脊节节凸起，兽爪孔武有力，毛发排列井然有序，抛光细润。相传獬豸通体皮毛黝黑，选用灰玉，利用矿石的天然特征和花纹恰如其分地表现獬豸的体貌特征。獬豸是中国古代神话传说中的神兽，它性情正直，懂人言，知人性，分善恶，辨忠奸，明是非，是勇猛无畏、清平公正的象征。

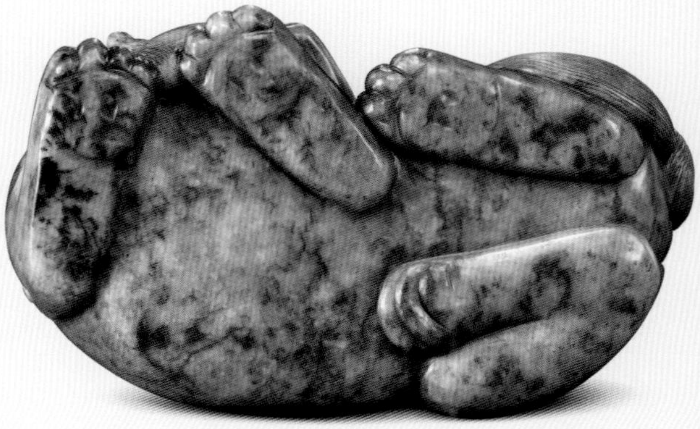

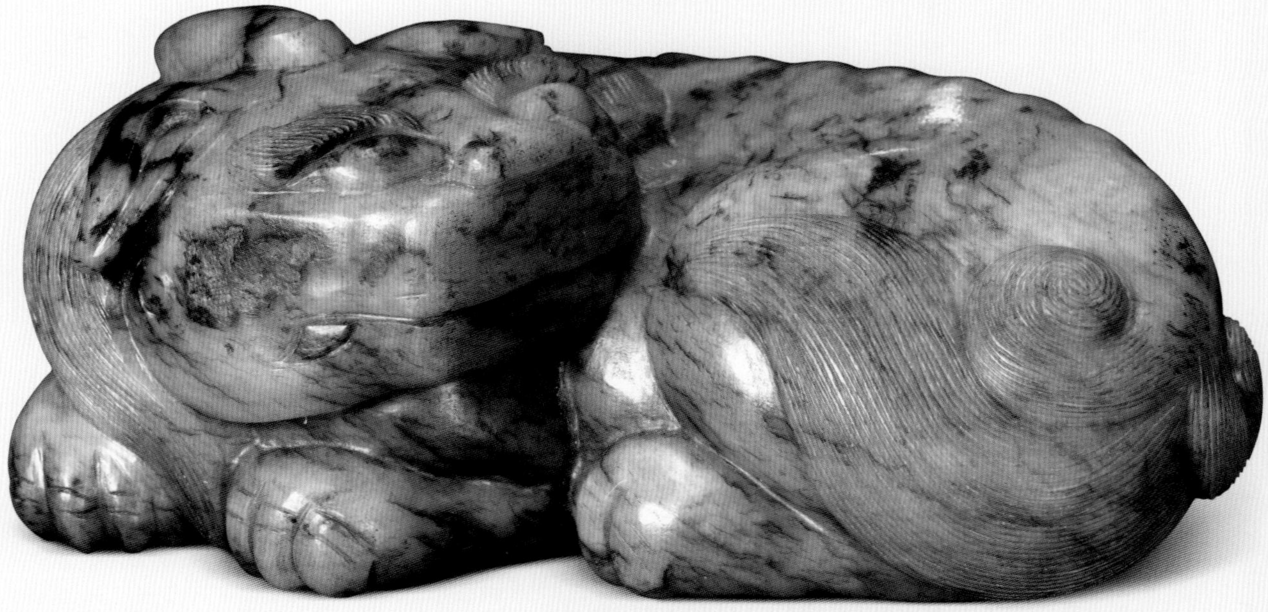

060 A pale celadon jade *xiezhi* group

Ming Dynasty (1368-1644)
Length 9.5cm, Width 7cm, Height 3.5cm
Provided by The Institute of Qing History Renmin University of China

Two recumbent xiezhi are carved in the round, a mother and her young. The xiezhi was an auspicious beast in Chinese traditional culture and the mother and child xiezhi confer the meaning of prosperity with numerous progenies.

青玉母子獬豸

明（1368—1644年）
长9.5厘米，宽7厘米，高3.5厘米
中国人民大学清史研究所提供

青玉质。整料圆雕母子獬豸呈卧态，两只瑞兽头向右倾，首尾相照，彼此对望。圆目凸鼻，双耳紧贴头部，独角垂于脑后，相互依偎憨态可掬。獬豸本是中国传统文化中主公正的瑞兽，母子獬豸寓意清白传家，世代清明。

061 A celadon and russet white jade "horse" belt buckle

Liao / Jin Dynasty (916–1234)
Length 5.4cm, Width 4.1cm, Height 0.6cm
The collection of Beijing Art Museum

The rectangular pale celadon jade belt buckle bears some brownish red rind markings. The front surface is a galloping horse carved in shallow relief. On top of the horse are three patches of clouds also in shallow relief carving with the center cloud blocking half of the sun. The brownish red rind markings are skillfully use to carved onto the body, hooves, and tail of the horse.

青白玉俏色奔马纹带饰

辽至金（916—1234年）
长5.4厘米，宽4.1厘米，厚0.6厘米
北京艺术博物馆藏

青白玉质，左下角有裂纹，表面有棕红色皮。带板近长方形，无边框，左上一角略呈圆弧，其他打磨较为平直。正面主体采用剔地浅浮雕手法雕一匹正在奔跑的骏马。马双耳竖起，嘴微张，眼睛圆睁，脖子略向前探出，前蹄双双弯曲，后蹄向后蹬踏，用阴刻线整齐地刻画出细密的鬃毛。马腿关节处突出，马蹄刻画逼真，马尾向上扬起。马蹄下端浅浮雕一排奔涌的波浪，翻起的浪花以未钻透的圆孔来表现，并以排列整齐的阴刻线来表示水的流动。奔马的上方浅浮雕三片云朵，正中的云朵遮住一半太阳。

值得一提的是这件带板还采用了俏色巧雕的手法，马的身体、马蹄、马尾都借以棕红色的皮色雕刻，巧妙传神。（高媛）

062 White jade carving of dragon-horse and dragon-turtle with books on backs

Qing Dynasty, Qianlong Period (1736–1795)
Length 15.5cm, Width 5cm, Height 6.6cm
Provided by The Institute of Qing History Renmin University of China

The white jade is carved with two mythical beasts, a dragon-horse and a dragon-turtle, both carrying books on their backs rushing out of the river. The mythical ancient belief of "dragon-horse carrying books and dragon-turtle presenting books" symbolizes the source of Chinese culture.

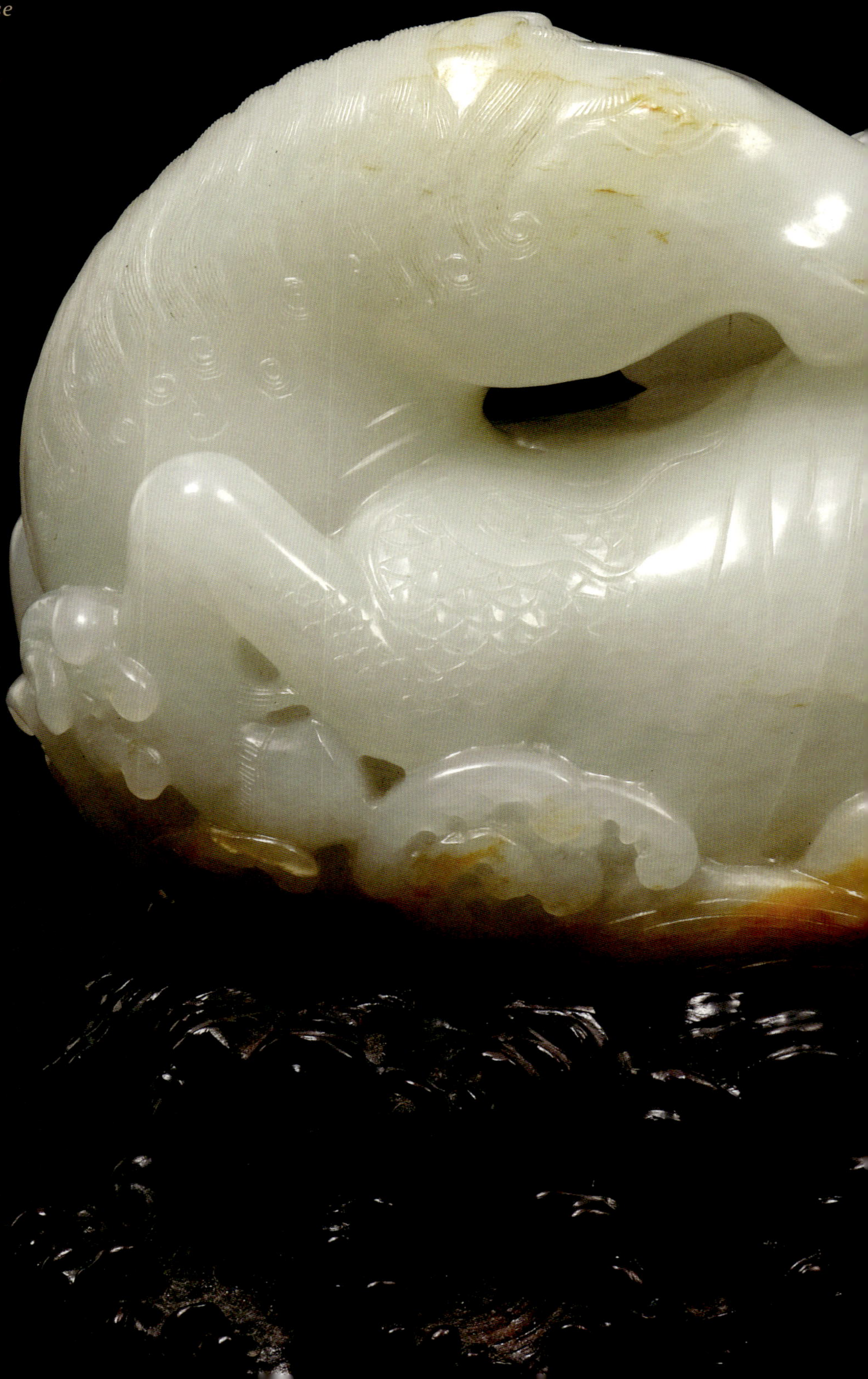

白玉龙马神龟摆件

清乾隆（1736—1795年）
长15.5厘米，宽5厘米，高6.6厘米
中国人民大学清史研究所提供

白玉质，留红皮。整料圆雕龙马与龙龟一组，四目相望，随河图洛书出水，龙马前蹄腾跃起伏，回首与龙龟相顾。绶带翻腾与双兽相系，一端系河图一卷，驮于龙马背上，另一端系洛书一部负于龙龟背上。龙龟颈部修长回首与龙马对望。龙马鬃毛卷曲似龙之毛发，四肢布满龙鳞，身体遒劲健硕，大有腾龙之势。龙龟龙鳞满布，甲上有八卦纹饰清晰可见。底部满雕海水江崖纹，一片皇家气象，红皮巧雕翻转的海水，泥沙翻滚，突出了『龙马负图，神龟贡书』的祥瑞之象。龙马双目留红皮一点，可谓画龙点睛之笔。

『龙马负图，神龟贡书』是关于河图洛书的最早传说，象征中华文明的起源。

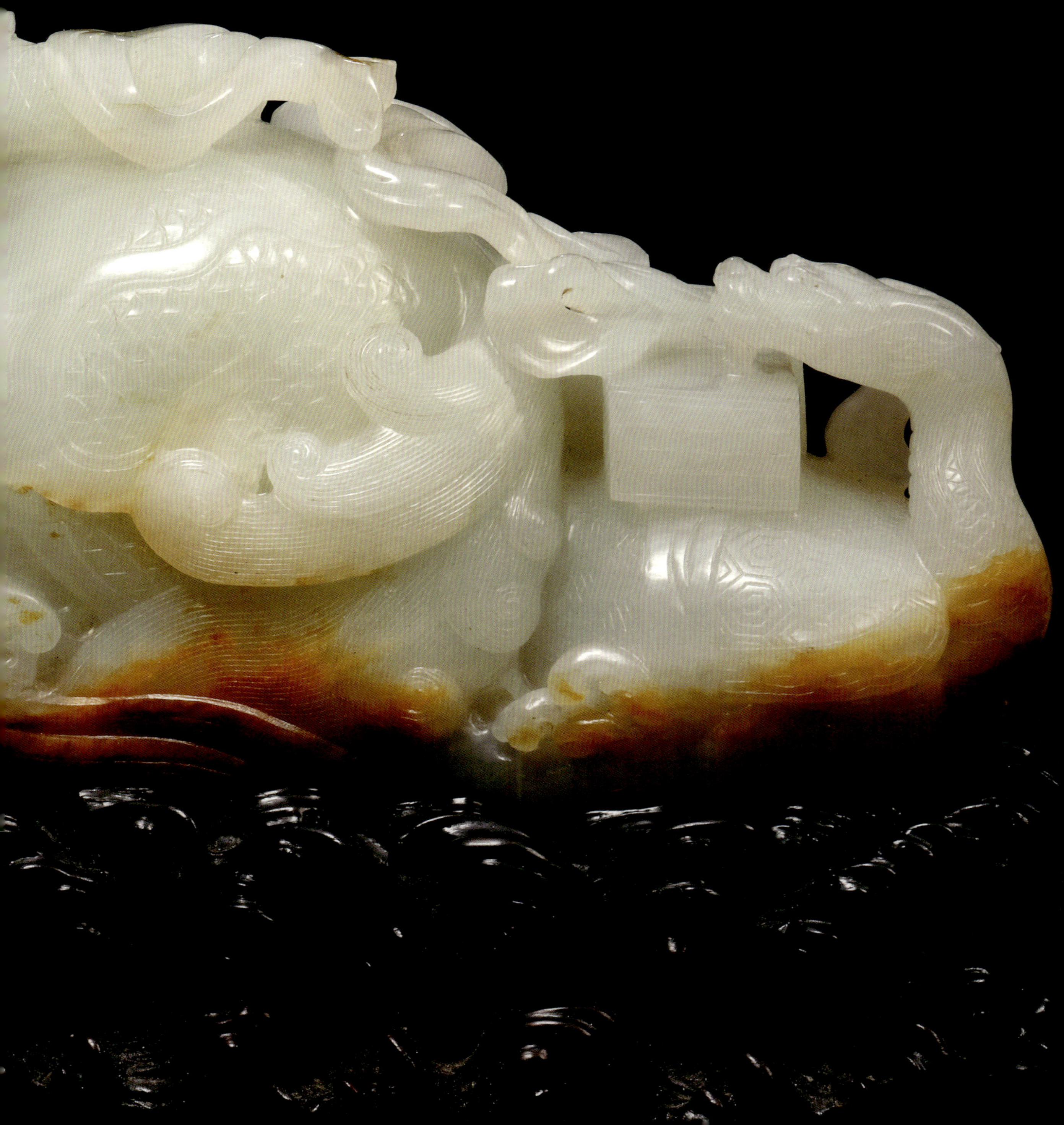

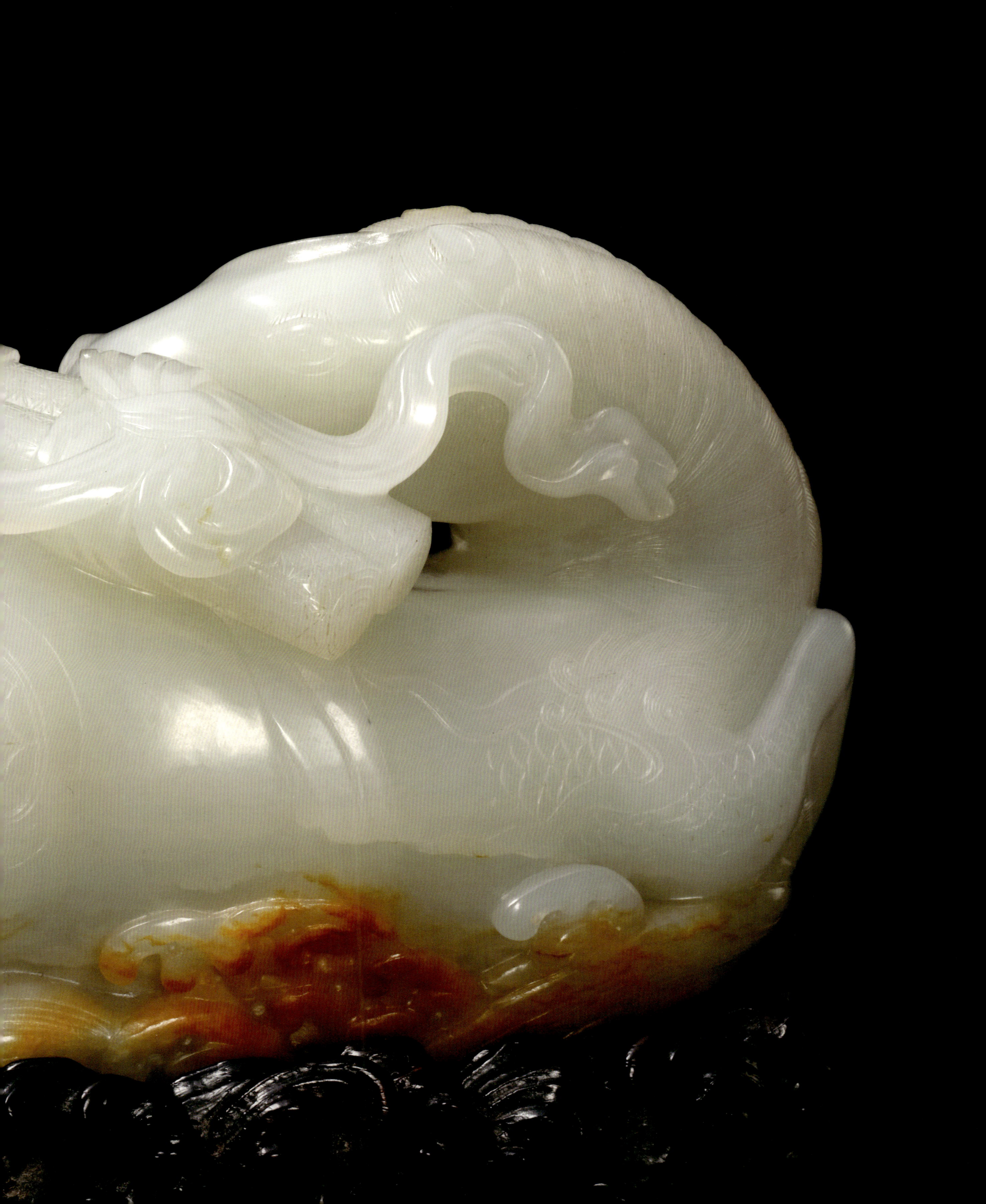

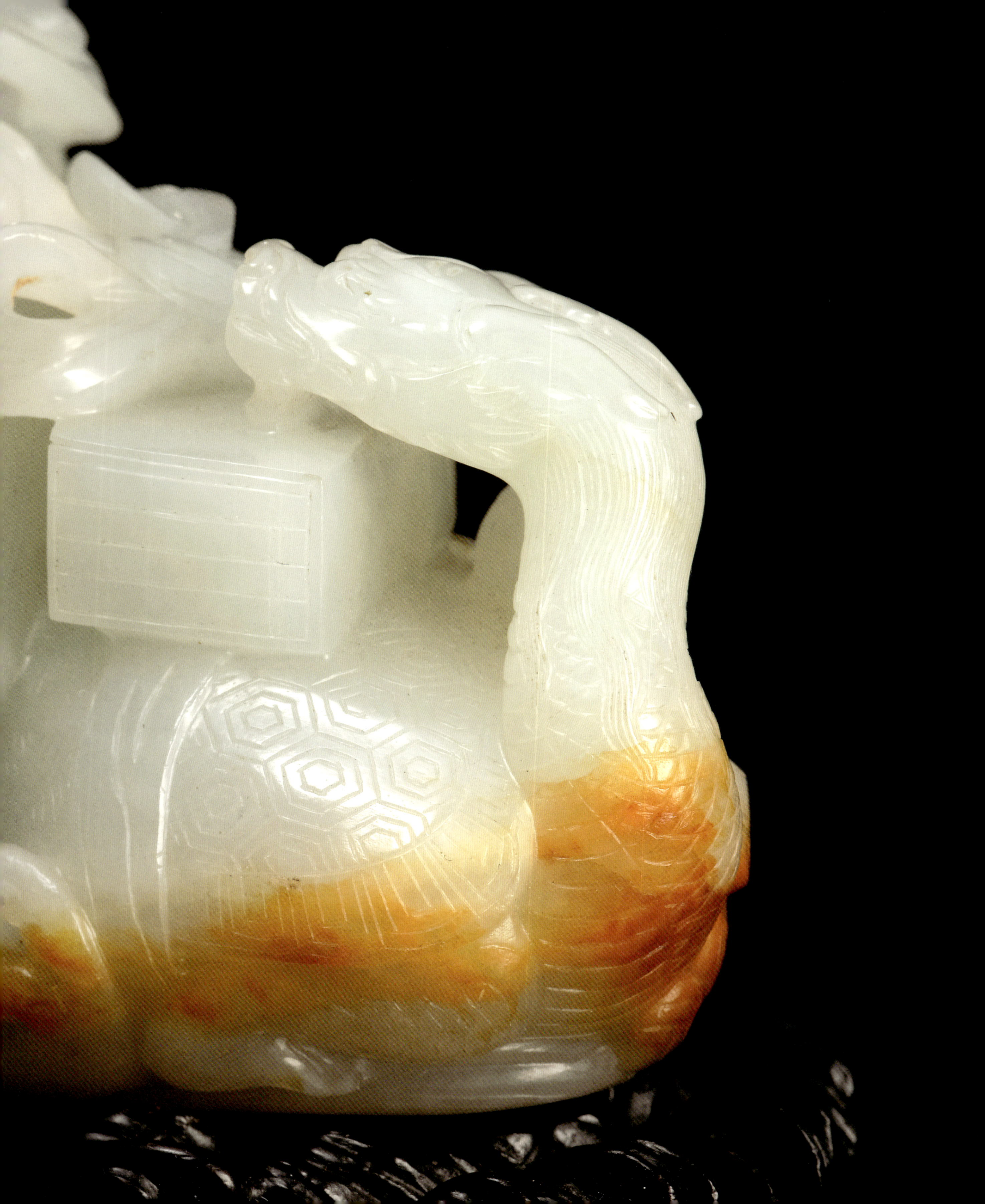

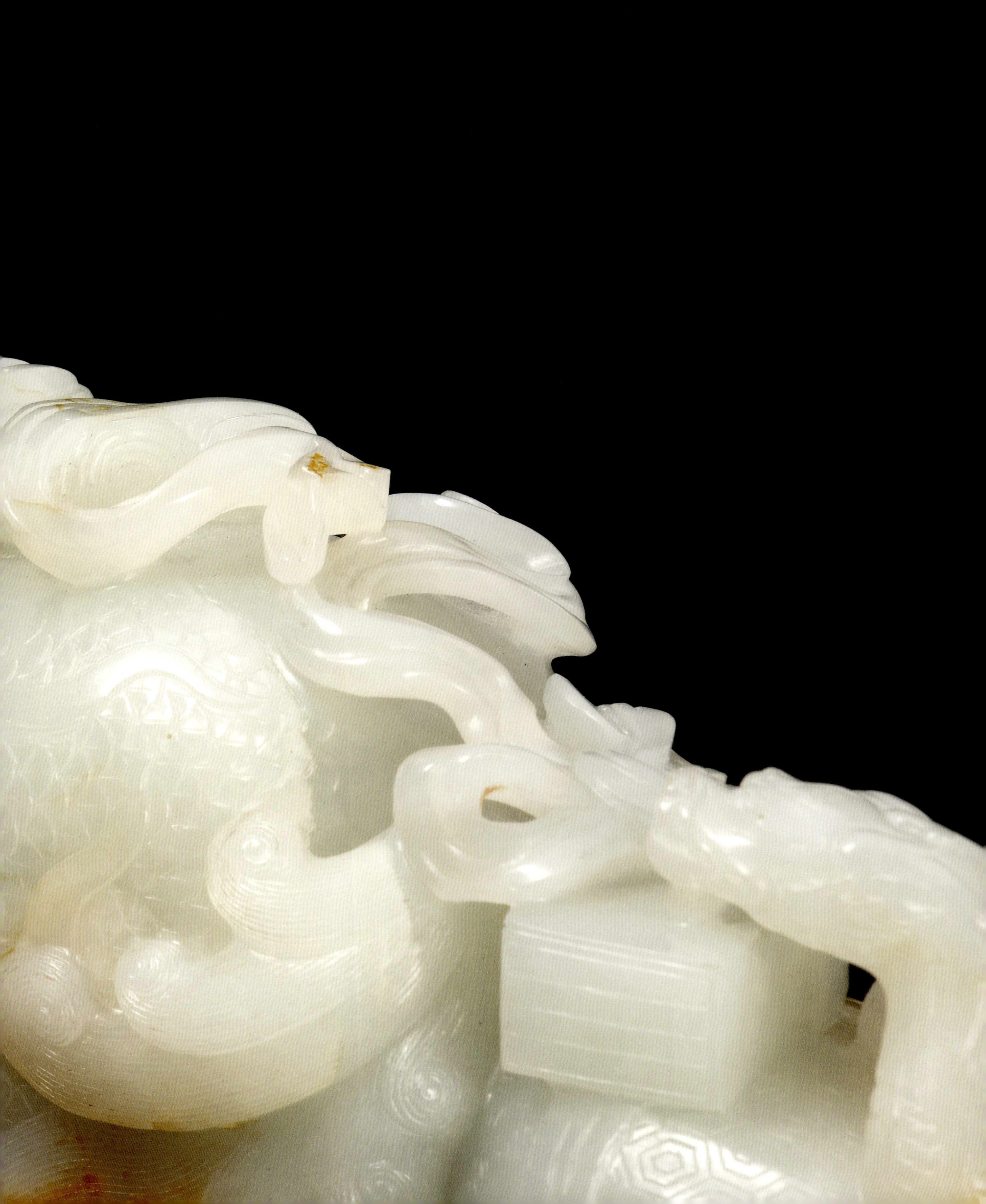

063 A white jade carving of a dragon-horse

Qing Dynasty, Qianlong Period (1736–1795)
Length 7.5cm, Width 3.5cm, Height 6cm
The collection of the Summer Palace

The recumbent dragon-horse is carved with its back carrying books on sea waves. The theme of dragon-horse carrying books symbolized the birth place of the Chinese culture.

白玉雕『龙马负图』

清乾隆（1736—1795年）
长7.5厘米，宽3.5厘米，高6厘米
颐和园藏

白玉质，带黄皮。整料雕琢，俏色巧雕白马回头伏卧，背上负图书，踏于海浪之上。题材取自『河图洛书』中的『龙马负图』。古时常把龙马、神龟与图、书结合一起作『河图洛书』，以象征中华文化的源头。

064 An archaistic white jade *gu*

Ming Dynasty (1368–1644)
Length 7.5cm, Width 7.5cm, Height 25.5cm
The collection of the Summer Palace

This is a fanggu (imitating antiquity; archaistic) jade rectangular gu with the foot carved with plantain-leaf patterns and the belly with beast-head patterns. The jade gu first appeared in the Ming dynasty as a studio object showing the elegant taste of the studio master.

白玉兽面纹方觚

明（1368—1644 年）
长 7.5 厘米，宽 7.5 厘米，高 25.5 厘米
颐和园藏

白玉质。该器造型仿古，敞口，长颈，方腹，撇足，平底。颈、足雕饰蕉叶纹，腹部刻兽面纹。觚的四角及四面中央雕饰有扉棱。器身分为上、中、下三段，共二十四条扉棱。玉制花觚始见于明朝，常置于案头，或插入如意，或插博古挂件，以体现物主人雅趣。

065 An archaistic spinach jade *gu*

Qing Dynasty, Qianlong Period (1736–1795)
Diameter 12.5cm, Height 25cm
The collection of the Summer Palace

The body of this spinach green jade Gu vessel has some black speckles and six rows of disrupted ridges with a short belly. This is a fanggu (archaistic) vessel with some modifications.

碧玉兽面纹觚

清乾隆（1736—1795 年）
直径 12.5 厘米，高 25 厘米
颐和园藏

碧玉质，有黑色斑点。器形仿古彝器略有变化；长颈，阔口，器身起六条间断的凸棱，觚腹较短，上下内敛似鼓式，足形与觚颈同，略矮。该器造型在仿古的基础上稍加变化，显得端庄大方。

066 An archaistic rock crystal *gu*

Qing Dynasty (1616–1911)
Diameter 12cm, Height 21.5cm
The collection of the Summer Palace

The Gu is an oval shape with a splaying mouth. The neck and foot are carved with plantain leaves and cloud-thunder patterns while the belly with low relief beast-face patterns.

水晶兽面纹觚

清（1616—1911 年）
直径 12 厘米，高 21.5 厘米
颐和园藏

水晶质。觚为海棠式，椭圆形，侈口，鼓腹，圈足。颈与足以阴线刻蕉叶纹和云雷纹。腹部减地浮雕兽面纹。

067 An archaistic white jade vase with cover and handles

Qing Dynasty, Qianlong Period (1736-1795)
Length 13cm, Width 8cm, Height 29cm
The collection of the Summer Palace

The vase is slightly oblate in shape with a lid. The neck is flanked by two dragon handles each attached with a loose ring. The belly is carved with beast-face and bat patterns.

白玉兽面纹双环瓶

清乾隆（1736—1795年）
长13厘米，宽8厘米，高29厘米
颐和园藏

白玉质。瓶体扁圆，由器盖和器身组成。小口，丰肩，鼓腹，下腹内收。颈部对称雕饰龙耳一对，口衔活环。中、下腹部以减地阳起的技法琢制兽面纹、蝙蝠纹。

068 A celadon jade carving of square *ding* vessel

With "Da Qing Qian Long Fang Gu" seal mark
Qing Dynasty, Qianlong Period (1736–1795)
Length 22.2cm, Width 14.7cm, Height 27.8cm
The collection of the Summer Palace

This is a fanggu ding vessel with a rectangular body carved with beast-face patterns. The base has a lishu (clerical script) inscription of "Daqing Qianlong Fanggu" (Imitating the Ancient Relics in the Qianlong Reign of the Great Qing)

青玉『大清乾隆仿古』款兽面纹方鼎

清乾隆（1736—1795年）
长22.2厘米，宽14.7厘米，高27.8厘米
颐和园藏

青玉质。仿古铜鼎造型，鼎身呈长方形，折沿，深腹，双立耳，四柱足；鼎腹四角及前后出扉棱；口沿及耳侧饰回纹，器身饰兽面纹，足饰蕉叶纹。底阴刻隶书『大清乾隆仿古』款识。

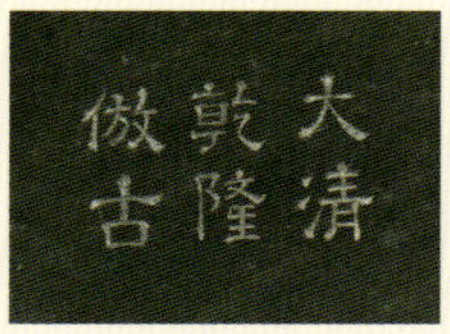

069 A jadeite carving of square *ding* vessel

The Republic of China (1912–1949)
Length 22cm, Width 10cm, Height 27cm
The collection of the Summer Palace

This is a jadeite carving of a lidded ding vessel with various mythical beast patterns. The body is flanked by two dragon handles each attached with a loose ring. The base has an apocryphal inscription of "Qianlong Nian Zhi" (made in the Qianlong Reign).

翡翠兽面纹龙耳活环方鼎

民国（1912—1949年）
长22厘米，宽10厘米，高27厘米
颐和园藏

翡翠质。由盖和器身组成，子母扣相合，采用减地浅浮雕、镂雕、透雕、线刻等技法。顶部雕有狻猊，形象生动，四周雕有夔凤等纹饰。鼎身两侧雕有龙耳、活环，正背面雕有饕餮纹。底阴刻伪托篆书『乾隆年制』款。

070 An archaistic pale green and russet jade ewer *gong*

Qing Dynasty, Qianlong Period (1736–1795)
Length 9.2cm, Width 5.3cm, Height 16.5cm
Provided by The Institute of Qing History Renmin University of China

This is a pale green jade carving of a gong vessel imitating the shape of the Shang bronze gong wine cup. The belly is embellished with taotie patterns. The handle is an openwork carving of phoenix dragon.

青白玉仿古饕餮纹觥

清乾隆（1736—1795年）
长9.2厘米，宽5.3厘米，高16.5厘米
中国人民大学清史研究所提供

青白玉质，带糖色。整料雕刻，器仿商周青铜器中酒器觥的造型。腹部饰仿古饕餮纹，上下侈口扩足以勾云纹、回纹装饰，手柄镂空圆雕仿古夔龙纹样。内膛掏挖工整，通体抛光细腻柔和，包浆厚重，是乾隆早期的宫廷仿古佳作。

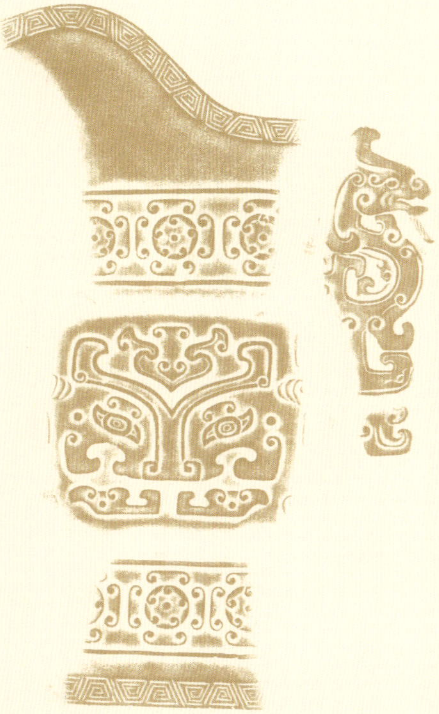

071 An archaistic white jade vessel, *zhi*

Song/Yuan/Ming Dynasty (960-1644)
Height 8.6cm, Diameter 6.8cm
Provided by The Institute of Qing History Renmin University of China

The white jade is carved into the shape imitating the Shang period bronze zhi vessel. The body is carved with taotie mask patterns. The zhi was one of the very old Chinese ritual wares for wine drinking popular in the late Shang to early Zhou period.

白玉饕餮纹觯

宋至明（960—1644年）
高8.6厘米，口径6.8厘米
中国人民大学清史研究所提供

白玉质，带糖色。整料雕琢，仿商周时期青铜酒器觯之造型，撇口、收颈、圆腹、圈足。腹部正、反面雕饕餮纹饰，其间以勾连云纹和如意纹相隔。口沿处饰仿古回纹。内膛打挖平整，打磨考究，器壁薄。觯乃中国古代传统礼器之一，是贵胄王尊在重要仪式上的行酒用器，形似尊而小，盛行于商代晚期及西周早期。

072 A celadon white jade carving of lion group

Qing dynasty, Qianlong Period (1711–1799)
Length 13.5cm, Width 10.5cm, Height 10.5cm
Provided by The Institute of Qing History Renmin University of China

The pale celadon jade is carved into two lions, an adult and a juvenile joined by a brocaded ball and the ribbon. The "adult with juvenile lion" group connotes the meaning of promotion to higher officialdom.

青白玉太狮少狮

清乾隆（1711—1799 年）
长 13.5 厘米，宽 10.5 厘米，高 10.5 厘米
中国人民大学清史研究所提供

青白玉质。整料随形圆雕太狮少狮，采用一大一小、一上一下、上下呼应的大胆构图，新颖别致。两狮之间用绣球与绶带相连，浑然一体，融汇贯通。工匠巧妙的利用玉料天然绺裂处通过高浮雕的手法细腻地融入狮子的各个部位，自然生动。尾部、眉毛拉丝工艺精湛，与狮身高浮雕交相呼应。太狮（师）少狮（师）是清代宫廷传统的吉祥纹饰，通常为大小双狮的形象。狮是尊贵和威严的象征，同时『狮』与『师』同言，谐音太师少师，寓意着辈辈高升，位高权重。

3 A white jade carving of lion

Qing Dynasty, Qianlong Period (1736–1795)
Length 11.2cm, Width 7.5cm, Height 6.3cm
The collection of the Summer Palace

The white jade bears some yellowish markings. A lion in a recumbent position is carved in the round with the front limbs holding a brocaded ball.

白玉狮子

清乾隆（1736—1795年）
长11.2厘米，宽7.5厘米，高6.3厘米
颐和园藏

白玉质，有黄色沁，狮圆雕卧式披发，环眼，阔嘴，四肢伏于地，前肢抱绣球，尾巴自身后向上冲。

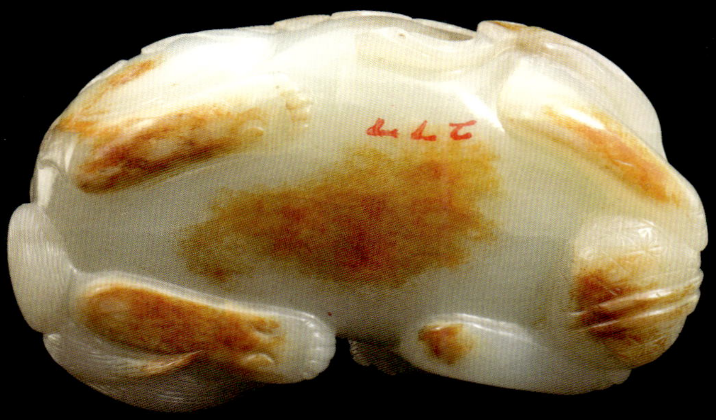

074 A white jade "Buddhist lion and cub" belt buckle

Qing Dynasty, Qianlong Period (1736-1795)
Length 8.8cm, Width 7cm, Height 1.7cm
Provided by The Institute of Qing History Renmin University of China

The white jade belt buckle is carved in the round with a mother lion carrying her cub on her back. The mouth of the mother lion holds a ribbon tied to a brocaded ball. The "lion with cub" connotes the meaning of getting promoted from junior to higher official ranks.

白玉太师少师带扣

清乾隆（1736—1795年）
长8.8厘米，宽7厘米，高1.7厘米
中国人民大学清史研究所提供

白玉质。以高浮雕和镂雕相结合的手法打造了一对母子狮形带扣。母狮背驮幼崽，呈侧首回望状，双目圆瞪，鬃毛卷曲，身姿矫健，尾如火焰。嘴中衔一绶带，下系一绣球，饰于母狮胸前。幼崽俯身与母狮呈对望状，活泼调皮。背面光素无纹，圆雕扣钮。『太狮少狮』与『太师少师』谐音，寓意世世为官，代代加爵。

075 A yellow jade carving of lion

Ming Dynasty (1368-1644)
Length 5.2cm, Width3.8 cm, Height 3.7cm
Provided by The Institute of Qing History Renmin University of China

A recumbent lion is carved in the round with its tail tucked under the body. The lion is believed to be the King of beasts with a noble and regal status.

黄玉狮

明（1368—1644年）
长5.2厘米，宽3.8厘米，高3.7厘米
中国人民大学清史研究所提供

黄玉质，带糖色。随形圆雕，狮子呈俯卧状，侧首凝视，双耳下垂，张口露齿，身躯饱满健硕，尾部回卷贴于腹侧。狮子乃百兽之王，玉狮寓意位高权重，地位尊贵。

76 A white jade lion

Qing Dynasty, Qianlong Period (1736-1795)
Length 11.5cm, Width 6.4cm, Height 9.3cm
Provided by The Institute of Qing History Renmin University of China

A half recumbent lion is carved in the round playing a brocaded ball. The lion with brocaded ball symbolized the getting rid of bad omens and bringing good luck.

白玉瑞狮戏球摆件

清乾隆（1736—1795 年）
长 11.5 厘米，宽 6.4 厘米，高 9.3 厘米
中国人民大学清史研究所提供

白玉质。整料圆雕，玉质洁白莹润，抛光打磨考究，包浆凝厚，刻画细腻传神。狮子半卧回首，双目圆瞪，张口露齿。身躯矫健，脊柱隆起，两前爪擎一绣球，尾部呈火焰状，毛发卷曲丝丝入扣。狮子绣球寓意去除灾祸，吉祥绥福，加官进爵。

077 A celadon jade carving of "champion"

Song/Yuan Dynasty (960-1368)
Length 7.2cm, Width 6.8cm, Height 4.8cm
Provided by The Institute of Qing History Renmin University of C

A male lion is carved in the round in a recumbent posture with an eagle resting on its back. This is a common jade carving theme signifying yingxiong (eagle being the ying, and the male lion being the xiong; meaning "heroic") symbolizing grand visions and heroic ambitions.

青玉『英雄』摆件

宋至元（960—1368年）
长7.2厘米，高6.8厘米，宽4.8厘米
中国人民大学清史研究所提供

青玉质，通体黑褐色牛毛纹沁。随形圆雕，以镂雕、高浮雕、线刻等多种技法，琢飞鹰雄狮一组，狮伏卧于下，体态浑圆，四肢粗壮，尾部卷曲，曲颈回首，双目圆睁，与栖于后背的雄鹰相望。雄鹰振翅俯身与狮相呼应。这种鹰与雄狮的飞禽踏兽形象是汉唐以来中国玉雕常见的题材。在天为英，立地为雄，取其谐音『英雄』，以此寓意建功立业、雄霸一方的远大志向和宏伟愿景。

078 A white jade carving of "champion"

Liao/Jin Dynasty (916-1134)
Length 5.7cm, Width 2cm, Height 3.7cm
Provided by The Institute of Qing History Renmin University of China

A male bear is carved in the round utilizing the openwork technique. An eagle is resting on the back of the bear. This theme also signifies the meaning of yingxiong (heroic) symbolizing heroic and high ambitions.

白玉『英雄』坠

辽至金（916—1134年）
长5.7厘米，宽2厘米，高3.7厘米
中国人民大学清史研究所提供

白玉质，皮壳厚重，刀法爽利，雕工细腻传神，以立体圆雕与镂空透雕等技法相结合，公熊双臂相抱，呈伏卧状，后腿弯曲，跃跃欲试，躯体壮硕浑圆，回首侧望。背驮一只雄鹰，体态舒张，双爪遒劲，擒于熊背之上。双翅紧收，侧颈与熊相呼应，喙尖而锋利。鹰熊与『英雄』谐音，寓意志向高远，英明神武。

079 A white jade carving of dragon-fish

Qing Dynasty, Qianlong Period (1736–1795)
Length 12cm, Width 6.5cm, Height 1.6cm
The collection of the Summer Palace

The white jade is carved with a dragon fish which has a dragon head with a fish body. Wearing this dragon fish jade connotes the meaning of excellence and success in the imperial examination.

白玉鳌鱼

清乾隆（1736—1795 年）
长 12 厘米，宽 6.5 厘米，高 1.6 厘米
颐和园藏

白玉质。鳌鱼龙头鱼身，是鲤鱼误吞龙珠而变成。古代科举考试中第一名将有资格立于皇宫大殿雕刻鳌头之上，故佩戴白玉鳌鱼，有着独占鳌头，出类拔萃，才高八斗的美好寓意。

080 A white jade carving of fish shape flower vase

Qing Dynasty, Qianlong Period (1736–1795)
Length 13cm, Width 3.5cm, Height 19cm
The collection of the Summer Palace

The dragon fish is a beast with a dragon head and a fish body. Two dragon fish are carved with an adult followed by a juvenile. The dragon fish is a beast in Chinese mythology believed to be transformed from a carp accidentally swallowed a dragon pearl.

白玉鳌鱼花插

清乾隆（1736—1795 年）

长 13 厘米，宽 3.5 厘米，高 19 厘米

颐和园藏

白玉质。整料雕琢。瓶身雕琢为鳌鱼形，鱼头雕饰独角，瓶身内挖膛，大鱼翻身跃起，迎浪直上，口张目瞪，摇须摆尾。小鱼紧随其后，浮浪而出。鳞、鳍自然逼真。鳌鱼是古代中国神话传说中的动物，是鲤鱼误吞龙珠而变成，龙头鱼身。雄性鳌鱼金鳞葫芦尾，雌性鳌鱼银鳞芙蓉尾，终日遨游大海嬉戏。底座木质，呈波浪形态，与玉鱼相配得宜。

A white jade carving of toad

Qing Dynasty (1616-1911)
Length 4cm, Width 2.8cm, Height 2.9cm
The collection of the Summer Palace

The white jade with some minor cracks. A three-foot toad is carved in the round with its mouth holding a river lotus. The auspicious golden toad holding lotus construes the meaning of bringing continuous wealth.

白玉金蟾

清（1616—1911年）
长4厘米，宽2.8厘米，高2.9厘米
颐和园藏

白玉质，有绺裂。以圆雕手法琢三足金蟾一只，前脚相扣，双眼圆睁，口衔莲花，左后腿蹬地，脚蹼压于腹下。在中国古代传说中，金蟾被视为招财的神兽。此件蟾衔荷莲表示财运连连。

082 A celadon white jade carving of toad with two pomegranates

Qing Dynasty, Qianlong Period (1736-1795)
Length 8.2cm, Width 6.5cm, Height 5.5cm
Provided by The Institute of Qing History Renmin University of China

The pale celadon jade is carved with a golden toad carrying pomegranate on its back. Both the golden toad and pomegranate connote the meaning of "numerous progenies". The toad is also revered in the traditional Daoist culture.

青白玉石榴金蟾

清乾隆（1736—1795 年）
长 8.2 厘米，宽 6.5 厘米，高 5.5 厘米
中国人民大学清史研究所提供

青白玉质，有天然灰褐色斑。整料圆雕，灰玉雕金蟾在前，白玉雕石榴在后。金蟾背石榴一对，双目凝视前方，跃跃欲试，神态灵动，有呼之欲出之感。蟾与石榴皆多子，二者相连常有多子多福之意。石榴与蟾亦暗喻道教全真派北五祖之一刘海蟾。蟾是中国传统道教文化中的典型神兽。

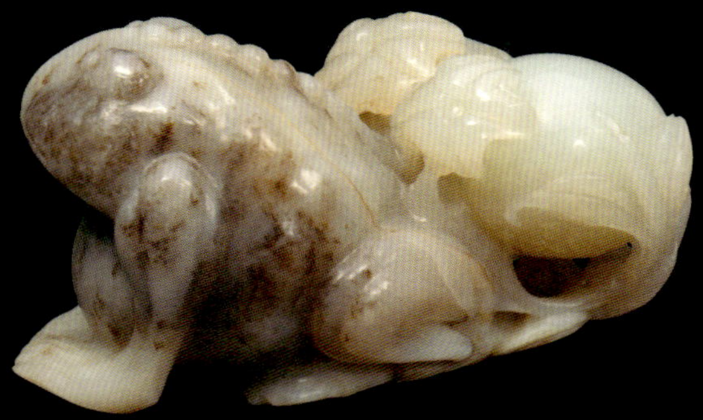

083 A chicken bone jade carving of toad

Yuan Dynasty (1206-1368)
Length 8cm, Width 5cm, Height 3cm
Provided by The Institute of Qing History Renmin University of China

This jigubai jade is carved with a toad in the round with its limbs bending in a crouching position. The jade toad conveys the meaning of a long and unaged life.

白玉蟾

元（1206—1368 年）
长 8 厘米，宽 5 厘米，高 3 厘米
中国人民大学清史研究所提供

鸡骨白玉质，整料随形圆雕，有牛毛沁。蟾蜍后腿紧绷，前腿撑地，作蹲踞状，好似蓄势待发。脖颈微曲，双目突出，凝视前方，四肢肌理清晰。腹部饰以阴刻线，突显其皮肤斑驳柔软之态。背部满布瘰疣，栩栩如生。玉蟾有长生不老，与天同寿之意。

084 A finely caved white jade elephant and boys group

Qing Dynasty, Qianlong Period (1736-1795)
Length 11.9cm, Width 5.6cm, Height 9.3cm
The collection of the Summer Palace

The jade has some cracks. It is carved with an elephant and a boy at the side while another boy at the back of the elephant. The "boys washing elephant" is an auspicious theme in jade carvings.

青白玉童子洗象

清乾隆（1736—1795年）
长11.9厘米，宽5.6厘米，高9.3厘米
颐和园藏

青白玉质，有绺裂。整料雕琢，采用圆雕技法雕琢象形。立象回首卷鼻体态肥硕，神态怡然。两童子一人伏于大象背，一人手持如意立于大象身侧。童子洗象是常见的吉祥题材的玉雕作品。『洗』与『喜』谐音，『洗象』寓『喜象』之意，也寓意气象更新。

085 A white jade table screen with elephant and boys

Qing Dynasty, Qianlong Period (1736–1795)
Length 14cm, Width 6cm, Height 20cm
The collection of the Summer Palace

The table screen is carved in relief with boys washing an elephant while the base is carved with lotus petals and auspicious cloud patterns. "The Washing of elephant" connotes the meaning of "washing and cleaning anew".

白玉雕『洗象图』座屏

清乾隆（1736—1795年）
长14厘米，宽6厘米，高20厘米
颐和园藏

白玉质。座屏式样，由底座和屏芯组成。该器运用圆雕和高浮雕的技法，屏风顶部雕饰祥云，屏芯主体纹饰为童子洗象，大象低身俯首，形态灵动，童子手持洗具，憨态可掬。莲瓣纹底座上雕饰祥云纹饰。洗象图有『喜象更新』之寓意。

086 A finely caved white jade elephant and boys group

Qing Dynasty, Qianlong Period (1736–1795)
Length 15cm, Width 7.1cm, Height 13.3cm
The collection of the Summer Palace

An elephant is carved in the round with two attending boys one holding a big peony while the other holding a precious vase. The elephant, the vase and peonies combination denote the Chinese belief of a peaceful world and good living.

白玉雕『太平有象』

清乾隆（1736—1795 年）
长 15 厘米，宽 7.1 厘米，高 13.3 厘米
颐和园藏

白玉质。圆雕立象，身披璎珞，回首卷鼻。两位童子，一人趴伏于象背，手捧大朵牡丹；另一人怀抱牡丹的宝瓶，立于象旁。象，厚重稳行，在中华文化中自古为瑞兽，与宝瓶、牡丹组合，有『太平有象』、『喜象升平』之说，寓意河清海晏、民康物阜。

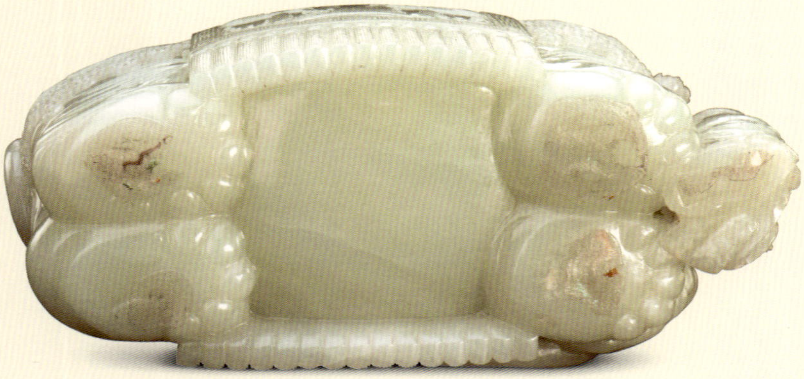

087 An olive-green and russet jade "elephant and boys" group

Yuan/Ming Dynasty (1206-1644)
Length 8cm, Width 4.5cm, Height 4cm
Provided by The Institute of Qing History Renmin University of China

The olive-green jade is carved with two boys playing with a recumbent elephant. The elephant is an auspicious animal in Buddhist beliefs. The cleaning or washing of elephant also denote spiritual cleansing in the Buddhist culture.

青玉『太平有象』摆件

元至明（1206—1644年）
长8厘米，宽4.5厘米，高4厘米
中国人民大学清史研究所提供

青黄玉质。立体圆雕，布满黄沁，大象侧首回望，身体呈伏卧状，长鼻翻卷，体态肥硕，双耳如扇，尾巴蜷收，安详恬适。臀部攀伏一童子，身着短衣长裤，手持象钩作戏象状。背部攀另一童子，憨态可掬。大象是佛教文化中寓意吉祥的瑞兽，素有太平有象、喜象升平的说法。洗象又称『扫象』，即『扫相』，寓意洗去蒙蔽心灵的尘垢，扫拂心中的执念，让真相得以显现。

088 A yellow jade carving of beast

Qing Dynasty, Qianlong Period (1736–1795)
Length 15cm, Width 7cm, Height 8cm
The collection of the Summer Palace

The yellow jade is carved with a recumbent Suanni, a mythical beast whose appearance is quite akin to a lion. The suanni signifies propitiousness in traditional Chinese culture.

黄玉狻猊

清乾隆（1736—1795 年）

长 15 厘米，宽 7 厘米，高 8 厘米

颐和园藏

黄玉质。采用圆雕、镂雕线刻等技法，整料雕琢一卧兽。从其造型判断，为龙生九子之一的狻猊。狻猊形似狮子，平生喜静不喜动，好坐，又喜欢烟火，是中国传统文化中象征吉祥的神兽。

089　A white jade carving of "parrot and peach" group

Qing Dynasty, Qianlong Period (1736–1795)
Length 9.5cm, Width 2.4cm, Height 4.9cm
Provided by The Institute of Qing History Renmin University of China

The jade bears some orange-red markings. A resting parrot is carved in the round with its beak holding a twig of peaches. The "parrot with peaches" traditionally signifies health and longevity.

白玉俏色鹦鹉衔桃

清乾隆（1736—1795 年）
长 9.5 厘米，宽 2.4 厘米，高 4.9 厘米
中国人民大学清史研究所提供

白玉质，带橘红色皮。立体巧雕，鹦鹉俯卧回首，口衔桃枝，圆目短喙，羽翼丰满回拢，双爪收于腹底。枝叶舒展灵动，双桃果实饱满圆润。鹦鹉在鸟类中以长寿著称，鹦鹉衔桃是乾隆宫廷常见题材，寓意英武长寿。

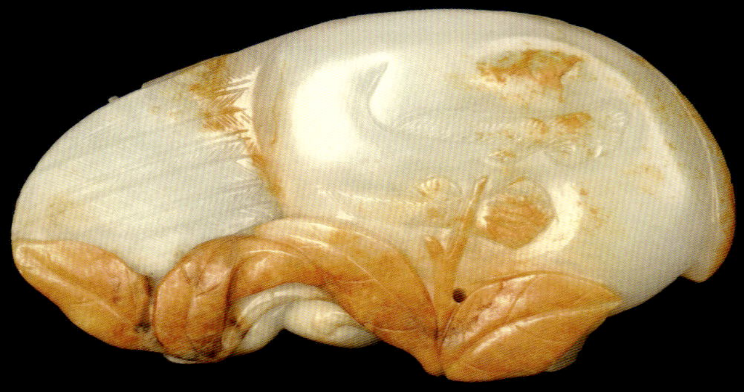

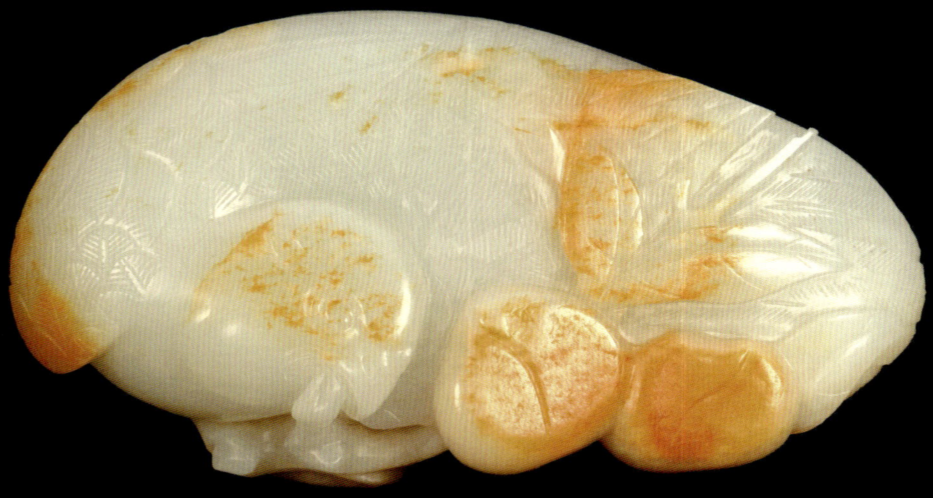

090 A pale green and russet jade "bird and peach" group

Qing Dynasty, Qianlong Period (1736-1795)
Length 9cm, Width 4.6cm, Height 5.4cm
Provided by The Institute of Qing History Renmin University of China

The pale green jade has some orange-red markings. A recumbent parrot is carved in the round with its beak holding a twig with peach. The parrot with peach design symbolizes good health, good luck and longevity.

青白玉巧雕鹦鹉衔桃

清乾隆（1736—1795 年）
长 9 厘米，宽 4.6 厘米，高 5.4 厘米
中国人民大学清史研究所提供

玉色白中闪青，带橘红色皮。立体圆雕，鹦鹉回首呈卧状，喙衔桃枝，长目短喙，翅尾紧收，双爪收于腹底，造型丰腴圆润。寿桃饱满圆润，桃枝舒展缠绕。鹦鹉衔桃暗喻英明神武，有健康长寿的吉祥寓意。

091 A white jade carving of "parrot and peach" group

Qing Dynasty, Qianlong Period (1736-1795)
Length 6.5cm, Width 5.3cm, Height 3.9cm
Provided by The Institute of Qing History Renmin University of China

The white jade carries some yellowish-brown markings. A recumbent parrot is carved in the round on top of the peach.

白玉鹦鹉衔桃

清乾隆（1736—1795年）
长6.5厘米，宽5.3厘米，高3.9厘米
中国人民大学清史研究所提供

白玉质，略带黄褐色沁。立体圆雕，鹦鹉卧姿回首，喙衔桃枝，身姿丰满，翎羽细腻传神，双翅拢于体测，下擒寿桃一枝。有英武长寿之寓意。

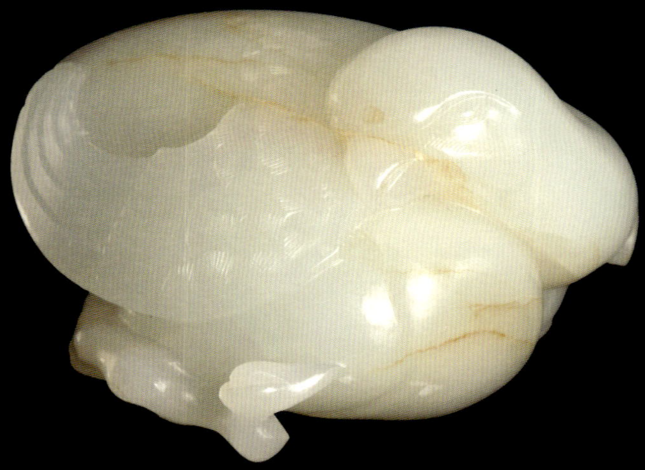

092 A white jade carving of QiLin carrying books from heaven

Early Qing Dynasty (1636-1795)
Length 10cm, Width 3.9cm, Height 9cm
Provided by The Institute of Qing History Renmin University of China

The jade bears some orange-gold color rind markings. A qilin, an auspicious mythical beast, is carved in the round with its back carrying books. The qilin carrying books symbolize the birth of a son and the family's well wishes for the son.

青白玉麒麟负书

清早期（1636—1795 年）
长 10 厘米，宽 3.9 厘米，高 9 厘米
中国人民大学清史研究所提供

青白玉质，洒金皮，间有白瑕。籽玉随形圆雕，麒麟昂首挺胸，双目凸起，粗颈微张，双蹄欲腾云而起，口吐祥云缠绕于身，背负宝书绶带，四肢雄壮，局部浮雕龙鳞。『麒麟负书』，亦称为『麒麟送书』，『麒麟吐书』。传说孔子降生之时天降麒麟于孔府，口吐玉书。因此，麒麟负书不仅代表了望子成龙的吉祥寓意，更包含了家出圣贤的美好期望。

093 A gray jade carving of Qilin carrying the Heavenly Book

Ming Dynasty (1368–1644)
Length 13cm, Width 5.8cm, Height 5cm
Provided by The Institute of Qing History Renmin University of China

The grayish white jade carries some black markings. A qilin with its head gazing back is carved in the round with its back carrying books. The body of the qilin is fully carved with scales.

灰白玉麒麟吐书摆件

明（1368—1644年）
长13厘米，宽5.8厘米，高5厘米
中国人民大学清史研究所提供

灰玉质，灰中闪青，带黑灰色沁。立体圆雕，麒麟负书造型。侧首回望，眉宇深邃，圆目龙鼻，口吐祥云，上托天书。麒麟造型肃穆，身形健硕，满饰龙鳞，四肢蜷缩于腹下，牛蹄龙尾，有望子成龙之寓意。

094 A rare pale green jade carving of a Qilin carrying the Heavenly Book

Qing Dynasty, Qianlong Period (1736-1795)
Length 10cm, Width 4.8cm, Height 7.8cm
Provided by The Institute of Qing History Renmin University of China

This is a Hetian (Khotan) pale green jade. A recumbent qilin is carved in the round with its back carrying books. The auspicious beast has a scaly body.

青白玉麒麟负书摆件

清乾隆（1736—1795年）
长10厘米，宽4.8厘米，高7.8厘米
中国人民大学清史研究所提供

青玉质，籽玉白中闪青，色泽纯净。随形圆雕，作麒麟负书造型。雕工细腻，毛发排线丝丝入扣，抛光打磨精良。麒麟昂首回望，双目圆睁，眉宇宽厚呈锯齿状，如意形鼻，口吐天书。长角卷曲，鬃发自然垂于两侧。体态健硕，四肢蜷卧，身饰龙鳞，龙尾牛蹄，有望子成龙之意。

095 A rare pale white jade "champion" vase

Song/Yuan Dynasty (960–1368)
Length 9cm, Width 5cm, Height 7.5cm
Provided by The Institute of Qing History Renmin University of China

It is a two-cylinder combination cup with some light russet markings. A bear and an eagle are carved in the middle of the two-cylinder cup. The combination of bear and eagle also connotes the meaning of yingxiong (heroic). It is used by the newlyweds in the wedding ceremony.

白玉『英雄』合卺杯

宋至元（960—1368 年）
长 9 厘米，宽 5 厘米，高 7.5 厘米
中国人民大学清史研究所提供

青玉质，满红沁。双筒相连均为圆口，深圈足薄胎。口沿和腹部刻谷纹，间以夔凤纹及如意纹相连。鹰熊在双筒之间，取谐音『英雄』之吉意。『合卺』指新婚夫妻在新房之内共饮合欢酒。此种双联杯是古代婚礼上用来喝交杯酒的专用酒具，又称合卺杯。

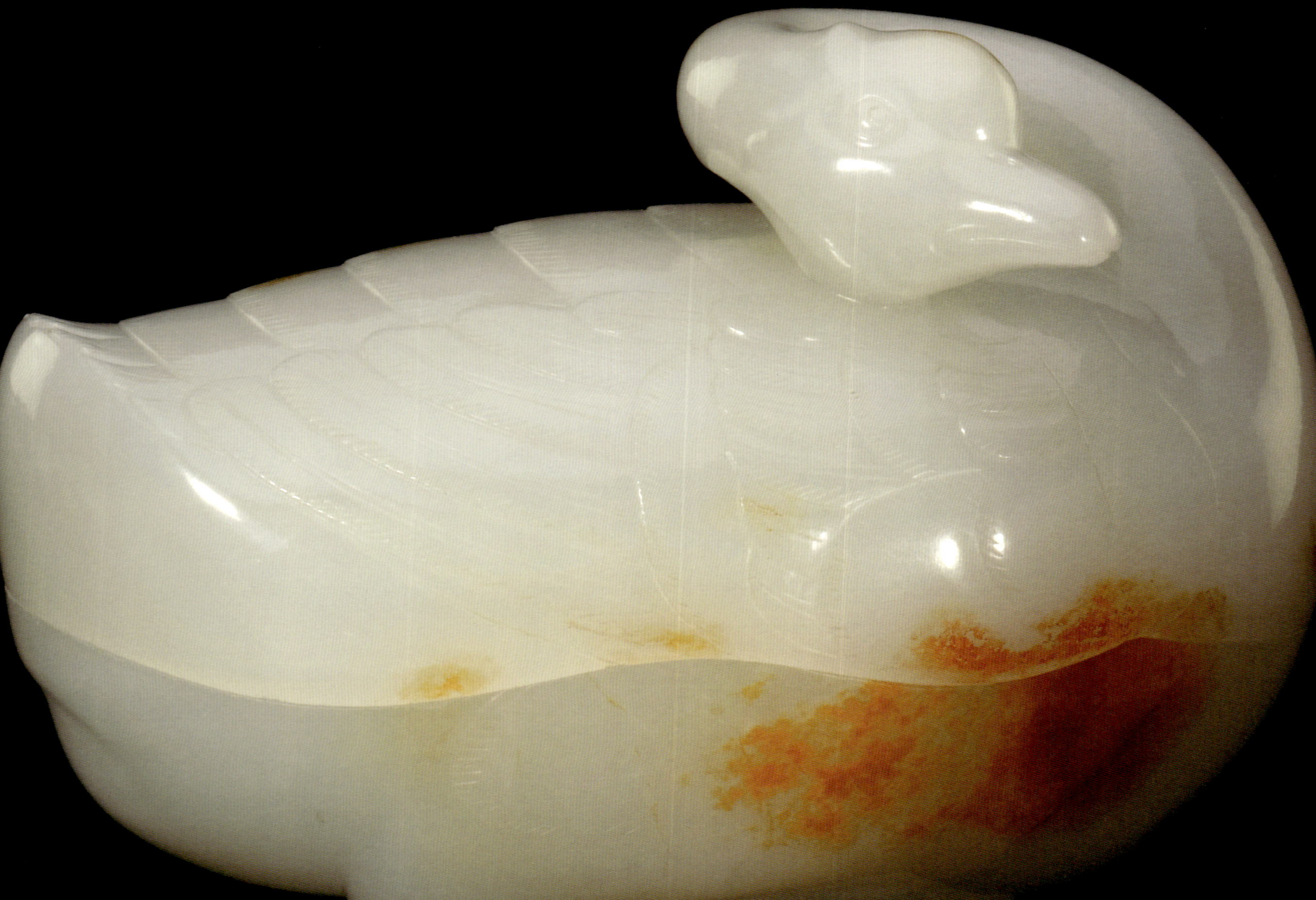

家豢天养

Domestic and Wild Animals

After the Tang and Song periods, Chinese jade culture slowly moved to become more secular and approachable to the commoners. These were shown quite profoundly in the trendy jade animal carvings depicting the world of nature and in real life. Animals in the wild such as flying birds and butterflies, fish and insects; domestic chickens, geese, dogs and cats, could all be the subject of jade carvings. Even the fierce and mighty lions, tigers, bears and other mythical beasts had been depicted as more docile and gentle. This clearly reflects men's progress in the ability to handle and manage the natural world.

唐宋以来，中国玉文化逐渐走向世俗化和写实性，客观反映自然界和现实生活中动物形象的玉器大行其道。天养之蝶燕鱼虫，家豢之鸡犬鹅猫，品类万端，皆可为器，原有威猛神性的狮虎熊貔也开始变得温顺可爱，反映了人类对自然的征服能力的进一步增强。

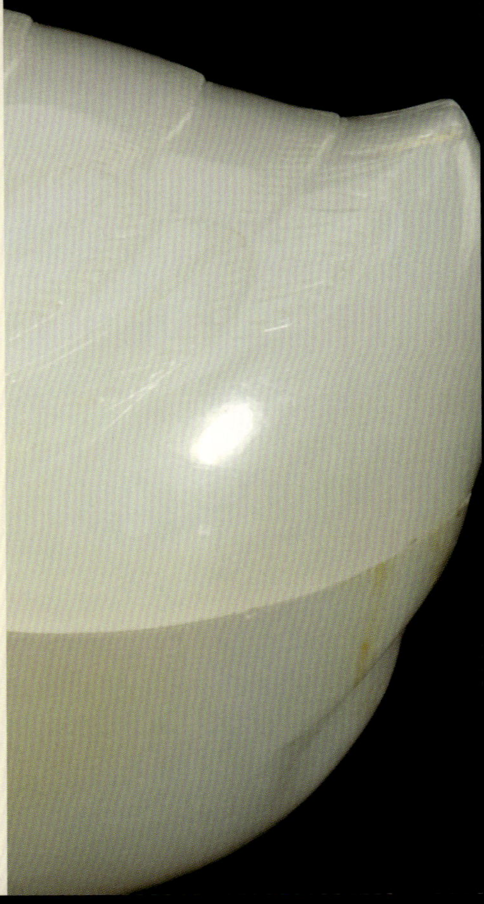

096 A celadon jade carving of ram

Han Dynasty (206 BCE–220)
Length 9cm, Width 4cm, Height 7cm
Provided by The Institute of Qing History Renmin University of China

There are some brown markings on the jade. A recumbent ram is carved in the round. There are many mythical beliefs regarding the ram. It also connotes the birth of the sage who could provide great help to the ruler.

青白玉公羊

汉（公元前 206—公元 220 年）
长 9 厘米，宽 4 厘米，高 7 厘米
中国人民大学清史研究所提供

玉质温润致密，局部有褐色沁闪灰皮，立体圆雕。玉羊四肢蜷缩呈跪卧状，引颈昂首，目视远方，双耳紧贴，头顶双角曲于耳旁，脖颈粗壮有力，身体健硕强悍。『羊』通『祥』，在中国古文字中有大吉祥之意。关于玉羊在中国传统文化中的传说由来已久，相传玉羊是华山之灵，当玉羊现世，意味着有辅佐君主的圣贤降世。

097 A jade carving of ram

Song/Yuan Dynasty (960–1368)
Length 7.8cm, Width 2.7cm, Height 4.8cm
Provided by The Institute of Qing History Renmin University of China

The jade has some russet markings with a ram carved in the round in a recumbent position. The ram has been a traditional auspicious animal. This ram carving has a pair of exaggerated long horns conferring the meaning of "leading ram of the flock".

玉卧羊

宋至元（960—1368 年）
长 7.8 厘米，宽 2.7 厘米，高 4.8 厘米
中国人民大学清史研究所提供

玉质温润细腻，皮壳凝重，局部有深褐色沁。立体圆雕，玉羊呈跪卧状，低首微垂，头顶弯曲状角，四肢蜷卧收于腹下，尾紧收。整体线条舒朗，雕工爽利，有宋元玉雕写实精简之特点。羊在中国古代文化中有祥瑞之意，此玉雕有意夸张公羊的角，有『领头羊』的寓意，凸显了威望和权力。

098 A celadon jade carving of ram

Song Dynasty (960–1279)
Length 5.5cm, Width 3cm, Height 3.4cm
Provided by The Institute of Qing History Renmin University of China

There are some brownish-red markings on this pale celadon jade. A recumbent ram is carved in the round with its four limbs tucked under the body. The ram "yang" rhymes the Chinese character "xiang" meaning good luck and happiness.

青白玉羊

宋（960—1279年）
长5.5厘米，宽3厘米，高3.4厘米
中国人民大学清史研究所提供

青白玉质，带棕红色沁。立体圆雕，玉羊呈跪卧状，四肢蜷缩收于腹下，昂首引颈，目视前方。羊角镂空雕刻，躯干圆润饱满，尾短而圆。羊性格温顺，与『祥』谐音，因此寓意吉祥大利。

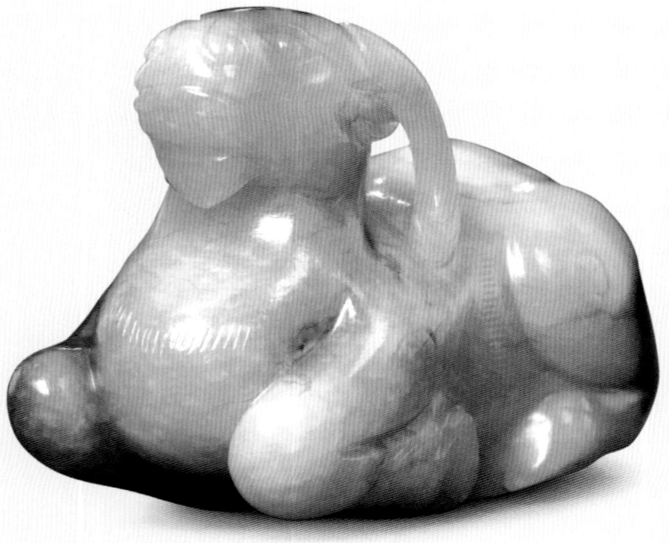

099 A small pale celadon jade carving of recumbent ram

Qing Dynasty, Qianlong Period (1736–1795)
Length 4.1cm, Width 2cm, Height 2.9cm
Provided by The Institute of Qing History Renmin University of China

This small white jade has some light-caramel markings at the base. A recumbent ram is carved with its mouth holding a lingzhi. The "ram with lingzhi" motif signifies propitiousness and happiness.

白玉羊衔灵芝

清乾隆（1736—1795 年）
长 4.1 厘米，宽 2 厘米，高 2.9 厘米
中国人民大学清史研究所提供

白玉质，玉色白中闪青，底部略带糖色。立体圆雕，玉羊呈伏卧昂首状，头顶一双弯角，双耳贴于脑后。口衔灵芝一束展转蜿蜒，背有祥云缠绕。羊衔灵芝寓意吉祥如意。

100 A white jade carving of three rams

Qing Dynasty, Qianlong Period (1736–1795)
Length 10cm, Width 5.5cm, Height 4.5cm
The collection of the Summer Palace

The white jade is carved in the round with ewe and two lambs. The ewe with lamb combination alludes to the Chinese characters "Sanyang Kaitai" conveying the meaning of auspiciousness and good luck with the coming of Spring.

白玉雕『三阳开泰』

清乾隆（1736—1795 年）
长 10 厘米，宽 5.5 厘米，高 4.5 厘米
颐和园藏

白玉质。圆雕三羊造型，一大二小，大羊侧卧于地，右前肢踏于地上，其余三肢屈起收于腹下；其上卧伏两只小羊，小羊居前，侧头转向大羊，另一只小羊紧伏于大羊身后。该器以三羊为饰，寓意『三阳开泰』。

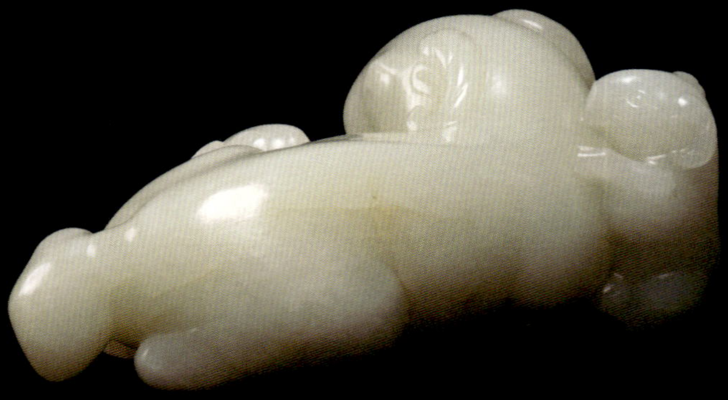

101 A white jade carving of three rams

Qing Dynasty, Qianlong Period (1736–1795)
Length 10cm, Width 4cm, Height 3cm
The collection of the Summer Palace

The white jade is carved with a group of three sheep, an adult ewe and two lambs. This group carving of sheep implies the traditional Chinese meaning of "sanyang kaitai": the ending of winter with the coming of spring and everything is booming and thriving.

白玉雕『三阳开泰』

清乾隆（1736—1795 年）
长 10 厘米，宽 4 厘米，高 3 厘米
颐和园藏

白玉质。整器圆雕三只羊，一大两小，头上皆有角，口衔青草，侧卧于地，四只蜷于腹下。三只羊寓意『三阳开泰』，指冬去春来、阴消阳长，吉亨兴盛之象。

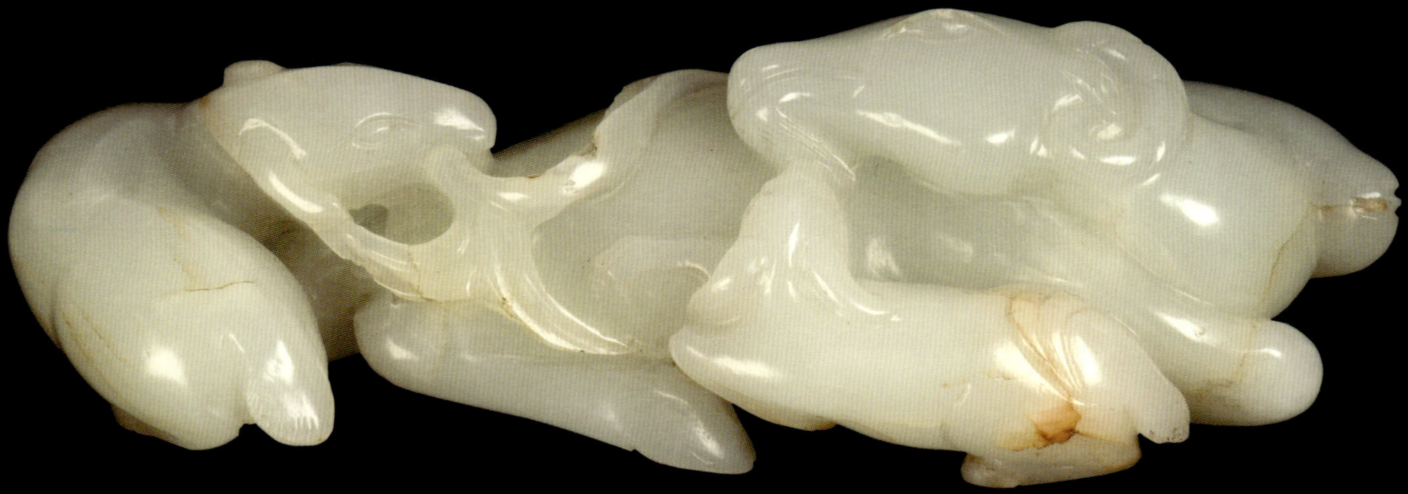

102 A gray jade carving of a ram

Qing Dynasty, Qianlong Period (1736-1795)
Length 5.5cm, Width 3cm, Height 4.6cm
Provided by The Institute of Qing History Renmin University of China

A strong and stout goat is carved in the round in a kneeling position. Its head looks backwards and it bears a beard. The Chinese word "goat" rhymes with the word xiang which means great happiness and good luck.

墨玉大吉羊

清乾隆（1736—1795 年）
长 5.5 厘米，宽 3 厘米，高 4.6 厘米
中国人民大学清史研究所提供

灰玉质。立体圆雕，打磨细腻，玉羊跪卧回首，双角垂于脑后，双耳贴于两侧，胡须置于一侧。身型丰满健硕，四肢卷曲于身下，尾宽而平有细排线。羊谐音『祥』，古有大吉祥之寓意。

103 A very rare pale green jade "ram and boy" group

Qing Dynasty, Qianlong Period (1736–1795)
Length 12.5cm, Width 2.8cm, Height 5.7cm
Provided by The Institute of Qing History Renmin University of China

This is a Hetian (Khotan) jade with a light greenish tone. It is carved in the round with a boy climbing the back of a recumbent goat. The goat in Chinese (yang) rhymes with the character xiang which means jixiang (peace and happiness). Boy riding a goat was a popular theme of the Three Kingdom period.

青白玉骑羊童子大摆件

清乾隆（1736—1795 年）
长 12.5 厘米，宽 2.8 厘米，高 5.7 厘米
中国人民大学清史研究所提供

和田玉，玉色白中闪青，选料大而整。立体圆雕，玉羊跪卧，首微右倾，头顶双角，双耳如叶，身形丰满健硕。背部攀伏一童子，头顶双髻，身着短衣长裤，憨态可掬，右手牵缰绳，左手抚羊首。

羊与『祥』谐音，玉羊不仅寓意吉祥，更有温和孝顺等品质。童子乘羊的题材在三国时期较为流行，表达了人们对天降祥瑞，圣贤出世的美好向往。

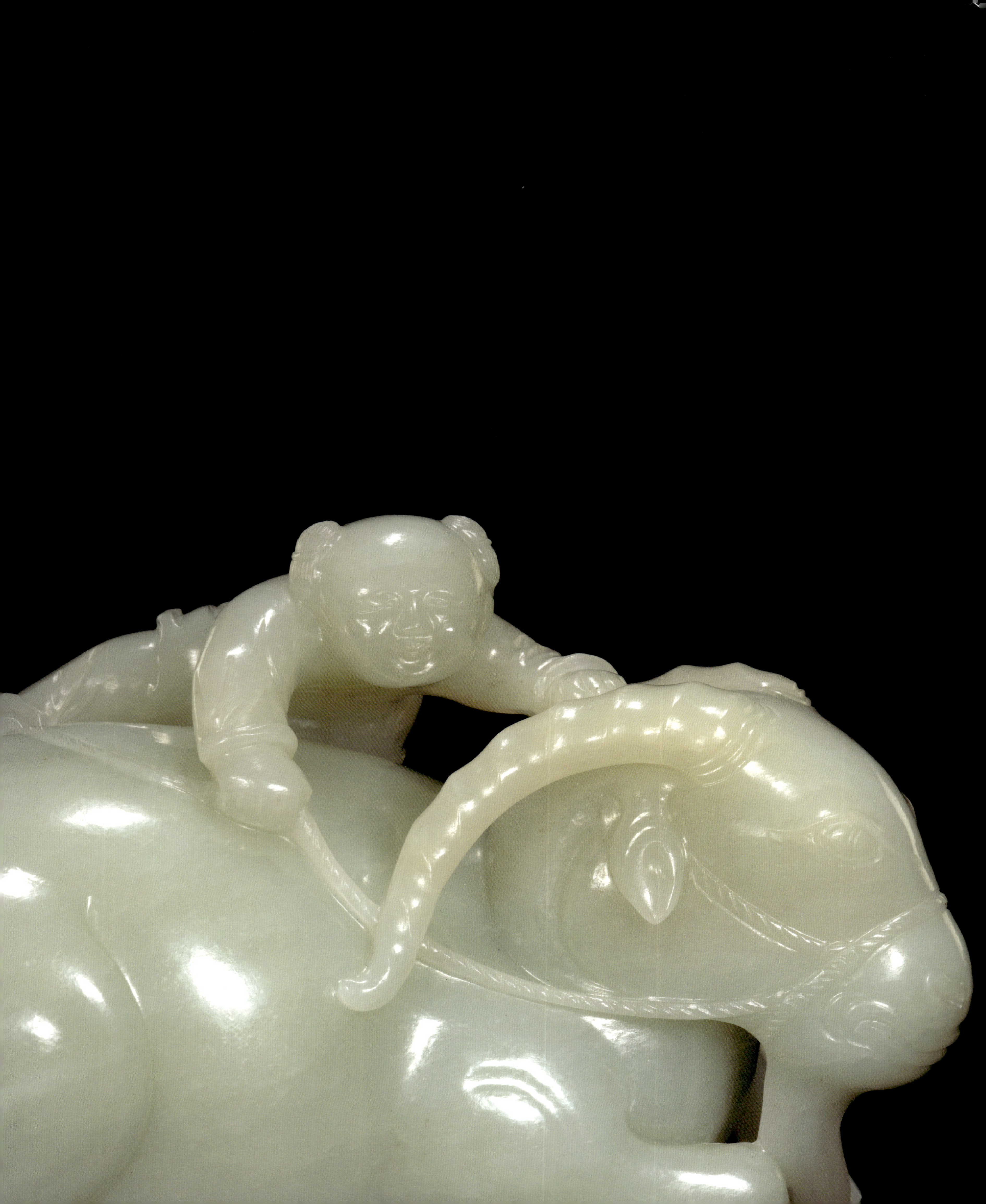

104 A rare jade carving of a camel

Song Dynasty (960–1279)
Length 12.5cm, Width 8cm, Height 5cm
Provided by The Institute of Qing History Renmin University of China

A recumbent camel is carved in the round with its head looking back and its four limbs tucked under the body. The camel is always portrayed as an animal able to work hard and withstand hardships.

灰玉骆驼

宋（960—1279年）
长12.5厘米，宽8厘米，高5厘米
中国人民大学清史研究所提供

灰色火烧玉质，有棕黄沁斑，包浆凝重。立体圆雕，骆驼回首蜷卧，背部驼峰隆起，四肢收于腹下，尾部回勾。头部棱角鲜明，两腮隆起，双目深挖，鼻吻浅琢，双耳紧贴于脑后。体态优美，比例谐调。唐宋时期的骆驼常有颈首回望的卧式造型，十分贴近自然。骆驼生性沉稳，坚忍不拔，有沙漠之舟的称号，是北方少数民族重要生产工具，常用来表现吃苦耐劳、甘心奉献的优良品质。

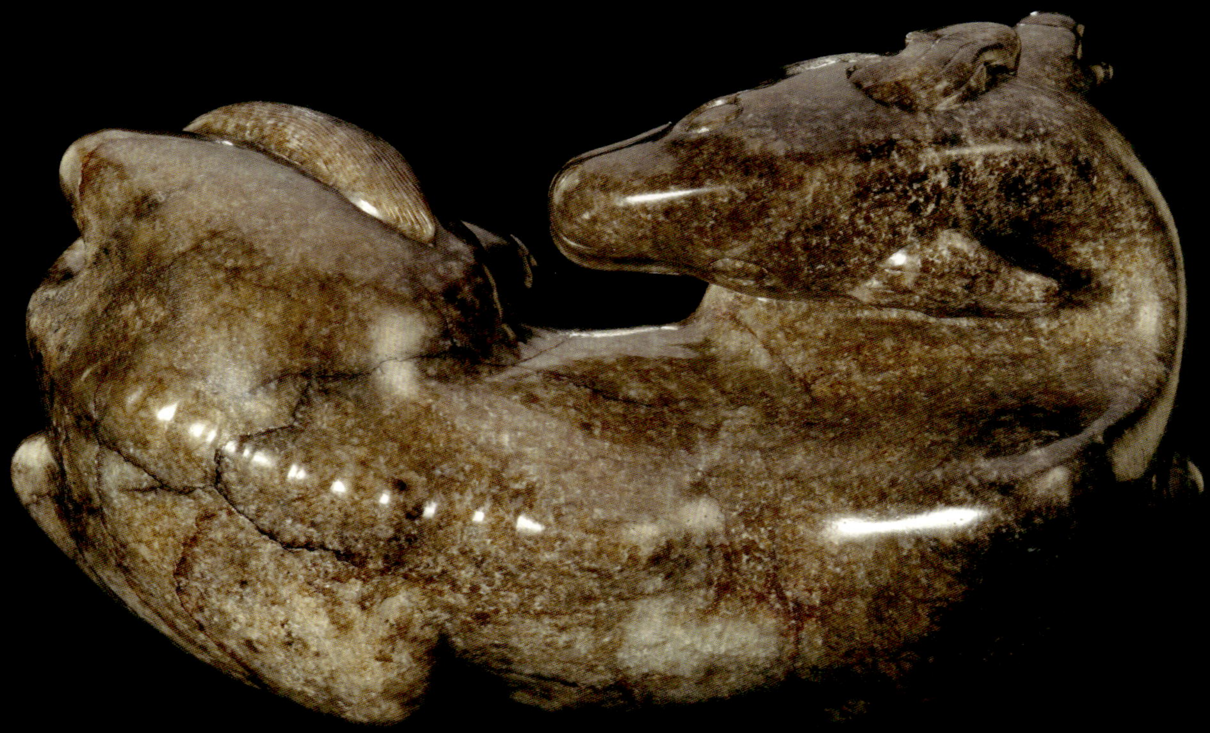

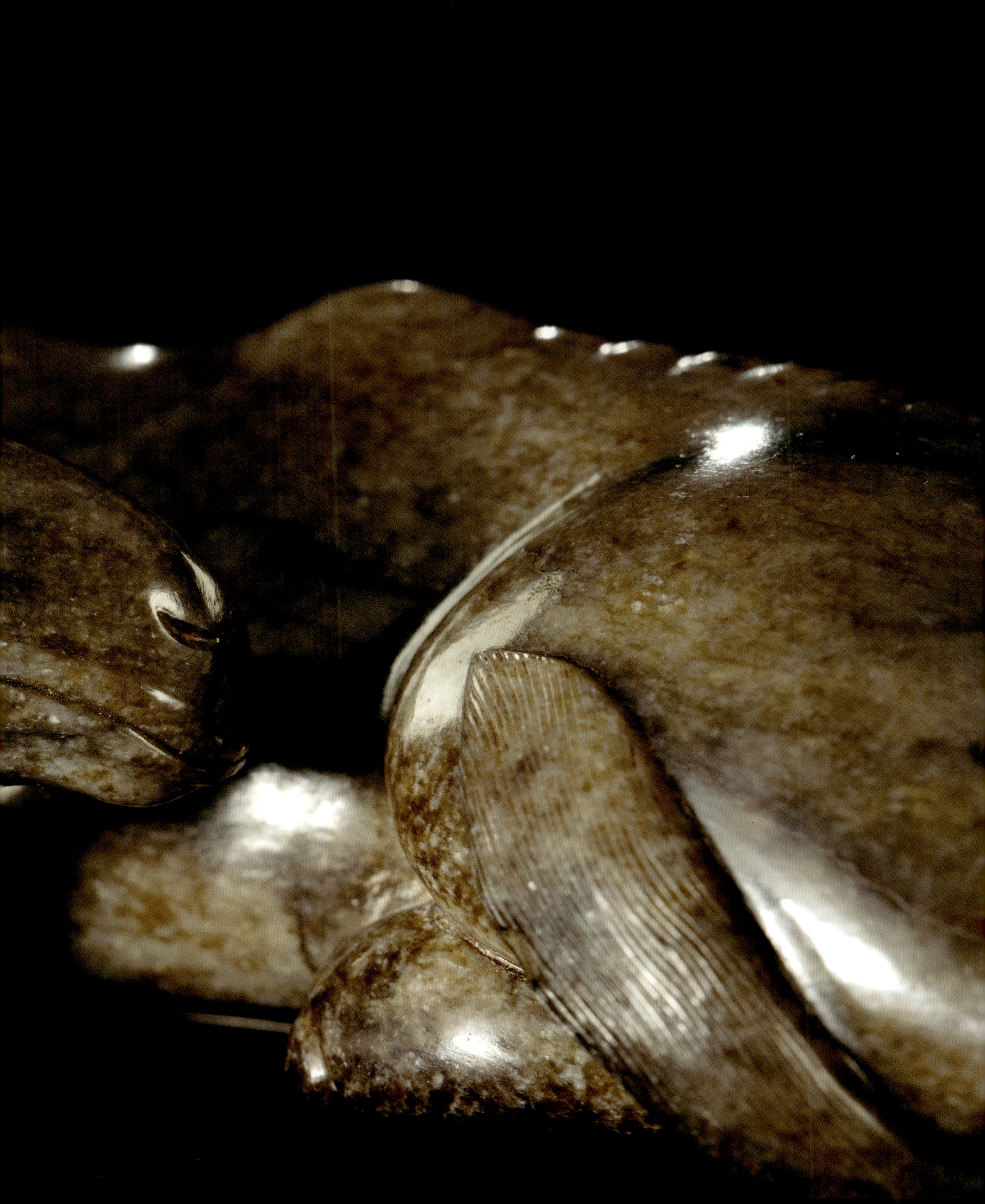

105 A small white and russet jade camel

Song Dynasty (960-1279)
Length 4.5cm, Width 1.5cm, Height 2.8cm
Provided by The Institute of Qing History Renmin University of China

The white jade bears some red-brownish inclusions and a recumbent camel is carved in the round. Its head gazes forward and the back bears two humps.

白玉骆驼

宋（960—1279 年）
长 4.5 厘米，宽 1.5 厘米，高 2.8 厘米
中国人民大学清史研究所提供

白玉质，有赤褐色沁斑。立体圆雕，中穿孔，颈部有细阴刻线。骆驼呈跪卧状，昂首注视前方，双耳树立，背部隆起两驼峰，鬃毛垂于两侧，四肢收于身下。

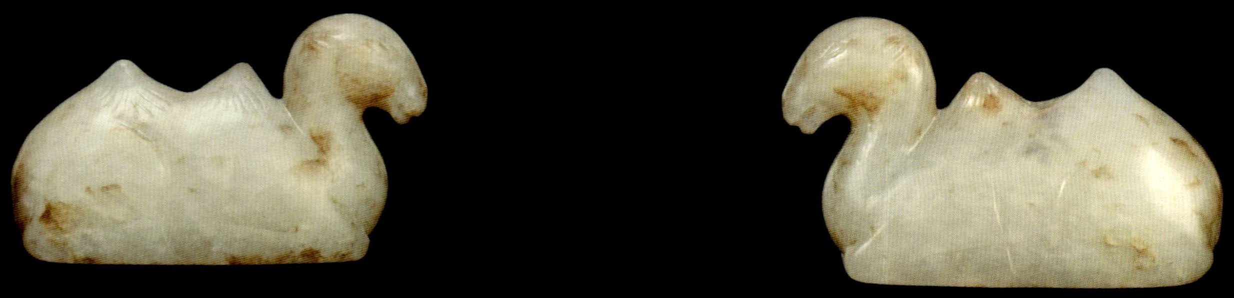

106 A white jade goose belt hook

Song Dynasty (960–1279)
Length 10cm, Width 1.2cm, Height 2.3cm
Provided by The Institute of Qing History Renmin University of China

The white jade bears some pale brownish tone inclusions. A goose head is carved in the round with its long neck. The back of the neck bears a button for use as a fastener or hook. The carving is simple yet very elegant.

白玉鹅首带钩

宋（960—1279 年）
长 10 厘米，宽 1.2 厘米，高 2.3 厘米
中国人民大学清史研究所提供

白玉质，器身多处有棕色沁。一端圆雕鹅首，钩身光素。背琢圆纽，便于穿系。此件带钩以最简洁的方式雕琢，并巧用玉质本色，充分体现了宋人『大道至简』的审美取向。

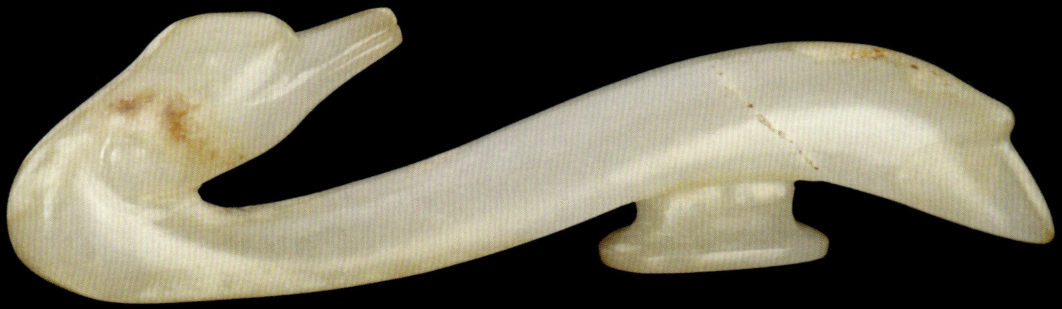

107 A pair of very finely carved white jade goose shape boxes

Qing Dynasty, Qianlong Period (1736-1795)
Length 10.6cm, Width 6.2cm, Height 8.8cm
Provided by The Institute of Qing History Renmin University of China

The white jade has some orange-red rinds with the interior hollowed out for use as storage boxes with accompanying lids. The geese, just like mandarin ducks, also signify a long and lasting love.

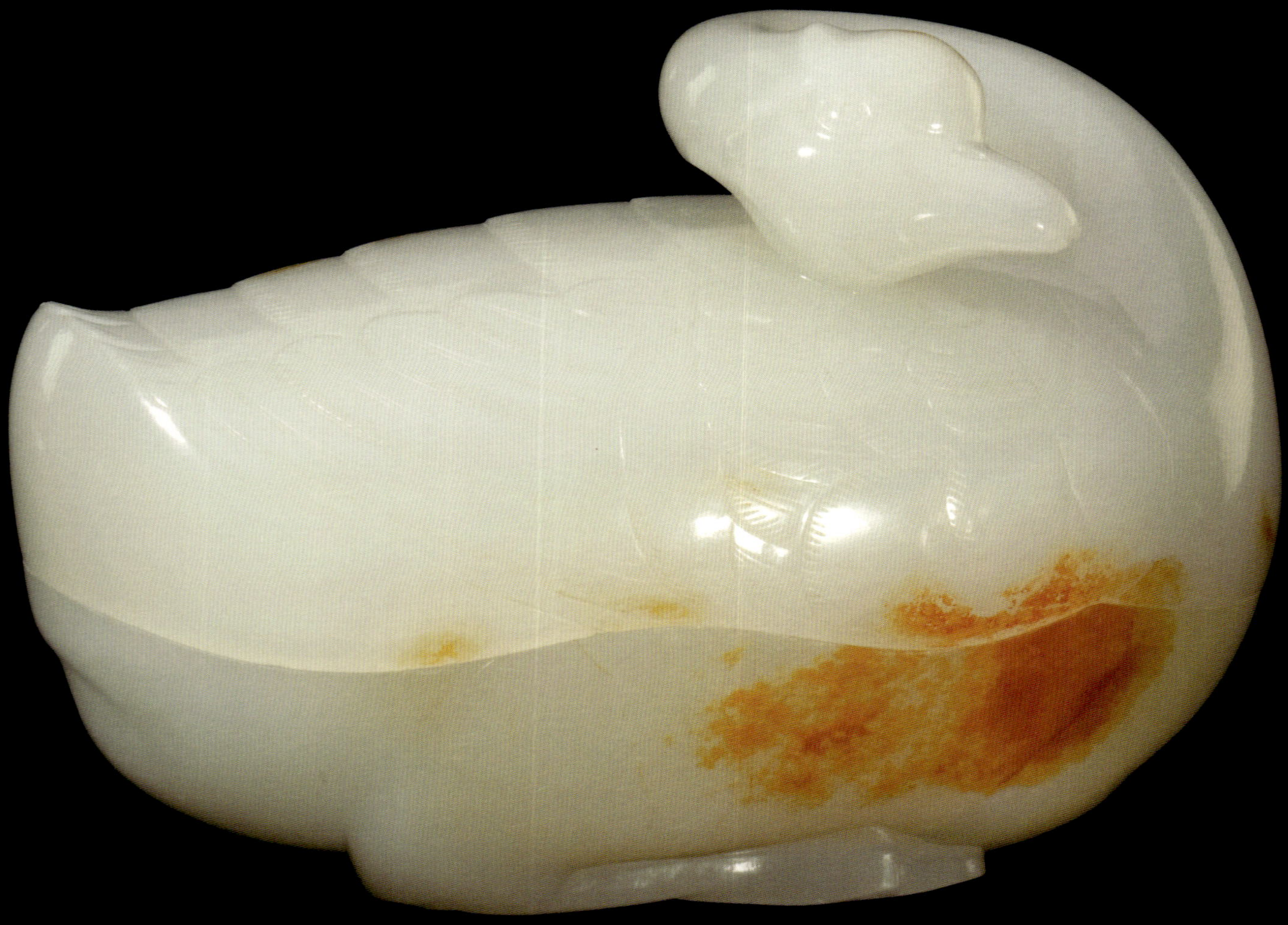

白玉鹅型盖盒（一对）

清乾隆（1736—1795年）
长10.6厘米，宽6.2厘米，高8.8厘米
中国人民大学清史研究所提供

白玉质，留红皮，抛玻璃光。选料硕大，籽料整挖，上下子母口琢成盖盒一对，饰琥珀色与原皮相配。两只白鹅曲颈对望，憨态可掬。盒内掏膛干净利落，盖盒严丝合缝，皮色明艳，位置恰到好处，羽毛刻画丝丝入扣，整体造型张弛有度、栩栩如生。鹅因其羽毛洁白、性情温顺而被古人视为一种清新脱俗、温情和善的瑞禽，深受古代文人墨客喜爱。鹅如鸳鸯一般，也是忠贞爱情的代表，因此，双鹅亦寓意双宿双飞、忠贞不渝的爱情。古有王羲之爱鹅之典故，文人常用此暗寓于文房雅器之上。此对玉鹅盒与天津博物馆收藏的宋代灰玉鹅盒如出一辙，应为乾隆宫廷仿古之佳作。

108　A white jade carving of goose

Qing Dynasty, Qianlong Period (1736–1795)
Length 6.5cm, Width 3cm, Height 4.3cm
Provided by The Institute of Qing History Renmin University of China

A recumbent goose is carved with its long neck bending over and resting on its back. The goose signifies peace and blissfulness in Chinese traditional folklore.

白玉卧鹅

清乾隆（1736—1795 年）
长 6.5 厘米，宽 3 厘米，高 4.3 厘米
中国人民大学清史研究所提供

白玉质。圆雕卧鹅，雕工细腻入微，线条流畅，曲颈侧眠，倚于背上，羽翼丰满，两脚蜷缩于身下，恬静祥和。白玉鹅象征吉祥如意，有『羲之爱鹅』之暗喻。

109 A white jade carving of goose

Qing Dynasty, Qianlong Period (1736-1795)
Length 8.6cm, Width 2cm, Height 6.8cm
Provided by The Institute of Qing History Renmin University of China

The white jade bears some russet markings. It is carved with a goose in the round with its neck and head turning back. The beak holds an ear of grain. This goose with grain theme conveys the message of a good harvest and peace throughout the year.

白玉衔穗鹅

清乾隆（1736—1795年）
长8.6厘米，宽2厘米，高6.8厘米
中国人民大学清史研究所提供

玉质白中闪青，留棕红皮。整料圆雕鹅呈回首状，曲颈于背脊，喙衔谷穗，体态丰盈，圆臀阔胸，羽翼饱满，双蹼置于底端。谷穗颗粒饱满，有吉庆有余、岁岁平安之意。

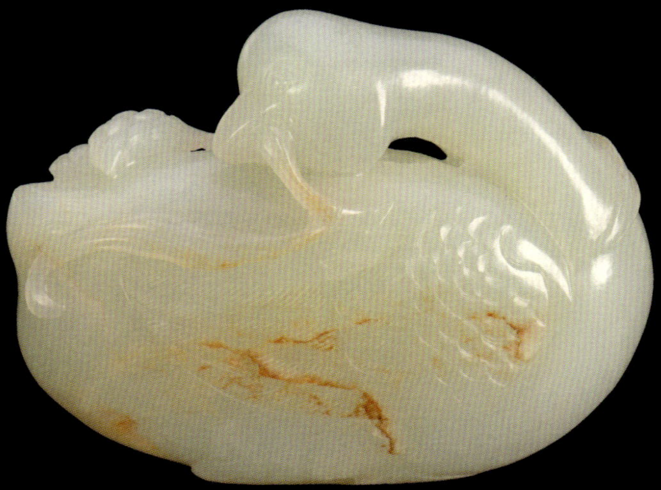

110 A white jade carving of goose

Qing Dynasty, Qianlong Period (1736–1795)
Length 13cm, Width 6cm, Height 11cm
The collection of the Summer Palace

The pale celadon jade is carved in the round with a wild duck with a long neck and its head turning backwards. Its beak holds an ear of grain. This wild duck with grain also alludes to the meaning of a good harvest accompanied by a peaceful year.

青白玉凫鸟

清乾隆（1736—1795年）
长13厘米，宽6厘米，高11厘米
颐和园藏

青白玉质。整料圆雕，口衔谷梗，作回首状，长颈，短翅，翅及身有排列整齐的羽毛，身肥硕，圆臀阔胸。双蹼向后作划水状。背负谷穗有岁岁平安之意，又有五谷丰登之祈。

111 A white jade carving of a couple of magpies

Song Dynasty (960-1279)
Length 6.7cm, Width 3.2cm, Height 3.2cm
Provided by The Institute of Qing History Renmin University of China

The white jade is infused with some orange-red markings. Two magpies are carved in the round, a mother magpie perching on a prunus stem with her fledgling on her back. The theme of two magpies with prunus connotes the arrival of peace and happiness.

白玉『喜上加喜』双喜鹊把件

宋（960—1279年）

长6.7厘米，宽3.2厘米，高3.2厘米

中国人民大学清史研究所提供

白玉质，留红皮，整料圆雕母子鹊一对。母鹊拢翅擒于枝上，回首望子，幼鹊俯首伏于其项背，双翅微张，神态亲昵。母子鹊身下擒梅枝，沿鹊尾伸出，枝头饰数朵含苞待放的梅花。俏红色玉皮巧作翅羽、梅花，构思巧妙绝伦。双鹊梅花有喜上眉梢、喜上加喜之吉祥寓意。

112 A celadon white jade carving of a turtle

Yuan/Ming Dynasty (1271–1644)
Length 10cm, Width 3.5cm, Height 5cm
Provided by The Institute of Qing History Renmin University of China

A turtle dove is carved in the round with archaic line patterns on the body. It comes with a wood stand at the base. The turtle dove is a Spring bird signifying bliss, happiness and wishing the aged for longevity.

青白玉鸠首

元至明（1271—1644年）
长10厘米，宽3.5厘米，高5厘米
中国人民大学清史研究所提供

青白玉质，带棕红色牛毛沁，皮壳厚重。立体圆雕，斑鸠呈立状，昂首平视，喙短而回勾，翅羽拢于体侧，尾羽丰满下弯。底部打挖掏膛可供镶嵌。体态圆润饱满，采用浮雕、线刻等技法，饰仿古纹。古人视鸠为春鸟、善鸟，象征着吉祥幸福。鸠鸟进食时不易噎食，亦有祝福老者长寿顺遂之意。

113 A white jade "magpie" box and cover

Qing Dynasty, Qianlong Period (1736-1795)
Length 12.5cm, Width 4.5cm, Height 5.9cm
Provided by The Institute of Qing History Renmin University of China

The white jade has a recumbent magpie carved in the round with its beak holding a lingzhi. The oval shaped interior is hollowed out. The magpie connotes the coming of happiness and is also revered by Confucianists alluding the men of virtue.

白玉喜鹊型盒

清乾隆（1736—1795 年）
长 12.5 厘米，宽 4.5 厘米，高 5.9 厘米
中国人民大学清史研究所提供

白玉质。立体圆雕，喜鹊呈坐卧状，圆目直视，喙中衔灵芝仙草，翅羽拢于体侧，双爪收于腹底，尾羽刻画细腻传神。玉盒椭圆型腹，内膛打挖平滑均匀，子母口相交。喜鹊寓意喜事临门，儒家常用喜鹊象征圣贤。

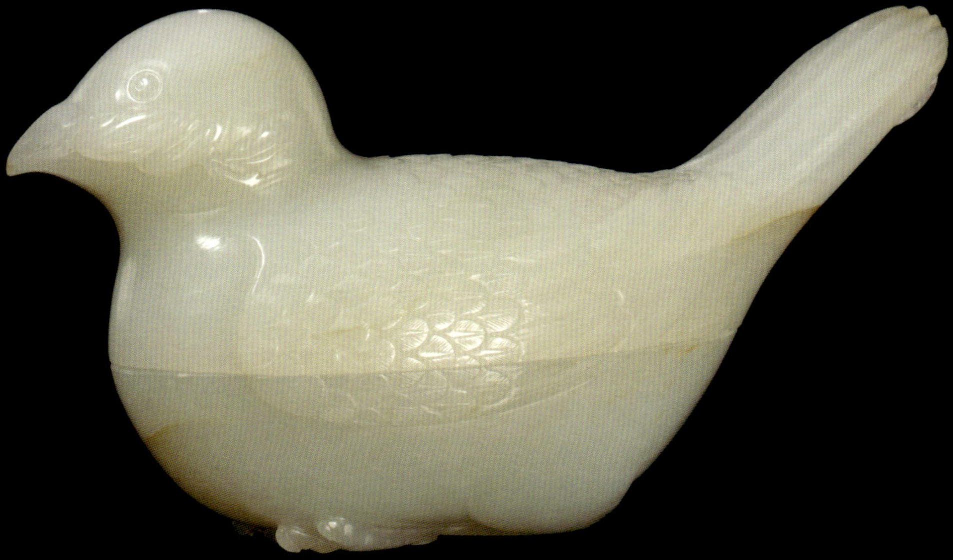

114 A russet and celadon jade rosefinch

Song Dynasty (960–1279)
Length 6cm, Width 1.9cm, Height 4cm
Provided by The Institute of Qing History Renmin University of China

The jade has some orange-red markings. A rosefinch is carved in the round in a recumbent position. Such designs are mainly found in the Song period artworks. The rosefinch is an auspicious bird bringing peace and happiness to the south.

青白玉朱雀

宋（960—1279年）
长6厘米，宽1.9厘米，高4厘米
中国人民大学清史研究所提供

青白玉质，带棕红色沁。立体圆雕，朱雀呈卧状，头顶绶带，昂首前望，双爪藏于身下，翅羽拢于两侧，尾内收下垂。此种造型朱雀多见于宋代仿汉玉雕中。朱雀乃主南方之神兽，有安定南方的吉祥寓意。

115 A jade carving of phoenix

Liao Dynasty (907–1125)
Length 4.7cm, Width 1.9cm, Height 2.9cm
Provided by The Institute of Qing History Renmin University of China

The jade has some russet markings with a recumbent phoenix carved in the round. The Liao dynasty had its unique nomadic aesthetic taste with some influence from the Tang and Song culture.

青白玉凤鸟

辽（907—1125 年）
长 4.7 厘米，宽 1.9 厘米，高 2.9 厘米
中国人民大学清史研究所提供

青白玉质，质地温润细腻，包浆厚重，器表布满深褐色牛毛沁斑。立体圆雕，凤鸟呈伏卧状，首小而圆，眼部以双圈法刻画，曲颈阔胸，身型丰满圆润，尾羽内卷。辽代承袭了唐宋艺术的审美基调，在自身粗犷豪迈的游牧民族格调中，不乏一丝古朴秀丽，形成了独特的艺术风格。中国古代文化对会飞翔的鸟怀有好奇与尊敬，尤其辽人对于凤鸟的崇尚更是在中国历史上十分突出。

116 A black and white jade carving of mandarin duck

Yuan Dynasty (1206-1368)
Length 5.8cm, Width 2.8cm, Height 4.9cm
Provided by The Institute of Qing History Renmin University of China

A recumbent mandarin duck is carved from this huoshaoyu (burnt jade). The back of the bird has a horizontal pierced hole. The mandarin duck is a symbol of love and alludes to a long and lasting love between husband and wife.

旧玉提油鸳鸯

元（1206—1368年）
长5.8厘米，宽2.8厘米，高4.9厘米
中国人民大学清史研究所提供

火烧玉质，局部有沁，有黑褐色提油。依料俏色圆雕，层层递进。鸳鸯呈卧态，昂首顶冠，圆眼短喙，翅羽丰满，细密有致，身型圆润，颈后有一横向穿孔。鸳鸯是忠贞不渝的象征，寓意夫妻恩爱，幸福美满。

117 A white jade carving of a mandarin duck

Qing Dynasty, Qianlong Period (1736-1795)
Length 6.5cm, Width 2.5cm, Height 5cm
Provided by The Institute of Qing History Renmin University of China

The jade pendant has some yellow rind. It is carved in the round with a mandarin duck turning back its head and holding a lotus spray with its beak. The carving is quite exquisite. The mandarin duck with lotus in beak connotes the love of husband and wife. This is a standard pattern for the Qianlong imperial pendants.

白玉衔莲鸳鸯形坠

清乾隆（1736—1795年）
长6.5厘米，宽2.5厘米，高5厘米
中国人民大学清史研究所提供

白玉质，间有黄皮。随料圆雕，鸳鸯回首衔莲花一束。双目灵动有神，羽翼雕琢细腻精巧，所衔莲花、莲叶、莲蓬均线条优美流畅，栩栩如生。鸳鸯衔莲寓意夫妻恩爱，百年好合，连生贵子，是乾隆时期典型宫廷玉坠。

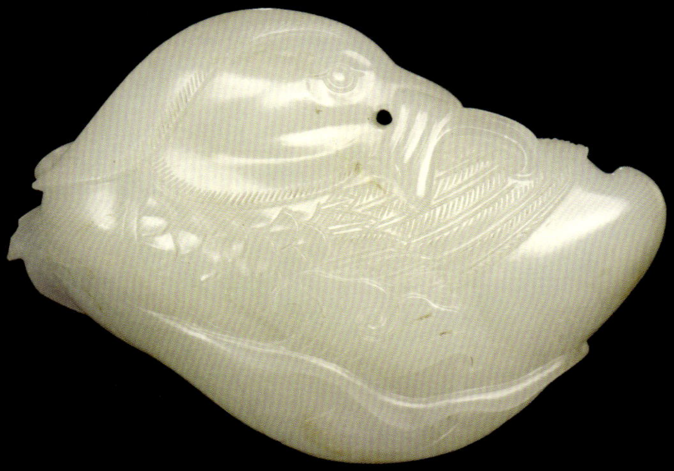

118 A white jade carving of mandarin duck with a lotus

Qing Dynasty, Qianlong Period (1736-1795)
Length 9.3cm, Width 3cm, Height 6.4cm
Provided by The Institute of Qing History Renmin University of China

The white jade possesses some grayish brown markings. A recumbent mandarin duck is carved with its head turning back and its beak holds a spray of lotus. The carving style is that of the Qianlong imperial imitation of the Han period style. The mandarin duck with lotus symbolizes a long and lasting love between husband and wife.

白玉衔莲鸳鸯

清乾隆（1736—1795 年）
长 9.3 厘米，宽 3 厘米，高 6.4 厘米
中国人民大学清史研究所提供

白玉质，间有灰褐色皮。随形圆雕鸳鸯呈俯卧状，回首衔莲花一束驭于项背之间，双翅饰有仿汉青铜纹，整体刀法利落，构图精巧，线条流畅，抛光极好。其雕刻风格具有典型的乾隆宫廷仿汉工艺。鸳鸯有夫妻比翼之意，莲蓬常寓多子多福，鸳鸯衔莲亦有夫妻恩爱、百年好合之美意。

119 A white jade carving of mandarin duck

Qing Dynasty, Qianlong Period (1736-1795)
Length 7.8cm, Width 4.3cm, Height 6cm
Provided by The Institute of Qing History Renmin University of China

A pair of mandarin ducks are carved in the round snuggling close together. Their beaks hold together a spray of lotus. A pair of mandarin ducks is a traditional auspicious emblem in Chinese culture and connotes the harmonious love between husband and wife.

白玉鸳鸯衔莲

清乾隆（1736—1795 年）
长 7.8 厘米，宽 4.3 厘米，高 6 厘米
中国人民大学清史研究所提供

白玉质，间闪白瑕，抛光细腻温润。整料圆雕两只鸳鸯，紧紧依偎，共衔白莲一簇，形态灵动和谐，周身饰仿汉勾连云纹，有慕古之意。鸳鸯是中国传统文化中典型的吉祥禽鸟。因鸳鸯总是形影不离，雄左雌右，栖息于池沼之上，意喻夫妻和睦，相亲相爱，忠贞不渝。

120 A white jade carving of mandarin duck

Qing Dynasty, Qianlong Period (1736-1795)
Length 5.5cm, Width 2.4cm, Height 3.2cm
The collection of the Summer Palace

The white jade is carved with a mandarin duck resting on a lotus leaf. Its beak holds a lotus sprig. The lotus rhymes with the Chinese character "he" (harmony) and connotes the meaning of a harmonious living between husband and wife.

白玉鸳鸯

清乾隆（1736—1795年）
长5.5厘米，宽2.4厘米，高3.2厘米
颐和园藏

白玉质。圆雕一鸳鸯，眼部浑圆，口衔荷叶梗，双持收拢于腹下，悠然自得，卧于荷叶之上，阴刻表现羽毛。『荷』与『和』谐音，此类题材寓意夫妻和和美美，白头偕老。

121 A white jade carving of mandarin duck

Qing Dynasty, Qianlong Period (1736-1795)
Length 6.1cm, Width 2.5cm, Height 4.2cm
The collection of the Summer Palace

A pair of mandarin ducks are carved in the round. One is slightly in front of its partner. The beaks of the pair share the holding of lotus.

白玉鸳鸯

清乾隆（1736—1795 年）
长 6.1 厘米，宽 2.5 厘米，高 4.2 厘米
颐和园藏

白玉质。圆雕双鸳鸯呈划水姿态，一只头向前，一只回首，两只鸳鸯共衔荷花。

122 A superb yellow russet jade carving of egret

Qing Dynasty, Qianlong Period (1736-1795)
Length 7.3cm Width 4.5cm, Height 5.3cm
Provided by The Institute of Qing History Renmin University of China

The yellow jade possesses some brown markings. A recumbent egret is carved in the round with its head turning back and the long beak holds a lotus. The egret holding lotus is a theme symbolizing continuous success in the imperial examinations.

黄玉鹭鸶衔莲

清乾隆（1736—1795 年）
长 7.3 厘米，宽 4.5 厘米，高 5.3 厘米
中国人民大学清史研究所提供

黄玉质，有褐色沁。圆雕鹭鸶，敛翅收足而卧，作回首姿态，长喙衔莲花，高额圆眼，风格古雅。『鹭』谐音『路』，『莲』谐音『连』，鹭鸶衔莲取『一路连科』之意，祝颂科场得意，仕途坦荡。

123 A jade carving of dog

Yuan/Ming Dynasty (1206–1644)
Length 8.2cm, Width 3cm, Height 3.3cm
Provided by The Institute of Qing History Renmin University of China

There are some orange-red markings on the white jade. A recumbent dog is carved in the round with crossing front paws and a curling tail. The dog is viewed as a symbol of loyalty and wealth.

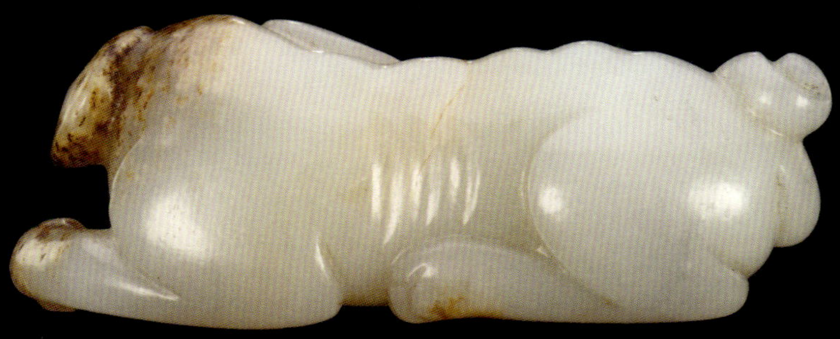

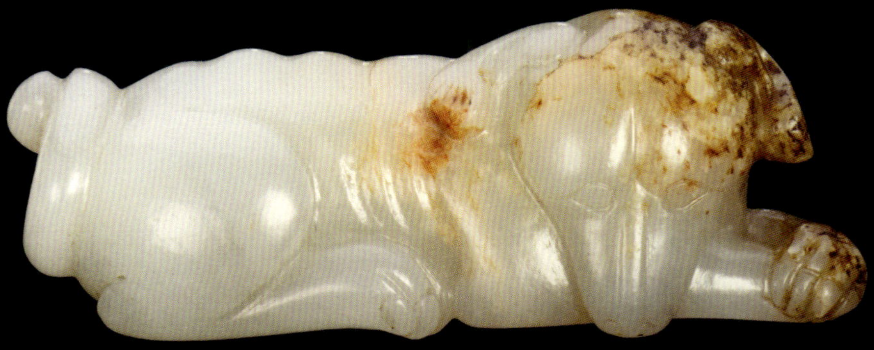

白玉卧犬

元至明（1206—1644年）
长8.2厘米，宽3厘米，高3.3厘米
中国人民大学清史研究所提供

白玉质，带橘红色沁。圆雕卧犬，呈蹲伏状，侧首垂耳，前爪交错，后腿卷屈，螺旋形尾。狗素以忠诚著称，亦有家门富贵吉祥之意。

124 A jade carving of dog

Ming Dynasty (1368-1644)
Length 6.3cm, Width 4.4cm, Height 6.5cm
Provided by The Institute of Qing History Renmin University of China

The white jade has some light caramel tone. A sitting hunting dog is carved in the round with its body turning back in an S shape. The dog is an agile animal and it also symbolizes loyalty and happiness.

白玉犬

明（1368—1644年）
长6.3厘米，宽4.4厘米，高6.5厘米
中国人民大学清史研究所提供

白玉质，玉质白中闪青有糖色。着棕黄色皮，圆雕猎犬伏地而坐，后肢卷曲，前肢撑地，上身回转呈S型，回首凝望。猎犬体型健硕，四肢修长，双耳下垂，双目有神。狗动作敏捷，性格忠诚，也有吉祥、欢喜的寓意。

125 A white jade carving of a couple of badgers

Qing Dynasty, Qianlong Period (1736-1795)
Length 8.1cm, Width 4.5cm, Height 3.2cm
The collection of the Summer Palace

Two badgers are carved in the round, one larger than the other on this piece of white jade. Two badgers in Chinese rhyme with the characters "shuanghuan" (double happiness) alluding a happy married life.

白玉双獾

清乾隆（1736—1795年）
长8.1厘米，宽4.5厘米，高3.2厘米
颐和园藏

白玉质，双獾一大一小，对望而卧。双獾，谐音『双欢』，寓意夫妻婚姻生活和和美美，欢欢喜喜。有祝福夫妻相生相依，欢爱甜蜜的传统寓意。

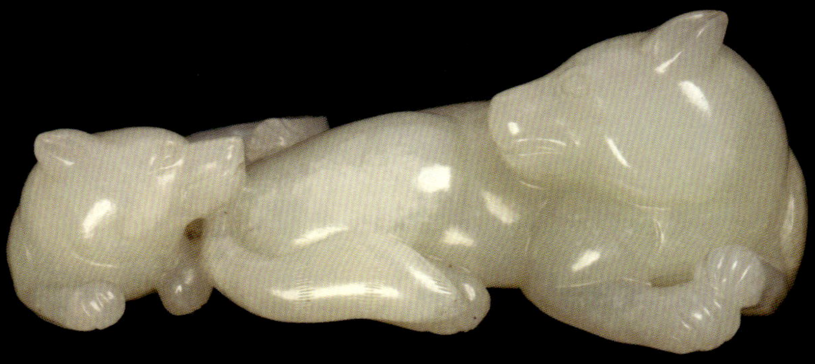

126 A white jade carving of dog

Qing Dynasty, Qianlong Period (1736–1795)
Length 5.3cm, Width 2.6cm, Height 2.1cm
The collection of the Summer Palace

In Chinese culture and folklore, the dog symbolizes loyalty. The ancients also view the dog as an auspicious animal bringing good luck and wealth.

白玉卧犬

清乾隆（1736—1795年）
长5.3厘米，宽2.6厘米，高2.1厘米
颐和园藏

白玉质。犬，在中华民族文化习俗里，象征着忠义。古人也把狗作为吉祥和财富的象征。

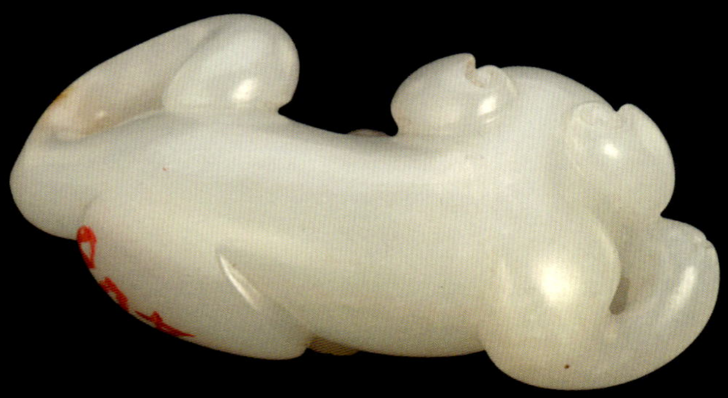

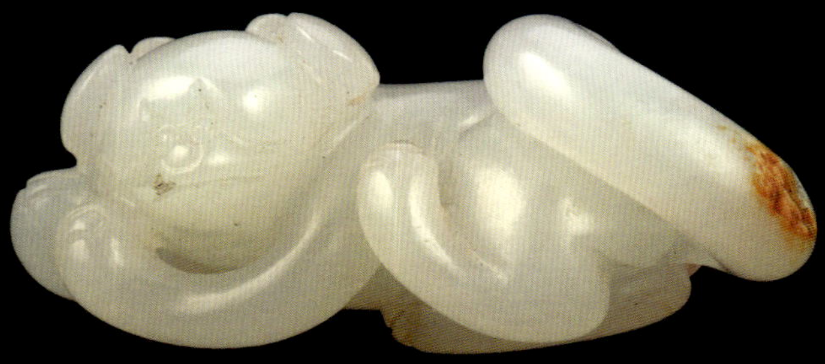

127 An agate carving of "horse and monkey" group

Ming Dynasty (1368–1644)
Length 7.5cm, Width 4.5cm, Height 4.5cm
The collection of the Summer Palace

The agate is skillfully carved into a kneeling horse with its head turning back. A little monkey clambers on the back of the horse. The horse with monkey group confers the meaning of "mashang fenghou" (immediate promotion in peerage rank).

玛瑙『马上封侯』

明（1368—1644 年）
长 7.5 厘米，宽 4.5 厘米，高 4.5 厘米
颐和园藏

玛瑙材质，巧色雕琢。用圆雕手法琢卧马跪伏于地，曲颈回首，菱形眼，鬃毛茂密贴于后颈，肢体健硕，体态优美。小猴攀附于马背，似与马儿嬉戏。『猴』与『侯』同音双关，泛指达官权贵。猴子骑于马背，取『马上』立刻之意。『马上封侯』比喻事业即将飞黄腾达的愿望。

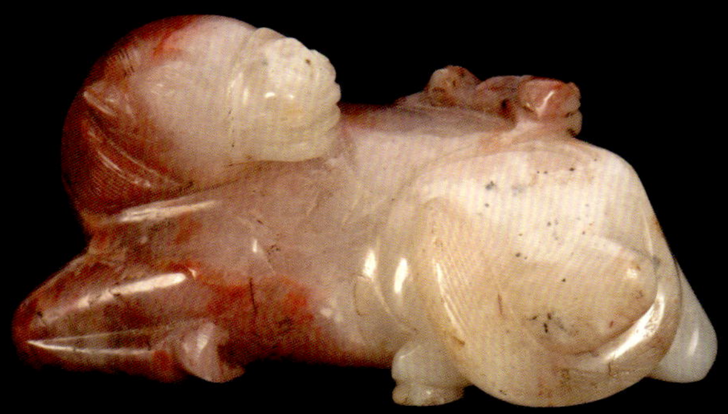

128 An agate carving of "horse and monkey" group

Qing Dynasty, Qianlong Period (1736–1795)
Length 9cm, Width 4cm, Height 4.5cm
The collection of the Summer Palace

The agate has some red markings. The carving of a monkey on the back of a horse connotes the meaning of "mashang fenghou" which alludes to the immediate promotion in aristocratic peerage.

玛瑙『马上封侯』

清乾隆（1736—1795 年）
长 9 厘米，宽 4 厘米，高 4.5 厘米
颐和园藏

玛瑙质，器身有红色沁，马上封侯是中国传统寓意纹样。由猴子、骏马组成。『猴』与『侯』同音双关。猴子骑于马上，『马上』为立刻之意。侯为古代分五等贵族爵位的第二等级，这里泛指达观权贵。寓意功名指日可待。

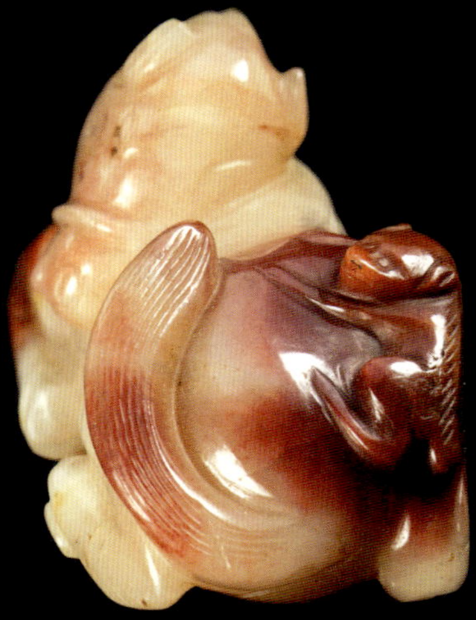

129 A white jade carving of "horse and monkey" group

Qing Dynasty, Qianlong Period (1736–1795)
Length 4.5cm, Width 2.6cm, Height 3.7cm
The collection of the Summer Palace

The white jade is carved with a recumbent horse with its four legs tucked under the body and its head turning back. A monkey rides on the back of the horse.

白玉雕『马上封侯』

清乾隆（1736—1795年）
长4.5厘米，宽2.6厘米，高3.7厘米
颐和园藏

白玉质。整器圆雕一马一猴，马为卧姿，四只蜷于腹下，反身回顾，嘴部有缰绳；猴骑于马背偏尾部，双手持缰绳。

A white jade carving of "horse and monkey" group

Qing Dynasty, Qianlong Period (1736–1795)
Length 5.3cm, Width 2.5cm, Height 3.7cm
The collection of the Summer Palace

A recumbent horse is carved with its head turning back. A monkey rides on the back of the horse. The base has a double layered foliage stand.

白玉雕『马上封侯』

清乾隆（1736—1795年）
长5.3厘米，宽2.5厘米，高3.7厘米
颐和园藏

白玉质。整器圆雕一马一猴，马为卧姿，四只蜷于腹下，反身回顾，嘴部有缰绳；猴骑于马背偏尾部，一手扶马嘴，一手持缰绳；底座为叶形，分上下两层，皆向中心翻卷。

131 A white jade carving of "horse and monkey" group

Qing Dynasty (1616-1911)
Length 5.5cm, Width 2.3cm, Height 4.2cm
The collection of the Summer Palace

The white jade bears some cracks. A recumbent horse with its head turning back is carved in the round. It has a monkey riding on its back. This connotes the meaning of "mashang fenghou" (immediate promotion in official ranks).

白玉雕『马上封侯』

清（1616—1911年）
长5.5厘米，宽2.3厘米，高4.2厘米
颐和园藏

白玉质，有绺裂。此玉以圆雕和透雕手法琢卧马一只，侧首回眸；马背上骑一猴，做抓耳张望之姿；马臀上伏一蜜蜂。此玉雕取『马上封侯』之意。

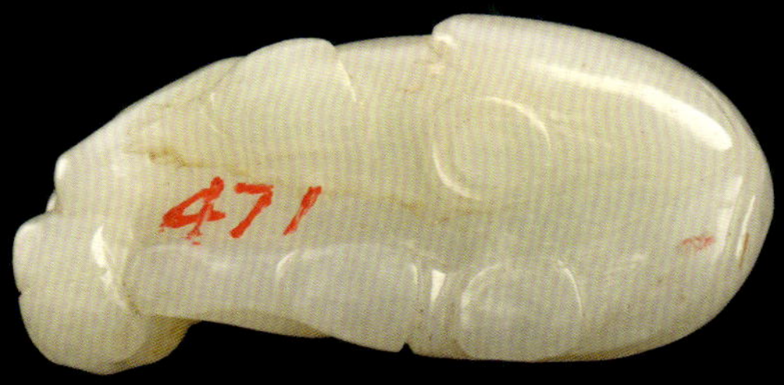

132 A celadon white jade carving of "monkey and lingzhi" group

Qing Dynasty, Qianlong Period (1736-1795)
Length 6.8cm, Width 3.7cm, Height 6.6cm
Provided by The Institute of Qing History Renmin University of China

Two monkeys are carved, one big and one smaller, in the round in this group. The big monkey presents a peach while the small monkey a sprig of lingzhi. The two monkeys presenting lingzhi and peach connote the meaning of wishing for felicity and longevity.

青白玉『双猴献瑞』

清乾隆（1736—1795年）
长6.8厘米，宽3.7厘米，高6.6厘米
中国人民大学清史研究所提供

青白玉质，洒金皮。整料随形圆雕大小玉猴，玉猴呈单膝跪卧状，大猴双手高举寿桃一枚，小猴双手擎灵芝一簇，大猴俯首，小猴昂首，两猴对视交谈。猴喜食桃，寿桃寓意长寿，灵芝寓意如意，大小双猴亦有代代封侯之意，双猴捧寿寓意福寿延绵，世代如意。

133 A white jade "horse and monkey" belt buckle

Qing Dynasty, Qianlong Period (1736-1795)
Length 8.3cm, Width 1.4cm, Height 5.8cm
Provided by The Institute of Qing History Renmin University of China

The white jade is carved on one side with a recumbent horse with head looking back while a monkey rides on its back. The reverse side is plain and bare.

白玉『马上封侯』带扣

清乾隆（1736—1795年）
长8.3厘米，宽1.4厘米，高5.8厘米
中国人民大学清史研究所提供

白玉质。依料圆雕『马上封侯』带扣，马呈跪卧状，回首凝望，背部攀伏一猴，紧握缰绳。背面光素，雕一对圆形纽，供在带上固定。

134 A white jade carving of rooster

Ming Dynasty (1368–1644)
Length 9cm, Width 4cm, Height 7cm
The collection of the Summer Palace

The white jade has some faint light brown inclusions. A recumbent rooster is carved with its head turning back. The pronunciation of rooster (ji) in Chinese rhymes with jixiang and jili which means auspiciousness and good luck.

白玉公鸡

明（1368—1644年）
长9厘米，宽4厘米，高7厘米
颐和园藏

白玉质，略有褐色沁。整料雕琢，公鸡呈卧姿，俯首回望，圆目短喙，鸡冠耸起；翅膀丰满，尾羽上翘，以阴线勾勒羽毛；双爪并合，收于腹下。鸡谐音『吉』，有吉祥、吉利之意。

135 A white jade carving of buffalo

Qing Dynasty, Qianlong Period (1736-1795)
Length 8.2cm, Width 5.8cm, Height 4.8cm
Provided by The Institute of Qing History Renmin University of China

A recumbent buffalo is carved in the round with its head gazing back. The buffalo wears a noseband tied with a string, showing it to be a farm animal. The farm buffalo signifies the coming of a good harvest and a fruitful year.

白玉牧牛

清乾隆（1736—1795 年）
长 8.2 厘米，宽 5.8 厘米，高 4.8 厘米
中国人民大学清史研究所提供

白玉质。随形圆雕，卧牛四肢蜷伏于身下，牛身线条简约，肌理均匀精准，细节处理丝丝入扣，玉牛昂首回望，背部贯穿一条细绳，勾画出了其牧牛身份，也暗示了牛的勤劳质朴。牛是农耕社会的重要生产工具，常寓意着身体力行、勤劳坚毅的美德。

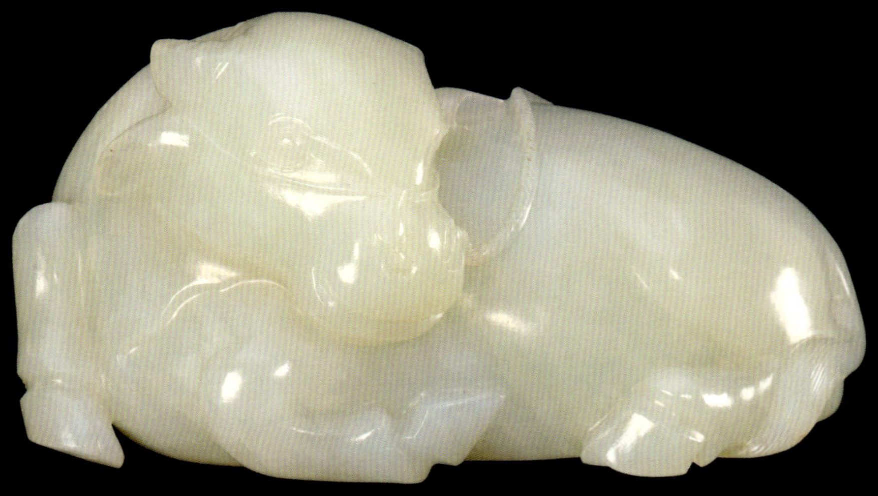

136 A white jade carving of "buffalo and boy" group

Qing Dynasty, Qianlong Period (1736–1795)
Length 13.5cm, Width 6.8cm, Height 10.5cm
Provided by The Institute of Qing History Renmin University of China

A recumbent farm water-buffalo is carved in the round. Its head turns back to gaze at the boy riding on its back. It wears a noseband tied with a string. This buffalo with boy theme connotes the meaning of wishing one's child to have a good and successful future.

青白玉童子牧牛

清乾隆（1736—1795 年）
长 13.5 厘米，宽 6.8 厘米，高 10.5 厘米
中国人民大学清史研究所提供

青白玉质。立体圆雕，雕工爽利，丝丝入扣，包浆凝重。水牛曲膝而卧，回首望向背上童子，牛角弯曲，目光温顺，眉部、耳侧均以阴刻线刻画毛发纹理。牛背上之小童身穿马褂，赤足而坐，右手轻抚牛背，左手持缰绳，缰绳一端从牛鼻中穿过，另一端从牛背上自然垂下。传说牛与龙育有一子为麒麟，牧童骑牛亦有『望子成龙』之寓意。

137 A white jade carving of buffalo

Qing Dynasty, Guangxu Period (1875-1908)
Length 5.9cm, Width 4.1cm, Height 2.5cm
The collection of the Summer Palace

The pale celadon jade has some cracks and carved in the round with a boy riding a water-buffalo. The animal turns back its head looking at the boy. The theme depicts a peaceful and idyllic pastoral scenery of the countryside.

青玉童子伏牛

清光绪（1875—1908 年）
长 5.9 厘米，宽 4.1 厘米，高 2.5 厘米
颐和园藏

青玉质，有绺裂。整料雕琢，以圆雕和透雕手法琢一水牛，口衔禾稻，四肢卧地，回首与伏在身上的童子相望。童子右手执鞭，肩背草帽。该器题材体现出一派其乐融融、纯真闲适的田园气息。

138 A white jade carving of buffalo

Qing Dynasty, Qianlong Period (1736-1795)
Length 5.1cm, Width 2.1cm, Height 3cm
The collection of the Summer Palace

The white jade is carved with a buffalo in the round. The buffalo is viewed by the Chinese as a hardworking, down to earth farm animal. It is also recognized as an animal bringing auspiciousness.

白玉牛

清乾隆（1736—1795 年）
长 5.1 厘米，宽 2.1 厘米，高 3 厘米
颐和园藏

白玉质。牛，从古至今，中华民族认为其是正直、勤劳的象征，雕刻玉牛象征着脚踏实地，是一种吉兽。

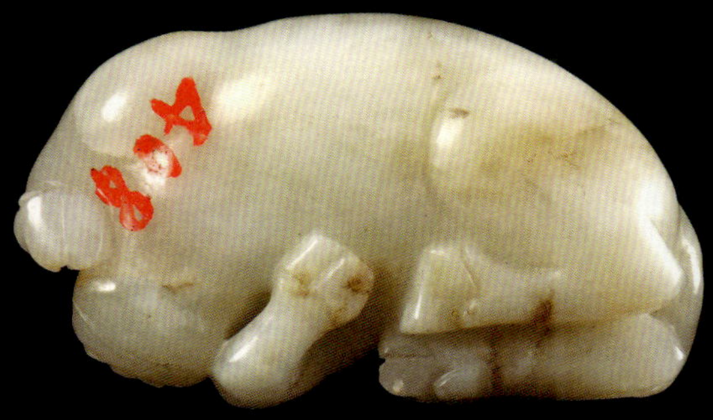

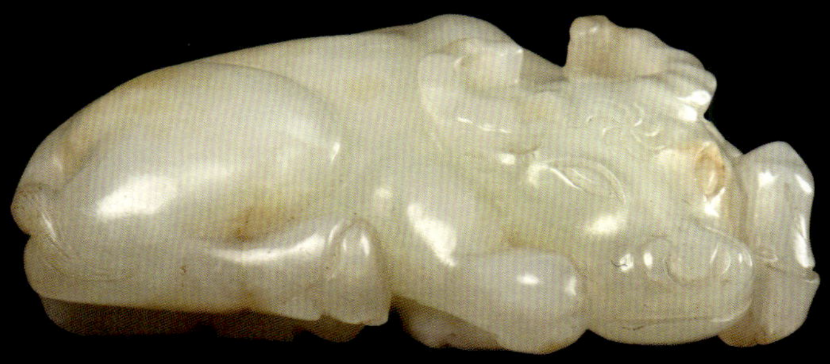

139 A celadon jade carving of buffalo

Qing Dynasty, Guangxu Period (1875-1908)
Length 6.3cm, Width 2.9cm, Height 2.2cm
The collection of the Summer Palace

The celadon jade is carved with a buffalo in the round, its mouth holding an ear of grain. The ear of grain conveys the message of a bumper harvest with a fruitful and peaceful year.

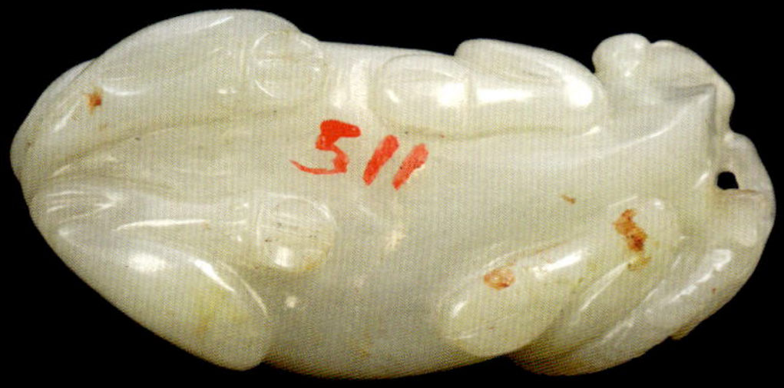

青玉牛

清光绪（1875—1908 年）
长 6.3 厘米，宽 2.9 厘米，高 2.2 厘米
颐和园藏

青玉质，牛口衔麦穗，麦穗象征丰收，岁岁平安、年年安康，整体寄托了勤劳肯干，终获收获的美好愿景。

140 A celadon jade carving of buffalo

Qing Dynasty, Qianlong Period (1736-1795)
Length 58cm, Width 40cm, Height 20cm
The collection of the Summer Palace

This large celadon jade has some cracks. A buffalo is carved in the round resting at ease in a recumbent position with its head turning back.

青玉卧牛

清乾隆（1736—1795年）
长58厘米，宽40厘米，高20厘米
颐和园藏

青玉质，有绺裂。用料硕大，采用圆雕、线刻等技法，将玉绺巧做，置于牛蹄、口、腹身等部位，生动自然。卧牛团身、俯卧、回首，神态怡然，似在小憩。

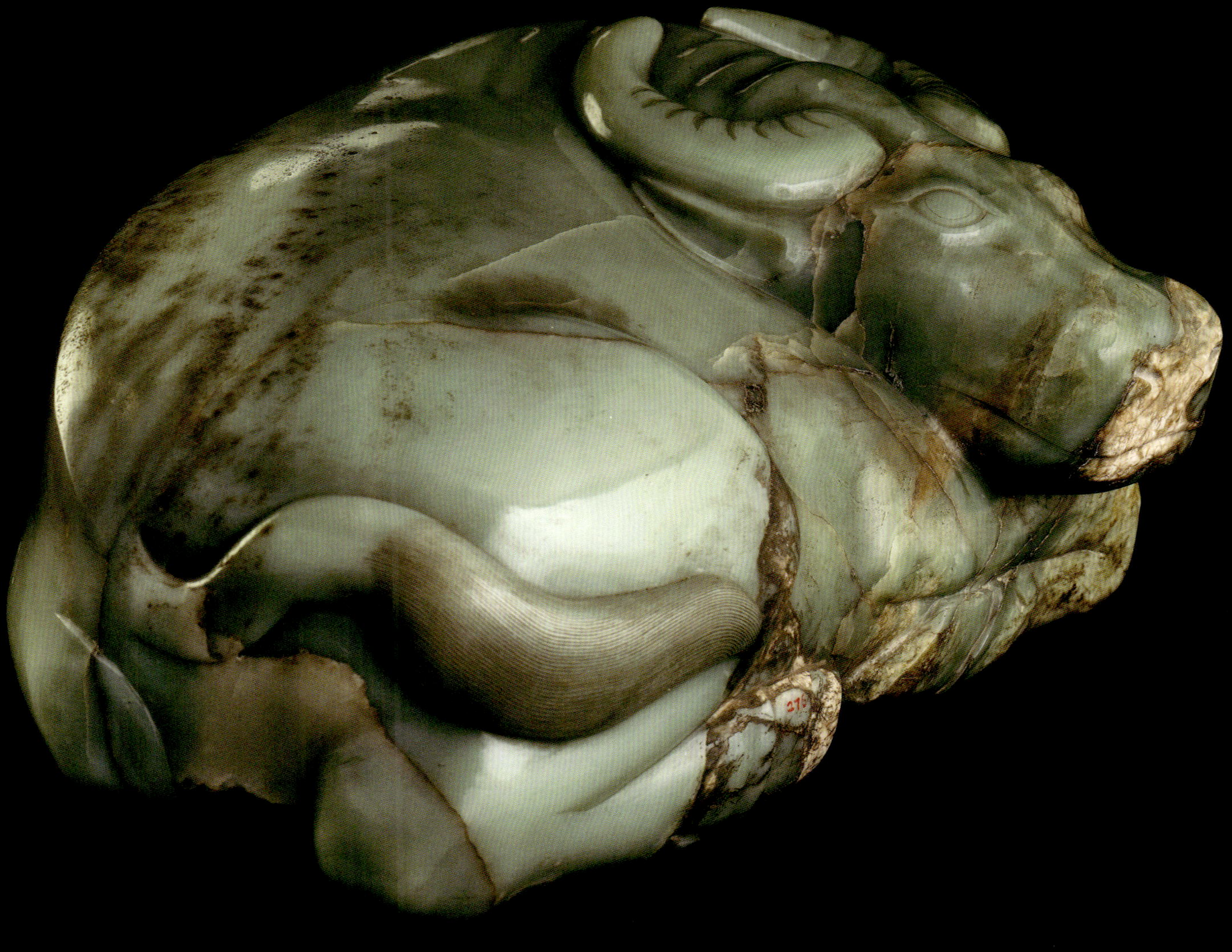

141 A white jade carving of catfish group

Qing Dynasty, Qianlong Period (1736-1795)
Length 9.5cm, Width 1.8cm, Height 7.2cm
Provided by The Institute of Qing History Renmin University of China

Two catfish are carved with the heads joining the others tail and share holding a lingzhi in the mouth. This catfish jade group conveys the auspicious wish for a fruitful and happy year and is usually used as a paperweight in the study room.

白玉衔灵芝双鲶鱼把件

清乾隆（1736—1795 年）
长 9.5 厘米，宽 1.8 厘米，高 7.2 厘米
中国人民大学清史研究所提供

白玉质，留红皮。籽玉随形圆雕鲶鱼一对，头尾相连，共衔灵芝。鲶鱼头扁阔丰满，嘴留长须，鱼身肌理分明，线条流畅，尾部微收，互相缠绕。寓意年年有余，长年大利。此类把件常用作文房镇纸。

142　A grayish white jade carving of carp

Qing Dynasty, Qianlong Period (1736–1795)
Length 9.5cm, Width 6cm, Height 4.8cm
Provided by The Institute of Qing History Renmin University of China

This grayish jade has some reddish inclusions with a Carp in a curling swimming posture carved in the round. The carp motif signifies a bumper year and also connotes the wish for success in the imperial examination.

灰白玉三色鲤鱼

清乾隆（1736—1795年）
长9.5厘米，宽6厘米，高4.8厘米
中国人民大学清史研究所提供

灰白玉质，满红皮。随形圆雕，鲤鱼口微张，双眼突出，肌理刻画细致入微，动感十足，整个鱼身呈弧形，底部有海水纹回旋环绕，可谓如鱼得水。鱼鳍和鱼尾利用籽料原有的朱红皮色进行巧雕，突显鲤鱼的生动活泼。『鲤』与『利』谐音，鱼与『余』谐音，因此，鲤鱼寓意着家家行利，年年有余。与此同时鲤鱼跃龙门的传说也广为流传，有金榜题名之意。

143 A white jade carving of fish and lotus

Qing Dynasty, Qianlong Period (1736–1795)
Length 7.5cm, Width 3cm, Height 5cm
The collection of the Summer Palace

The white jade has a lotus leaf and a fish carved in the round. The Chinese pronunciation for lotus and fish rhyme with the meaning of "liannian youyu" which means "good surplus of food every year".

白玉雕『年年有余』

清乾隆（1736—1795年）
长7.5厘米，宽3厘米，高5厘米
颐和园藏

白玉质。整料雕琢，器身主体为莲叶，鱼身呈腾跃状，如跃浪而出，双侧碾琢扇形鳍，鱼尾卷曲有力，另有鱼附身莲叶。『莲』与『连』谐音，『鱼』与『余』谐音，故寓意『连年有余』。

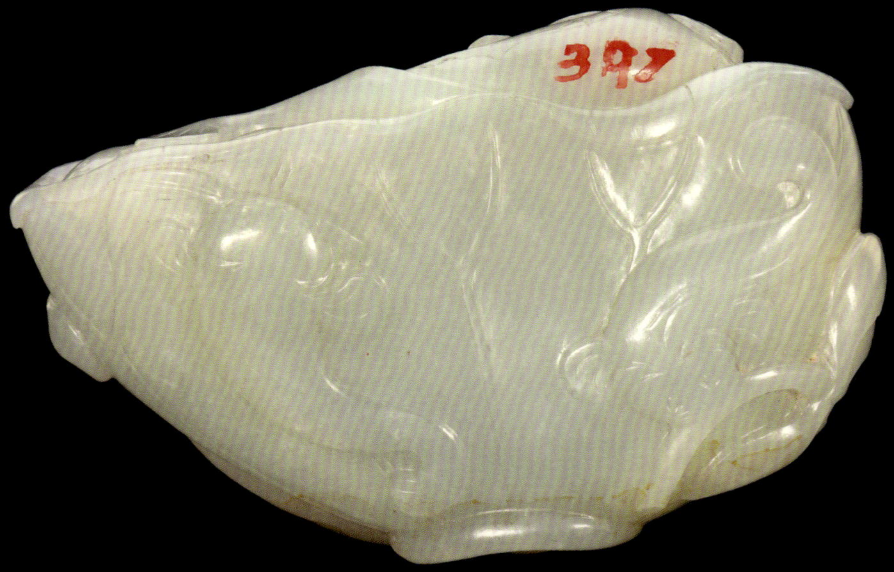
397

144 A white jade carving of fish and lotus

Qing Dynasty, Qianlong Period (1736-1795)
Length 21.3cm, Width 4.5cm, Height 10.3cm
The collection of the Summer Palace

The white jade bears some yellow rind. A large swimming gui fish is carved in the round with its mouth grasping a sprig of lotus. The fish and lotus connote the meaning of "liannian youyu" which means good surpluses every year.

白玉雕『连年有余』

清乾隆（1736—1795年）
长21.3厘米，宽4.5厘米，高10.3厘米
颐和园藏

白玉质，略带黄皮。整料雕琢，采用圆雕技法，琢刻一条游弋于水中的鳜鱼。鱼小头，宽身，扇面状尾，背鳍挺拔；鱼嘴上翘，口衔一束荷叶莲花，在鱼身右侧伸展绽放。『莲』与『连』谐音，『鳜』与『贵』谐音，『鱼』与『余』谐音，故寓意『连年有余』、『富贵有余』。

145 A white jade carving of fish

Qing Dynasty (1616–1911)
Length 7.3cm, Width 1.8cm, Height 4.1cm
The collection of the Summer Palace

The white jade is carved into a fish with mouth grasping a lotus. This fish with lotus is a traditional auspicious pattern and connotes a good life with surpluses of food every year.

白玉鱼

清（1616—1911年）
长7.3厘米，宽1.8厘米，高4.1厘米
颐和园藏

白玉质。鱼口衔莲花，莲花和鲤鱼组成的中国传统吉祥图案，寓意连年有余，祈盼生活富足。

146 A superb white and russet jade carving of a goldfish

Qing Dynasty, Qianlong Period (1736–1795)
Length 9cm, Width3.5cm, Height 7cm
Provided by The Institute of Qing History Renmin University of China

The white jade display object has some gold-orange rind. A goldfish is carved with its mouth holding a lotus sprig. The goldfish in Chinese rhymes with jinyu (gold and jade) and alluding to the auspicious meaning of "jinyu mantang" (a hall full of gold and jade).

白玉留皮『金玉满堂』摆件

清乾隆（1736—1795年）
长9厘米，宽3.5，高7厘米
中国人民大学清史研究所提供

白玉质，洒金皮。随料圆雕，金鱼衔莲一束，莲出鱼嘴，顺流而下至腹部，圆目突出，头肥身硕，有鱼戏莲间之意趣，鱼尾似欲摇曳，将『尾展拖轻縠』的游动之态雕刻的极为传神。『金鱼』与『金玉』同音，以表『金玉满堂』，『莲』谐『连』音，又暗含『连年有余』的美好祝福，满含浓郁的吉祥寓意。

147 A black and white jade carving of a goldfish group

Ming Dynasty (1368–1644)
Length 4cm, Width3cm, Height 2.5cm
Provided by The Institute of Qing History Renmin University of China

Some pond creatures are skillfully carved on this huoshaoyu (burnt jade) such as the goldfish, snail together with some water plants. This combination group also alludes to the meaning of "jinyu mantang": wealth in the form of "a hall full of gold and jade".

火烧玉巧雕『金玉满堂』坠

明（1368—1644）
长4厘米，宽3厘米，高2.5厘米
中国人民大学清史研究所提供

火烧玉质，皮壳厚重。巧雕塘中金鱼水族一组，金鱼体态肥硕圆润，双目圆突，乌目洁身，尾鳍修长飘逸，身下有慈姑、螺蛳、水草相饰。此一塘水族组合构思巧妙，雕工流畅，线条简洁明快，寓意金玉满堂，平安富贵。

A white jade carving of catfish and lotus

Qing Dynasty, Qianlong Period (1736–1795)
Length 10.7cm, Width7.5cm, Height 4cm
Provided by The Institute of Qing History Renmin University of China

The white jade has some russet markings. A catfish is carved with its mouth grasping a stalk of lotus with the flower in full bloom. This fish with lotus display object connotes the meaning of "liannian youyu" (good surpluses in every year).

白玉红皮『连年有余』摆件

清乾隆（1736—1795 年）
长 10.7 厘米，宽 7.5 厘米，高 4 厘米
中国人民大学清史研究所提供

白玉质，俏棕红色皮，间有原皮。随料圆雕，鲶鱼头部圆润饱满，圆目凸出，身型壮硕，双须微张于两侧，尾鳍飘逸洒脱。鲶鱼衔莲一束，莲枝上莲花盛开，茎叶蜿蜒曲折。整件玉雕极具动态，刻画出了鲶鱼在荷叶间嬉戏的景象。鲶鱼衔莲寓意连年有余，在川知乐。

149 A white jade carving of brush pot with plum blossom and golden pheasant

Qing Dynasty, Qianlong Period (1736–1795)
Length 7.7cm, Width 3.6cm, Height 11.5cm
The collection of the Summer Palace

The white jade brush pot has some yellow inclusions. The outer wall has plant and rockery, flower and bird carved in relief. The paradise flycatcher with the plum blossom depicts the meaning of "changshou qimei" (health and longevity).

白玉梅花绶带鸟纹笔筒

清乾隆（1736—1795年）
长7.7厘米，宽3.6厘米，高11.5厘米
颐和园藏

白玉质，略带黄皮。该器随形琢碾，外壁以浮雕技法雕琢树石、花鸟纹饰；玉皮随色巧作，雕琢精细，造型拙朴，抛光较佳。绶带鸟又名寿带鸟，梅谐音『眉』，寓意『长寿齐眉』。

150 A white jade carving of vase with plum blossom and stones

Qing Dynasty, Qianlong Period (1736-1795)
Length 18cm, Width 5.4cm, Height 13.3cm
The collection of the Summer Palace

The white jade vase is oblate in shape and has a lid. Its two sides are carved with rockery, plum blossom and the flycatcher bird. This vase display object is carved in high relief with the openwork method.

白玉洞石梅花绶带鸟纹瓶

清乾隆（1736—1795 年）
长 18 厘米，宽 5.4 厘米，高 13.3 厘米
颐和园藏

白玉质。该器玉料呈扁平形，下部宽，上部窄。圆形盖顶，盖面光素。器身两侧雕琢山石、绶带鸟和梅树，树干沿瓶体攀援而上至肩部。幼枝上缀饰花朵和待放的蓓蕾，枝干伸展生动自然。摆件采用凸雕、镂刻技法。

151 A white jade carving of cats and dragonfly

Qing Dynasty, Qianlong Period (1736-1795)
Length 7.3cm, Width 5.2cm, Height 4cm
The collection of the Summer Palace

The white jade is carved with three cats, a mother cat with its two kittens. The mother cat is in a crouching position with its mouth grasping a dragonfly. One kitten snuggles on the mother's back while the other kitten is at its mother's tail.

白玉猫戏蜻蜓

清乾隆（1736—1795 年）
长 7.3 厘米，宽 5.2 厘米，高 4 厘米
颐和园藏

白玉质。整料雕琢，造型为一大两小三只猫。大猫呈匍匐状，口衔蜻蜓左翅；两小猫一只依偎于大猫之背，一只依偎于大猫之尾，呈三猫戏蜻蜓之状，惟妙惟肖。

152 A white jade carving of cat

Qing Dynasty (1616–1911)
Length 7.5cm, Width 4.8cm, Height 2.4cm
The collection of the Summer Palace

There are some cracks on this white jade. A recumbent cat is carved in the round lying on top of leaves. Its tail rolls in front of the body emanating a comfortable and leisurely look.

白玉卧猫

清（1616—1911年）
长7.5厘米，宽4.8厘米，高2.4厘米
颐和园藏

白玉质，有绺裂。以圆雕技法刻一猫卧于叶片之上，五官、毛发、脚爪几步雕刻到位。玉猫尾巴卷在身前，造型圆润可爱，浑身散发出一种慵懒、闲适之感。

153 A white jade hare

Qing Dynasty, Qianlong Period (1736–1795)
Length 4.8cm, Width 3.5cm, Height 3.3cm
Provided by The Institute of Qing History Renmin University of China

A rabbit is carved in the round in a half-recumbent position. The rabbit is one of the twelve animal signs in the Chinese zodiac. It is also an auspicious animal in the Chinese culture representing the moon.

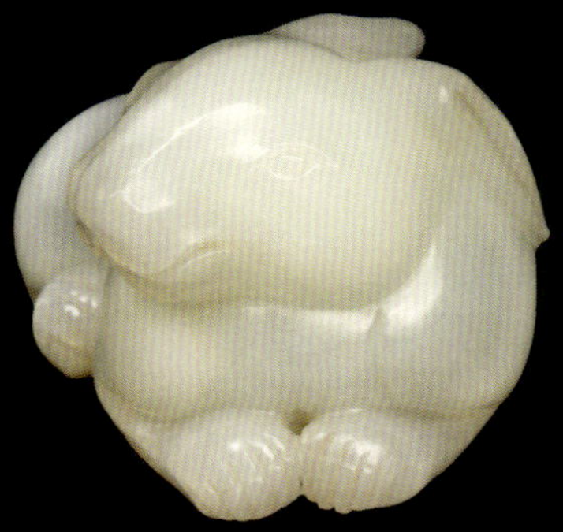

白玉兔

清乾隆（1736—1795 年）
长 4.8 厘米，宽 3.5 厘米，高 3.3 厘米
中国人民大学清史研究所提供

白玉质。圆雕玉兔，双耳修长垂于脑后，额头及鼻梁高耸，双目细腻有神，嘴角线条干净利落。玉兔身体呈半卧状，后腿蜷缩，前腿内弯，尾部短小圆润，毛发阴刻线清晰有序。兔是十二生肖之一，在中国传统文化中是代表月亮的神兽。

154 A white jade carving of butterfly and flower plaque button

Qing Dynasty, Qianlong Period (1736-1795)
Length 6.3cm, Width 1.2cm, Height 6.9cm
Provided by The Institute of Qing History Renmin University of China

This is a white jade carving of a round shaped jade plaque button with butterflies and peony patterns. The reverse side has sprig of peonies with layers of petals in light relief. It is used as a robe button for the traditional scholars' robe.

白玉『蝶恋花』纹鳖扣

清乾隆（1736—1795 年）
长 6.3 厘米，宽 1.2 厘米，高 6.9 厘米
中国人民大学清史研究所提供

白玉质。玉扣近圆形，采用浮雕阴刻的手法，正面雕蝴蝶一对上下团抱，中间饰高浮雕牡丹纹，蝴蝶婀娜多姿，花朵徐徐绽放，仿佛与蝶齐舞。背面高浮雕牡丹花蒂，花瓣层层叠叠，花蔓花萼清晰疏朗，叶脉上阴刻线丝丝入扣。取材中国传统题材『蝶恋花』，暗喻缠绵悱恻的情感。

此扣名鳖扣，为古时道袍或吉服之玉扣，是中国传统文人配饰中的重要品种，常置于胸前，兼可把玩。

155 A white jade carving of mantis

Qing Dynasty, Qianlong Period (1736–1795)
Length 6.3cm, Width 2.5cm, Height 2.7cm
Provided by The Institute of Qing History Renmin University of China

The white jade is carved in the round with a praying mantis. A Chinese trumpet vine flower is attached to the back of the mantis. This mantis theme conveys the message of intrepid bravery and flourishing growth.

白玉螳螂凌霄花

清乾隆（1736—1795年）
长6.3厘米，宽2.5厘米，高2.7厘米
中国人民大学清史研究所提供

白玉质。依料圆雕，螳螂双臂前伸有锯齿，肢爪蜷曲，头部呈三角状前倾微缩，圆眼微凸，前胸修长，大腹宽尾，腹部呈节状，两排后肢紧贴于腹部两侧，双翅折叠于腹上。螳螂身后饰凌霄花。螳螂通常寓意勇猛无畏，亦有『金玉满堂堆长廊』的吉愿。

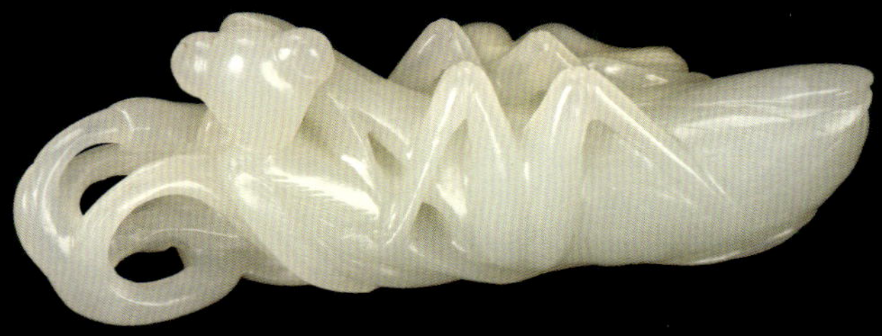

156 A white jade carving of "chunshui" belt buckle

Jin Dynasty (1115-1234)
Length 7.8cm, Width 7.4cm, Height 2cm
Provided by The Institute of Qing History Renmin University of China

The white jade is carved in the openwork technique showing a falcon hunting a swan. This chunshui (Spring Water) style of carving depicts the Spring hunting season of the Northern nomads much favored by the Jin period rulers.

白玉雕『春水』绦环

金（1115—1234年）
长7.8厘米，宽7.4厘米，高2厘米
中国人民大学清史研究所提供

白玉质，背砂底，间有金黄色皮，细微处有牛毛纹沁。采用透雕、镂雕、局部圆雕等技法，琢海东青自天而降，猎捕一只仓皇惊逃的天鹅，羽翅翻挣，生动鲜活，紧张氛围呼之欲出。绦环，绦带所系之环，始于宋辽时期，是十分流行的男性佩饰常系于胸前与腰间。

此纹饰称作『春水』，主要表现了北方游牧民族皇家春季围猎的景象。『春水』为主题的纹饰深受金代统治阶级的喜爱，海东青猎捕天鹅，表现出以小搏大、以弱胜强的犷悍精神，寄托其窥觎中原的野心，是对辽金时期北方游牧民族精神世界的精准写照。

157 A white jade carving of “quail and millet” group

Qing Dynasty, Qianlong Period (1736-1795)
Length 7cm, Width 2.9cm, Height 4.6cm
Provided by The Institute of Qing History Renmin University of China

The white jade has some brown inclusions. A recumbent quail is carved in the round with its beak holding an ear of millet and a sprig of lingzhi. The quail with millet and lingzhi convey the message of “peaceful every year” and “all’s well every year”.

白玉鹌鹑

清乾隆（1736—1795年）
长7厘米，宽2.9厘米，高4.6厘米
中国人民大学清史研究所提供

白玉质，内有棕色斑点。圆雕卧状鹌鹑，鹌鹑昂首向前，口衔麦穗与灵芝一束，体态圆润丰满，羽毛层叠鳞比，双爪藏于身下。鹌鹑衔麦穗，寓意岁岁平安，安居乐业，口衔灵芝更有岁岁如意之意。

嘉木良卉

Woods and Flowers

The Chinese people had also combined their culture of the plant world with jade carvings. The evergreen pine, the blooming flowers of prosperity, the gentlemen with bamboo, scholars with plum blossoms, all these subjects had created very profound cultural meanings in jade carvings. Since the Ming and Qing periods, the realistic usage of jade items had also been enhanced. Plant subjects had been utilized in carvings of scholarly studio items, boulder-shape shanzi, and table screens. These had opened up new trends and routes for ancient Chinese jade development.

松柏长青，花开富贵，君子居竹，高士倚梅。古人将植物文化与玉石雕刻相结合，创造出文化寓意深刻的植物类玉雕作品。特别是明清以来，玉器的实用性与陈设性进一步增强，在玉文房器、山子、插屏等器型上适宜开展雕刻植物类题材，为中国古代玉器的发展开辟了新路径。

158 A celadon jade carving of pine shape brush pot

Qing Dynasty, Qianlong Period (1736-1795)
Length 11.9cm, Width 8.4cm, Height 7.1cm
The collection of the Summer Palace

The body of this celadon jade brush washer is carved with pine branches in relief. The skill of work is quite detailed and exquisite portraying the classic ancient carving style.

青玉雕松随形洗

清乾隆（1736—1795年）
长11.9厘米，宽8.4厘米，高7.1厘米
颐和园藏

青玉质，器身采用圆雕技法，雕刻松枝，其雕琢极为精巧，树干及松针雕琢纹丝不乱，极具章法，古意盈盈，妙不可言。

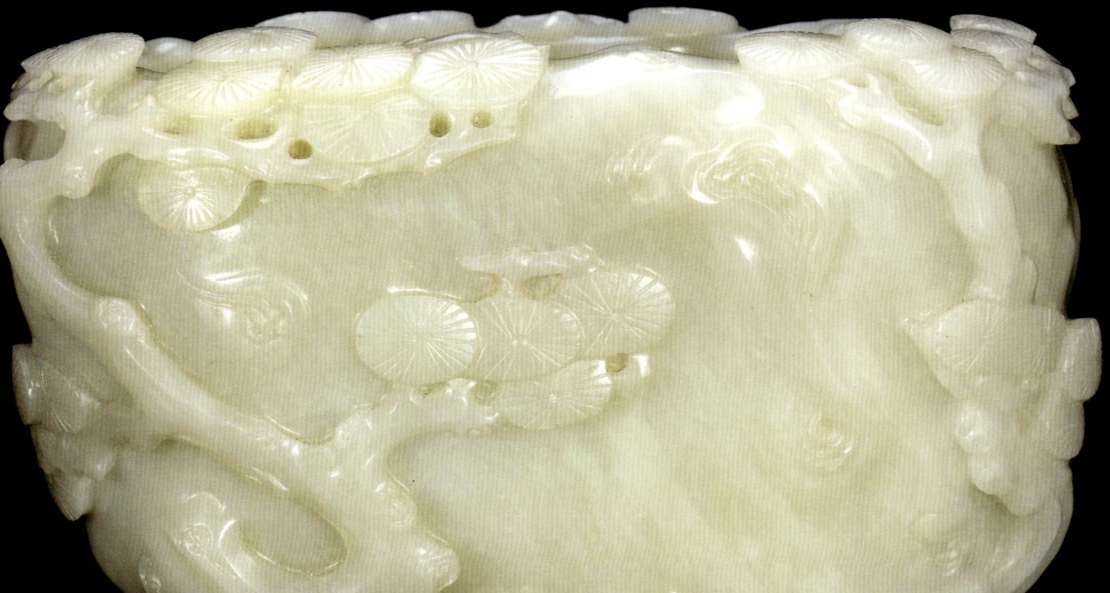

159 A celadon jade carving of brush pot with pine and plum blossom

Qing Dynasty, Qianlong Period (1736-1795)
Length 8cm, Width 6cm, Height 13cm
The collection of the Summer Palace

The celadon jade bears some russet rind inclusions. The body of the brush pot is carved with pine trees in low relief. The carving of this brush pot is natural and skillfully done enhancing the serene atmosphere of the study room.

青玉雕松倭角方笔筒

清乾隆（1736—1795 年）
长 8 厘米，宽 6 厘米，高 13 厘米
颐和园藏

青玉质，有少许黄褐皮色。该器用整料雕出海棠口形笔筒，筒身随形浅浮雕遒劲苍松。器形规整而不失自然之趣，散发着浓郁的书卷气息。

160 A white jade carving of pine and plum blossom

Qing Dynasty (1616–1911)
Length 4.5cm, Width 1cm, Height 5.2cm
The collection of the Summer Palace

The white jade display object is carved with pine, bamboo and plum blossoms with rockeries. The pine tree, bamboo and the plum tree are evergreen plants and lauded by the Chinese as the "three friends of Winter". This display object characteristically exudes the righteous quality much admired by the Chinese intelligentsia.

白玉松梅摆件

清（1616—1911年）
长4.5厘米，宽1厘米，高5.2厘米
颐和园藏

白玉质。以透雕技法雕出怪石嶙峋，一面盘状松枝与竹叶交错，另一面两朵寒梅绽放在石壁之中。松、竹、梅三者因具有四季常青、宁折不屈、傲雪凌霜的品格被中国古人视为『岁寒三友』。此玉件涵盖了中国文人崇尚的几种高洁美好的品格。

161 A white jade carving of vase with pine, bamboo and plum blossom

Qing Dynasty, Qianlong Period (1736-1795)
Length 6.5cm, Width 5.5cm, Height 13.3cm
Provided by The Institute of Qing History Renmin University of China

The white jade bears some reddish inclusions. It is carved as a flower receptacle in the form of a pine stem. The rest of the body are carved in light relief with bamboo and plum flower and a standing crane. These construe the message of "songhe yannian" (pine and crane bringing a long life).

白玉岁寒三友花插

清乾隆（1736—1795 年）
长 6.5 厘米，宽 5.5 厘米，高 13.3 厘米
中国人民大学清史研究所提供

白玉质，留红皮。随形圆雕，以苍劲的松干为主体，掏膛匀称，可插花。四面以浮雕手法饰以松、竹和梅。松下仙鹤独立，竹边一簇山石灵芝。整件花插寓意松鹤延年，亦饱含文人高风亮节的情怀。

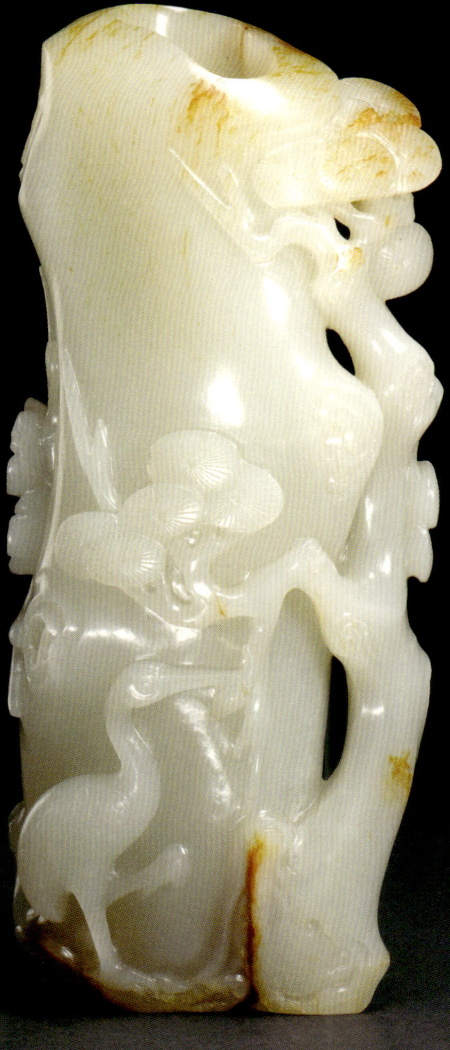

162 A spinach jade carving of table screen

Qing Dynasty, Qianlong Period (1736–1795)
Length 35cm, Width 16cm, Height 40cm
The collection of the Summer Palace

The front side of this table screen is carved with a poem by Emperor Qianlong in lishu (clerical script). The reverse side has carving of an idyllic country landscape with farm houses and farmers.

碧玉刻御制诗插屏

清乾隆（1736—1795年）
长35厘米，宽16厘米，高40厘米
颐和园藏

碧玉质。此器正面琢刻隶书乾隆御制诗：『东郭还西墅，山家接水村。春朝庆老幼，丰岁足鸡豚。三代遗风在，一时深意存。治民无别术，饥饱俾寒温。』背面阴刻雕琢出房屋村舍、人物等田野农庄图案与御制诗相应。

163 A lapis lazuli carving of landscape group

Qing Dynasty, Qianlong Period (1736-1795)
Length 14.2cm, Width 5.3cm, Height 16cm
The collection of the Summer Palace

This blue lazurite stone is carved with a shanzi (boulder) with light relief of rockeries and pine tree. The front is engraved with a royal poem of Emperor Qianlong.

青金石御题翠云岩山景

清乾隆（1736—1795 年）
长 14.2 厘米，宽 5.3 厘米，高 16 厘米
颐和园藏

青金石质，颜色湛蓝。此件山子根据石料纹理走向雕琢成山形，山景之上浮雕山石、松柏。正面刻有乾隆御题诗《御题翠云岩》，诗文曰：叶姿枝态锁层峰，织翠流青色正浓。习习天风拂岩落，人间烦暑觅何从。

御題翠雲巖
葉姿枝態鎖層
峯織翠流青色
正濃習習天風
拂巖落人間煩
暑覓何從

御
題搬雲巖
葉婆枝態鎖層
峰織搬流青色
正濃習習天風
拂巖落人間煩
暑覓何從

164　A white jade carving of "fishing felling farming and reading" group

Qing Dynasty, Qianlong Period (1736-1795)
Length 10cm, Width 5cm, Height 14.6cm
The collection of the Summer Palace

The white jade has some orange-yellow markings. It is carved in low relief of a boulder (shanzi) with hills, pine trees, a bridge with two farm boys and a scholar reading in a pavilion.

白玉雕『耕读图』山子

清乾隆（1736—1795 年）
长 10 厘米，宽 5 厘米，高 14.6 厘米
颐和园藏

白玉质，局部有橘黄色玉皮。以浮雕、透雕等雕刻技法琢刻出群山、苍松、亭台、小桥，近处两小童手持鞭子赶牛过桥，远处半山腰亭台上一儒士手持书卷正在读书。该器随形巧雕，借用中国传统绘画中远山近景的技法，层次分明，人物琢刻栩栩如生。

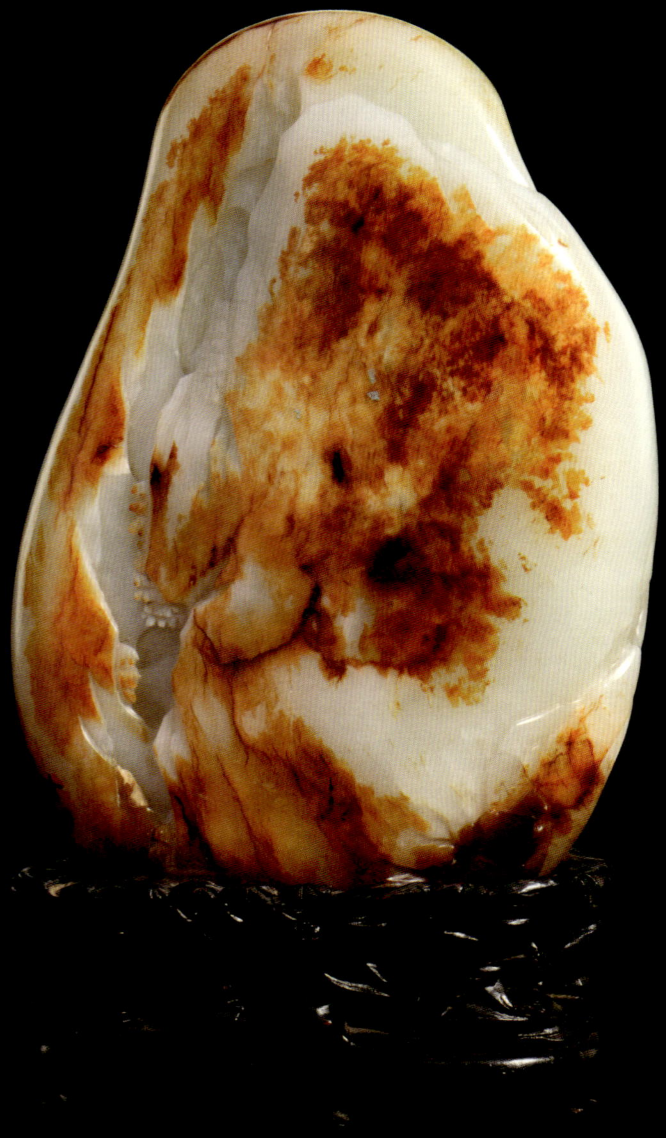

165 A turquois carving of landscape group

Qing Dynasty (1616-1911)
Length 18.5cm, Width 11cm, Height 17cm
The collection of the Summer Palace

The turquois stone is carved in both high and low relief of deer, crane, pine tree, immortals, boys and pavilion. It connotes the message of "Luhe Tongchun" (deer and crane in Spring) signifying the prosperous Spring season.

松石雕『鹿鹤同春』山景

清（1616—1911年）
长18.5厘米，宽11厘米，高17厘米
颐和园藏

绿松石整料随形雕琢，采用圆雕、高浮雕、阴刻等多种技法，细琢鹤鹿、松树、仙人、童子、亭榭等，整幅画面富有层次感。『鹿鹤同春』又名『六合同春』，寓意天下皆春，万物欣欣向荣。

531

166 A gray jade water pot of catfish and lotus

Ming Dynasty (1368-1644)
Length 11.3cm, Width 6.4cm, Height 5.5cm
Provided by The Institute of Qing History Renmin University of China

The gray jade bears some russet markings and is carved as a waterpot with hollowed out body. The body has carvings of lotus leaves and two catfish in high relief. The catfish and lotus connote the auspicious meaning of Liannian Youyu (good surpluses in every year).

灰玉雕『年年有余』水盂

明（1368—1644 年）
长 11.3 厘米，宽 6.4 厘米，高 5.5 厘米
中国人民大学清史研究所提供

灰玉质，带棕色皮，间有黑色提油。依料立体圆雕，掏膛成一水盂，以莲叶为体，膛内打磨光滑，口沿处饰有莲花。右侧卷曲莲叶与之相连，两莲叶间高浮雕一鲶鱼，身体圆润，长须垂于叶上。另一尾鲇鱼翻游于荷叶底部，给人『鱼戏莲叶间』之感。莲叶鲶鱼寓意连年有余，以文房水具的造型出现暗喻了荷花『出淤泥而不染』的高尚品德。

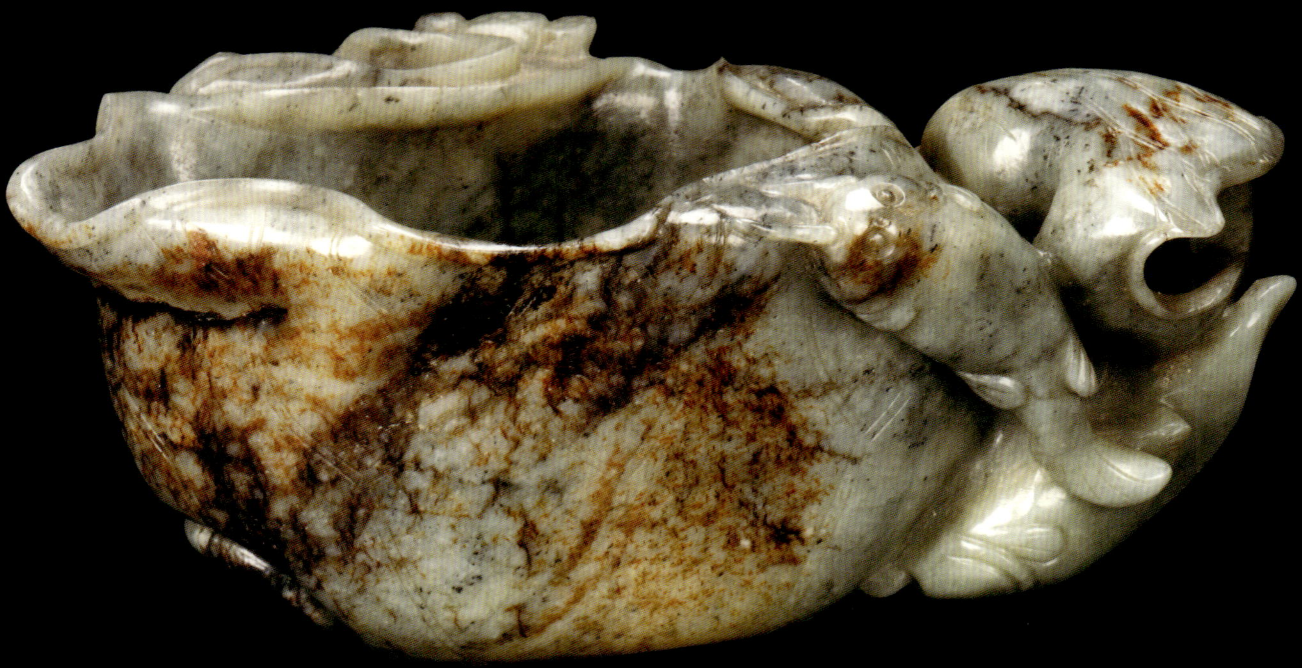

167 A celadon jade water pot of lotus

Qing Dynasty (1616–1911)
Length 13cm, Width 7cm, Height 3.5cm
The collection of the Summer Palace

The celadon jade is skillfully carved with lotus leaves at the base and two lotus flowers on the body. The center of body is hollowed out for use as waterpot.

青玉荷花水盂

清（1616—1911年）
长13厘米，宽7厘米，高3.5厘米
颐和园藏

青玉质。底部巧妙雕刻荷叶，器身雕双联荷花，芯部掏堂为水丞。

450

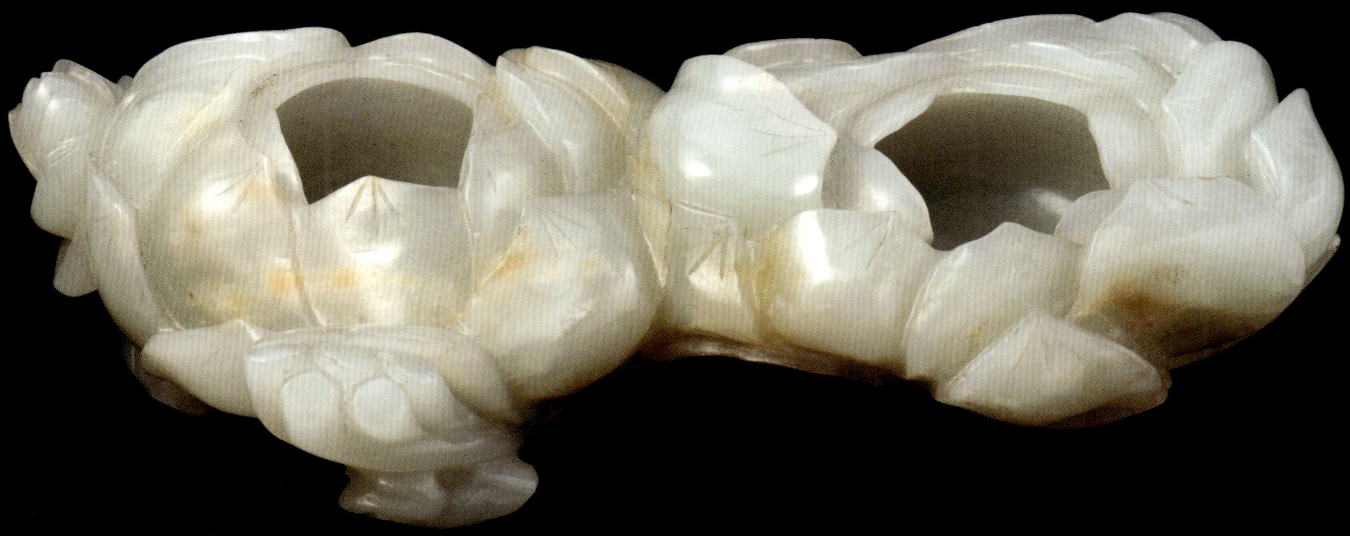

168 A white jade table screen with lotus

Qing Dynasty, Guangxu Period (1875-1908)
Length 7.8cm, Width 0.4cm, Height 14.6cm
The collection of the Summer Palace

The round table screen is carved with dragonfly and lotus on one side while the reverse side is carved with plum blossom and bamboo. The plum blossom confers a pure and noble character while the bamboo signifies longevity and peace.

白玉雕莲砚屏

清光绪（1875—1908年）
长7.8厘米，宽0.4厘米，高14.6厘米
颐和园藏

白玉质。圆牌一面雕刻蜻蜓莲花，谐音『清廉』，寓意居高位而不贪，公正廉洁。另一面雕刻梅花竹叶，梅花寓意圣洁、高尚，竹子寓意长寿安宁。

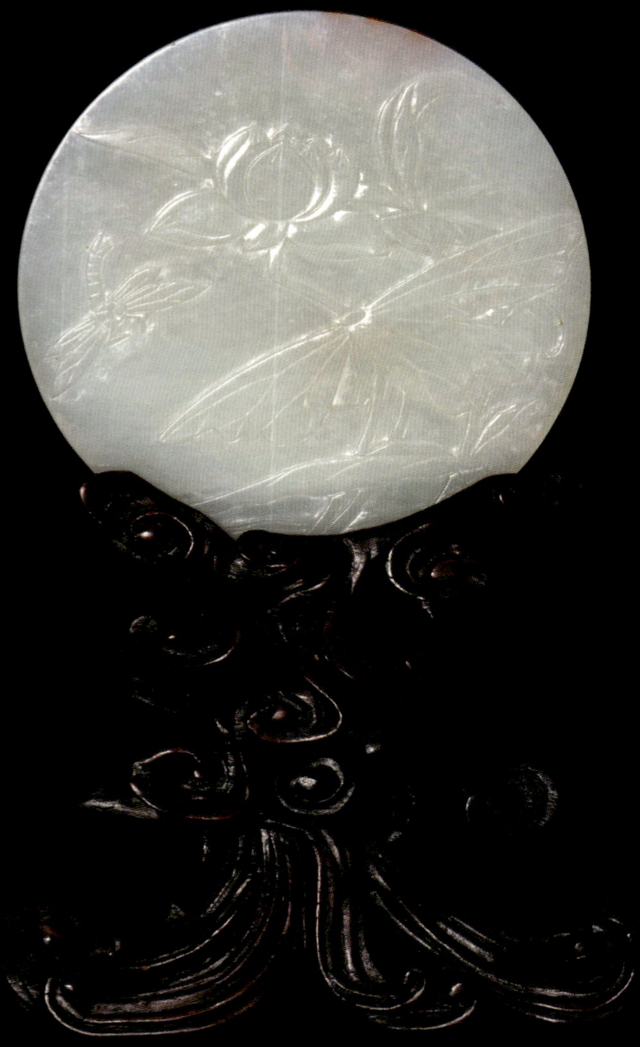

169 A celadon and russet white jade carving of mandarin duck and lotus

Jin / Yuan Dynasty (1115–1368)
Diameter 2.6cm, Height 1cm
The collection of Beijing Art Museum

This celadon jade round ornament is carved depicting mandarin ducks and lotus leaves in openwork form. Although this is only a small ornament, the skill of carving is exquisite with very distinctive layers. It is a standard example of the "ring supported high relief" carving popular in the Jin and Yuan periods.

青白玉俏色镂雕荷叶鸳鸯饰件

金至元（1115—1368年）
直径2.6厘米，厚1厘米
北京艺术博物馆藏

青玉质，有棕褐色沁斑。佩形状为周正的圆形，正面镂雕荷叶与两只鸳鸯。正中一片荷叶舒展，上缘与圆环上部相连，细阴刻线刻画出叶脉纹理与芯部，左下的荷叶作枯萎卷曲状，配合棕褐色的沁斑更显逼真，似有俏色的意图，叶片背面同样有细阴刻线刻画出叶脉。荷叶的茎镂雕卷曲在叶片之下，两片荷叶之间雕一对站立的鸳鸯。两只鸳鸯并行，其中一只，头有冠羽，回首背身，双翅并拢于身后，面部、颈部羽毛以人字纹阴刻线表现，翅膀上的羽毛则以平行的短阴刻线表现；另一只在造型上大部分被遮挡住，只有头部和前胸露出，头上冠羽略小，整体作曲颈颔首的姿态。两只鸳鸯并立，好似刚刚游上岸，以荷叶遮挡身体，正在整理羽毛。佩饰背面凹陷无纹饰，也无钻孔，且可以看到打磨的痕迹。整件佩饰虽小，但景物错落有致，层次分明，是一件典型的流行于金元时期的环托高浮雕形式的作品。

170 A white jade carving of lotus leaf shape brush washer

Qing Dynasty, Qianlong Period (1736–1795)
Length 15cm, Width 14cm, Height 7cm
Provided by The Institute of Qing History Renmin University of China

The white jade brush washer bears some russet inclusions. The body is hollowed out with the sides carved into lotus leaves and lotus flower in relief. The lotus connotes a pure and noble character.

白玉荷叶形洗

清乾隆（1736—1795 年）
长 15 厘米，宽 14 厘米，高 7 厘米
中国人民大学清史研究所提供

白玉质，带红皮。籽料整挖中空，随形雕琢蜷曲荷叶为洗，底部与周身以浮雕与圆雕相结合的方式饰以莲花，与莲叶相连，末端束于笔洗一侧，纹饰与线条流畅，贯穿始终。此笔洗寄托了清正廉洁、君子爱莲的寓意。

A white jade water pot of lotus

Qing Dynasty, Qianlong Period (1736-1795)
Length 6.5cm, Width 6.5cm, Height 3cm
The collection of the Summer Palace

The white jade is carved in the form of a lotus leaf with its center hollowed out. The outer body is carved with water grass surrounding the lotus leaf.

白玉荷叶水盂

清乾隆（1736—1795 年）
长 6.5 厘米，宽 6.5 厘米，高 3 厘米
颐和园藏

白玉质。随形雕刻一片翻卷荷叶之形。舒放内敛，内挖精细，形成洗池，外有水草、荷叶相绕。

172 An agate water pot of lotus

Qing Dynasty, Guangxu Period (1875-1908)
Length 10cm, Width 8.8cm, Height 5cm
The collection of the Summer Palace

The body of the waterpot is carved in the form of a lotus leaf. The outer body is very skillfully carved with lotus pod and toad.

红玛瑙池莲洗

清光绪（1875—1908年）
长10厘米，宽8.8厘米，高5厘米
颐和园藏

红玛瑙质。笔掭器身为荷叶形，外侧巧雕莲蓬、蟾等动植物，灵动传神，栩栩如生。

173 A white jade teapot with dragon handle

Qing Dynasty, Jiaqing Period (1796–1820)
Length 20cm, Width 12cm, Height 13cm
The collection of the Summer Palace

There are some yellowish markings on this white jade teapot with lid. The lid and belly of the teapot are carved with lotus petal patterns. It also has a dragon shaped handle.

白玉龙柄莲瓣纹壶

清嘉庆（1796—1820年）
长20厘米，宽12厘米，高13厘米
颐和园藏

白玉质，局部有黄皮色。该器由盖和壶身配套组成，盖和壶身有子母扣。盖顶为宝珠形纽，壶盖和壶身腹部有莲瓣纹。龙形柄，鼓腹，圈足。

174 A spinach jade carving of moon flask and cover with "Ba Ji Xiang" ornamentation

Qing Dynasty, Qianlong Period (1736–1795)
Length 15.5cm, Width 3.5cm, Height 27.5cm
Provided by The Institute of Qing History Renmin University of China

The spinach green jade moon flask bears some black speckles. Its lid has a floral finial. The two sides are flanked by phoenix head handles with loose rings. The body is carved with the auspicious Buddhist Bajixiang (Eight Buddhist Emblems) in relief. These eight emblems convey the message of long-lasting happiness and good luck.

碧玉西番莲八吉祥双凤首活环扁瓶

清乾隆（1736—1795年）

长15.5厘米，宽3.5厘米，高27.5厘米

中国人民大学清史研究所提供

碧玉质，带炭色斑点。整料掏膛圆雕，内膛均匀，瓶盖带纽，顶部饰莲瓣纹，与瓶身花卉纹饰相呼应。两侧镂雕凤首耳配活环。瓶身圆形开光，浮雕佛教八吉祥纹饰，即胜幢、法轮、法螺、宝伞、吉祥结、宝瓶、莲花、双鱼。中心饰牡丹纹，由八宝环绕周围。取富贵长春，吉祥如意之意。

175 A white jade plate with golden trace

Qing Dynasty, Jiaqing Period (1796–1820)
Diameter 26cm, Height 4.6cm
The collection of the Summer Palace

Both the inner and outer walls of this white jade dish are carved with chrysanthemum patterns which are then gilded. The chrysanthemum, being one of the sijunzi (the four gentry), is very much adored by the literati of the period.

白玉描金菊纹盘

清嘉庆（1796—1820年）
直径26厘米，高4.6厘米
颐和园藏

白玉质。此盘造型规整，壁薄体轻，口沿外撇，腹部渐收，底为圈足。盘内外壁皆雕刻形态各异的菊纹，花纹描金。菊与梅、兰、竹被称为四君子，因此菊纹深受文人的喜爱。

76 A white jade brush pot with orchid and stones

Qing Dynasty, Jiaqing Period (1796–1820)
Diameter 6cm, Height 7.7cm
The collection of the Summer Palace

This white jade brush pot is cylindrical in shape. The outer wall is carved with orchids and rockeries in low relief together with poems of the Qianlong emperor in the early Jiaqing period.

白玉圣制兰花诗文山石图笔筒

清嘉庆（1796—1820 年）
直径 6 厘米，高 7.7 厘米
颐和园藏

白玉质，笔筒呈圆筒形，外壁浅浮雕兰花山石及《圣制兰花诗》。圣制诗，特指年代为清嘉庆元年至三年即清乾隆六十一年至六十三年，乾隆归政之时所作诗文。该笔筒器形规整，玉质莹润，构图与诗文相应成趣。

177 A white jade carving of plum blossom vase

Qing Dynasty, Qianlong Period (1736–1795)
Diameter 13.7cm, Height 25.5cm
The collection of the Summer Palace

The white jade vase has a lid with a lion shaped finial. The vase is flanked by two handles with plum flower shaped loose rings. The plum blossom is seen to stand the cold of winter and very much adored by the Chinese.

白玉梅花活环耳盖罐

清乾隆（1736—1795年）
直径13.7厘米，高25.5厘米
颐和园藏

白玉质。该器由盖和瓶身组成，小口，折肩，长腹下收，圈足；盖为狮形纽。该器肩部两侧雕梅花形耳，耳为梅花活环。瓶腹部浅浮雕梅花。梅花傲立雪中，不畏严寒，不惧艰辛，自古就为中华民族优秀品格的完美象征。

A carnelian agate carving of "lily with bat and lingzhi" group

Qing Dynasty, Qianlong Period (1736–1795)
Length 9cm, Width 6.2cm, Height 5.6cm
Provided by The Institute of Qing History Renmin University of China

This carnelian agate is a unique agate from Yunnan. It is white interlaced with some red colors and a pair of lilies are carved. A lingzhi and a pair of bats are carved on the lilies. The lingzhi and the bat are both auspicious objects conveying good luck and propitiousness.

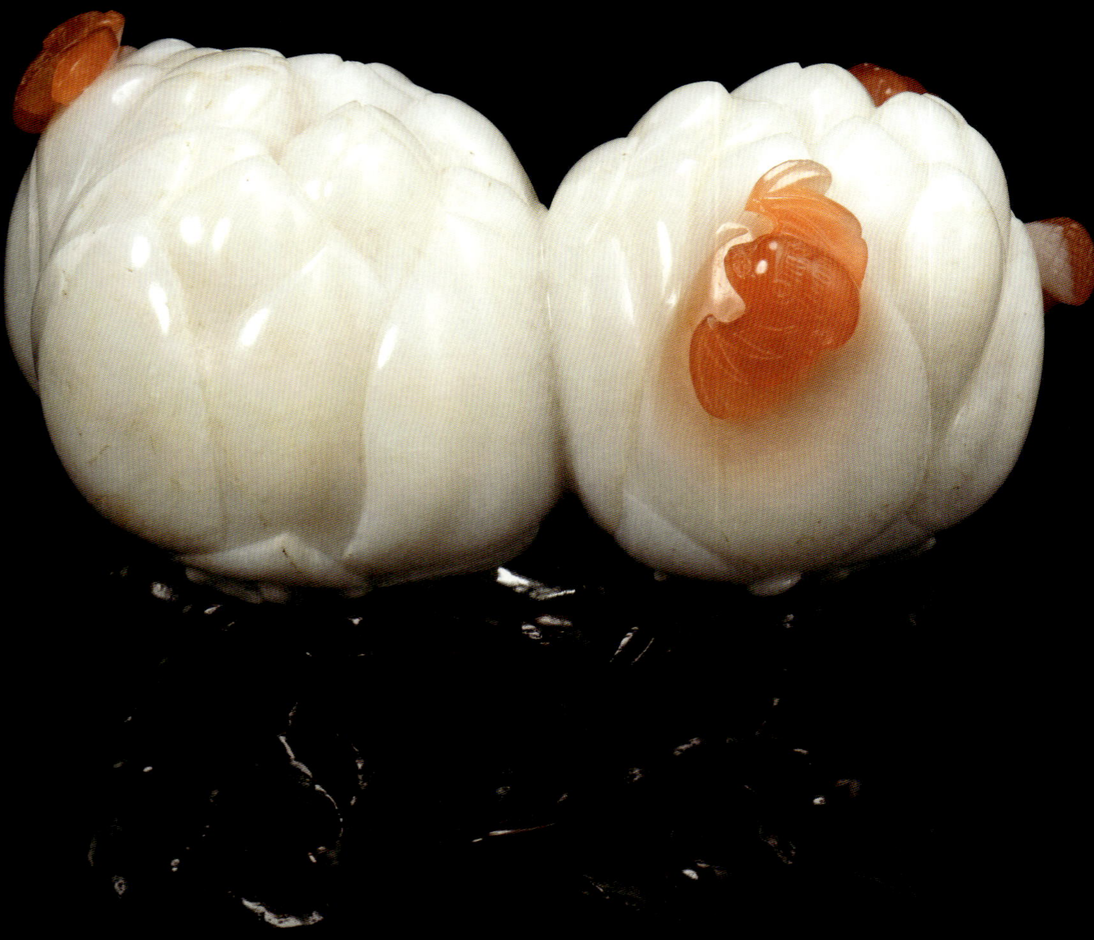

南红玛瑙红蝠灵芝纹百合

清乾隆（1736—1795年）

长9厘米，宽6.2厘米，高5.6厘米

中国人民大学清史研究所提供

南红玛瑙质，红白相间。随形圆雕，选玛瑙白色为主体，圆雕百合一对，层层叠叠，丰满细润；一侧取红色玛瑙浮雕灵芝如意一枚，系『卐』字纹绶带。另有红色蝙蝠一双饰于百合之上，尤为灵动。百合寓意百年好合；灵芝与『卐』字绶带寓意万代如意；朱红色蝙蝠寓意洪福齐天。南红玛瑙为中国独有的玛瑙品种，多产于云南宝山，产量稀少，为历代统治者所珍视。

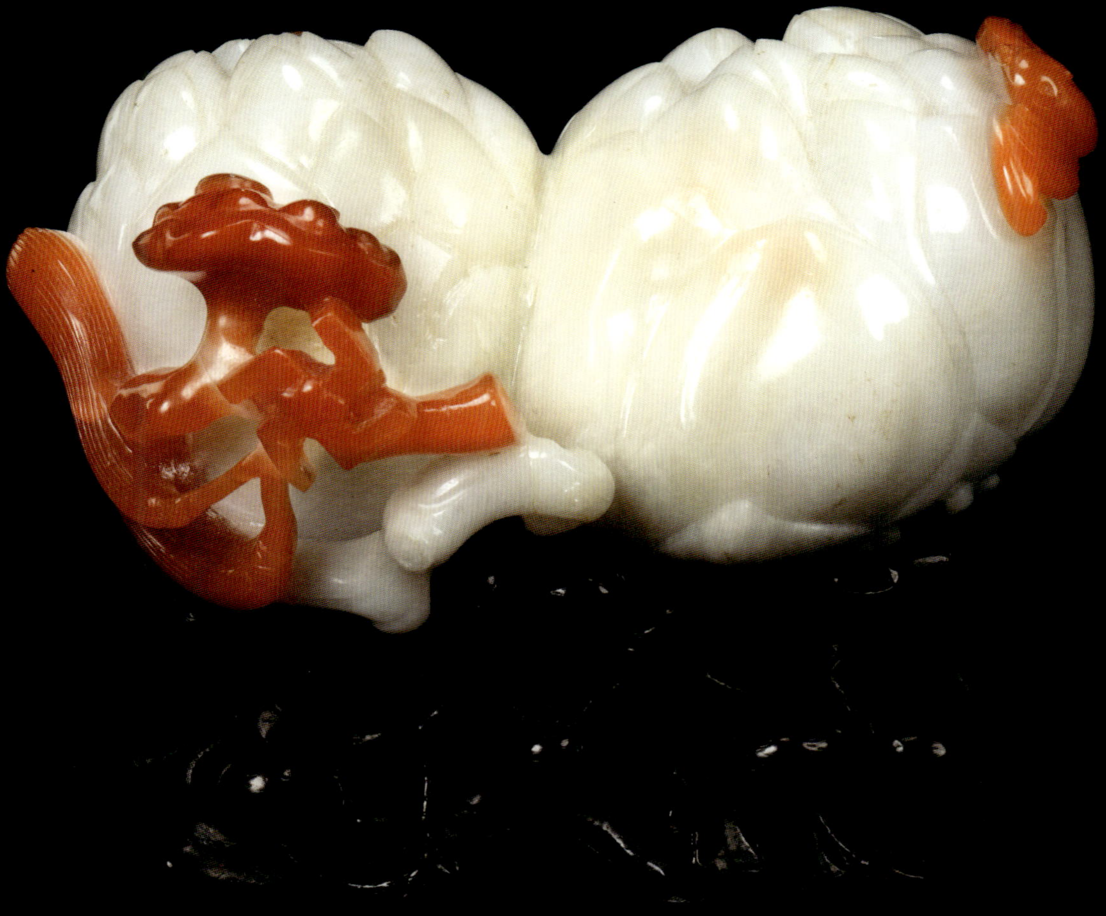

179 A white jade carving of magnolia

Qing Dynasty, Qianlong Period (1736–1795)
Length 6cm, Width 3cm, Height 11.5cm
The collection of the Summer Palace

The white jade is carved in the form of a magnolia flower. It has a strong three-dimensional effect with layers of splaying petals and a bending stalk.

白玉玉兰花

清乾隆（1736—1795 年）
长 6 厘米，宽 3 厘米，高 11.5 厘米
颐和园藏

白玉质。整料雕刻玉兰花形，花瓣向外敞开，层层包裹；花枝弯曲，立体感极强。

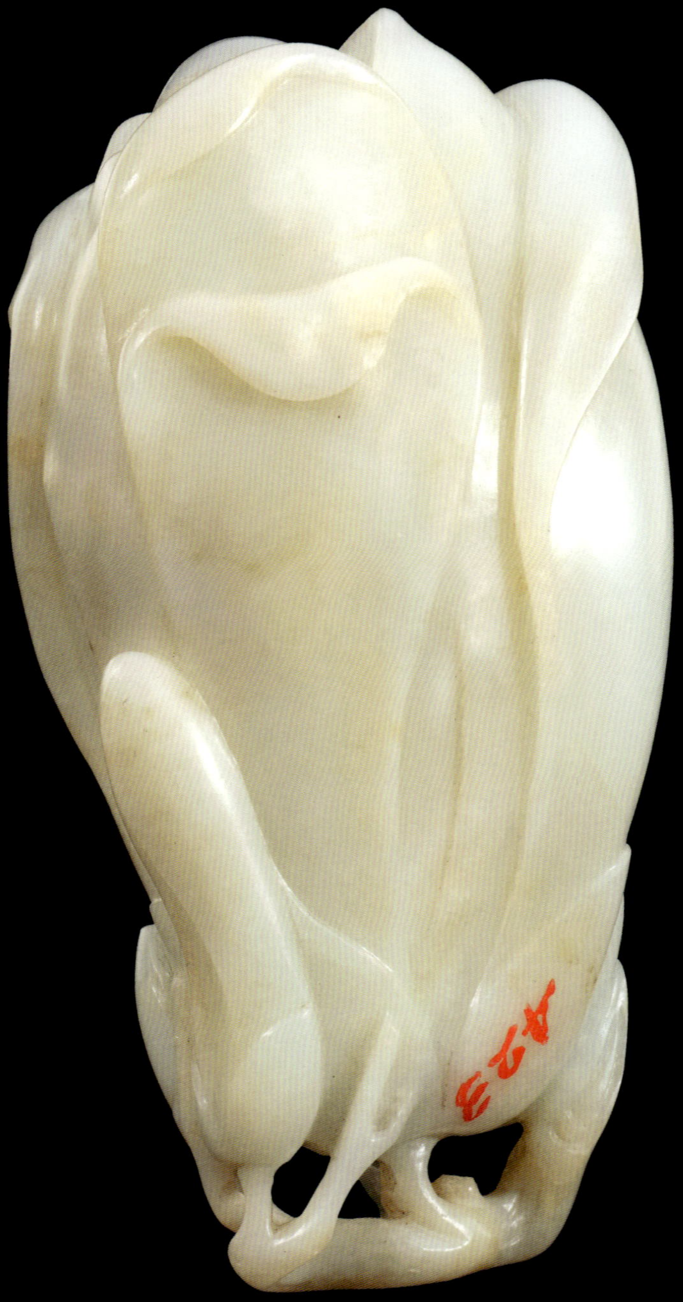

180 A white jade carving of magnolia

Qing Dynasty, Qianlong Period (1736-1795)
Length 6.5cm, Width 4cm, Height 11cm
The collection of the Summer Palace

The white jade has some light russet markings. A magnolia flower is carved with multilayers of splaying petals and a bending stalk.

白玉玉兰花

清乾隆（1736—1795年）
长6.5厘米，宽4厘米，高11厘米
颐和园藏

白玉质，局部黄皮色。整料雕刻玉兰花形，花瓣向外敞开，层层包裹；花枝弯曲，立体感极强。

181 A large jadeite carving of table screen

The Republic of China (1912–1949)
Length 44cm, Width 38cm, Height 81cm
The collection of the Summer Palace

The jadeite table screen is rectangular in shape with carvings of magnolia and begonia. The reverse side of the table screen is carved with a poem of the emperor Qianlong.

翡翠雕『玉堂富贵』仿乾隆御题插屏

民国（1912—1949年）
长44厘米，宽38厘米，高81厘米
颐和园藏

屏芯呈长方形，采用整块翡翠原料，以浮雕的手法琢刻而成。一面雕有玉兰、海棠等纹饰，寓意『玉堂富贵』。另一面表现的是战国时期『甘罗拜相』的场面，并附有乾隆皇帝的御制诗一首。

邈矣關雎化
龍漦禍水流
粲然傾國貌
一笑隕宗周
乾隆御題

邈矣關雎化
龍漦禍水流
粲然傾國貌
一笑隕宗周
乾隆御題

182 A celadon jade carving of brush pot with *"wan xiang"* mark

Qing Dynasty, Daoguang Period (1821–1850)
Diameter 14.3cm, Height 14.4cm
The collection of the Summer Palace

The celadon jade brush pot has some yellowish-brown speckles. The outer wall is carved in light relief with bamboo, orchid and rockeries. It also has a carving of a poem in lishu (clerical script) expressing the scholars love for the bamboo and orchid.

青玉『晚香』款兰竹图诗文笔筒

清道光（1821—1850年）
直径14.3厘米，高14.4厘米
颐和园藏

青玉质。玉呈青碧色，有黄褐色斑点。外壁采用浅浮雕和线雕技法表现竹、兰、山石等纹饰，图案纹饰之后刻隶书『竹兰诗』一首。竹、兰纹饰古往今来为文人雅士所喜爱，用以表达自己卓尔不凡的情趣，或作为自身品德的警戒，包含正直、虚心、纯洁而有气节的思想感情。

183 A red coral carving vase with peony and mantis

Qing Dynasty, Guangxu Period (1875–1908)
Length 10.2cm, Width 5.5cm, Height 21.2cm
The collection of the Summer Palace

The red coral is carved in the form of a flower receptacle with peony, stems and leaves, and a praying mantis. The peony and mantis on a flower receptacle convey the message of "wealth and peace" together with "a prosperous family".

红珊瑚雕『富贵平安』花插

清光绪（1875—1908 年）
长 10.2 厘米，宽 5.5 厘米，高 21.2 厘米
颐和园藏

红珊瑚质。以用圆雕、透雕、浮雕等多种技法，琢刻出牡丹花枝、花叶，花间雕一螳螂，形态生动。花瓶、花枝利用珊瑚天然的枝状随形琢刻而成，花枝沿瓶身呈缠绕状。牡丹被誉为百花之王，花之富贵，螳螂寓意家财兴旺，牡丹置于瓶间，取『富贵平安，家财兴旺』之意。

184 A white stone carving screen with peony and magpie

Qing Dynasty, Guangxu Period (1875–1908)
Length 23.5cm, Width 10cm, Height 35cm
The collection of the Summer Palace

The white stone is carved in the form of a round table screen and inlaid with various jades and other precious stones in the form of magpie and peonies. The magpie and peony construe the meaning of "happy to welcome wealth". It has an accompanying wooden stand.

白石嵌百宝『喜迎富贵』砚屏

清光绪（1875—1908 年）
长 23.5 厘米，宽 10 厘米，高 35 厘米
颐和园藏

屏芯以白石为地，其上以玉石、翡翠、青金石、芙蓉石等材质嵌喜鹊、牡丹等花鸟纹饰。喜鹊谐音『喜』，牡丹花语富贵，两者结合取『喜迎富贵』之意。附硬木屏座。

时蔬佳果

Vegetables and Fruits

Jade had also been carved to depict bumper harvest of the grains, the seasonal fresh fruits and vegetables. These jade carvings could be used for adornment and wearing purposes; and for the joy of pure appreciation and tactile touch. These carving shapes are rich with auspicious meaning. The pomegranates and lotus seedpods signified prosperity with many descendants; the bottle gourds, the fingered citron and peaches represented longevity and prosperity while the lively jade carvings of fruits and vegetables are still loved and admired until today.

五谷丰登，节令时鲜。琢玉为果为实，可佩、可赏、可玩，造型丰富，寓意美满。石榴、莲蓬等常常象征多子多福；葫芦、佛手、仙桃等代表福寿绵长。灵巧生动的蔬果形象玉器直到今时依然被人们喜爱与崇尚。

85 A gray jade carving of lotus seedpod

Song/Ming Dynasty (960–1644)
Length 5cm, Width 4.8cm, Height 2.7cm
Provided by The Institute of Qing History Renmin University of China

This gray burnt jade bears some black markings. A lotus pod is carved in the round with the lotus seeds clearly visible. The lotus pod signifies the concept of numerous progenies and also an upright and honest character.

火烧玉莲蓬

宋至明（960—1644 年）
长 5 厘米，宽 4.8 厘米，高 2.7 厘米
中国人民大学清史研究所提供

火烧玉质，带黑色提油，有棕黑色沁斑，立体圆雕，造型自然写实，莲蓬饱满圆润，莲子粒粒清晰，莲心颗颗突出，底部一把莲叶翻转承托莲蓬两侧。莲蓬寓意多子多福，亦有清廉之意。

186 A finely carved white jade lotus seedpod and toad group

Qing Dynasty, Qianlong Period (1736–1795)
Length 13.6cm, Width 5.5cm, Height 7.8cm
Provided by The Institute of Qing History Renmin University of China

The white jade has some amber colored inclusions. Two lotus pods, one large and one smaller with lotus flowers are carved. A golden toad is carved on the larger lotus pod. The lotus pod and the toad both convey the meaning of a prosperous life having numerous offspring.

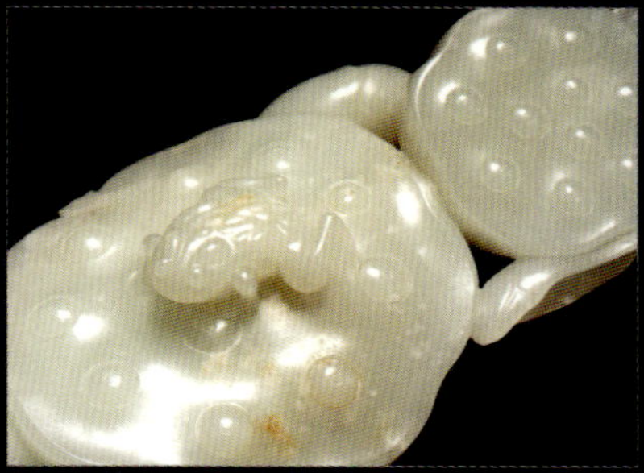

白玉金蟾莲蓬

清乾隆（1736—1795年）
长13.6厘米，宽5.5厘米，高7.8厘米
中国人民大学清史研究所提供

白玉质，琥珀色皮。随形圆雕大小莲蓬。大莲蓬饰蟾蜍一只，活灵活现，莲花绽放于一侧。大小莲蓬相邻处饰有莲花含苞待放，另一侧点缀蜷曲荷叶、莲蓬、莲花、花苞、荷叶集结于底部，蜿蜒一侧结为一束，末端可见叶茎的横切面，表现了莲花『中通外直』的特点。蟾蜍与莲蓬都是多籽之物，寓意早生贵子，多子多福，子孙满堂；同时，莲花有『出淤泥而不染』之美寓，象征洁身自好、清廉自持。

187 A white jade carving of lotus with dragonfly group

Qing Dynasty, Qianlong Period (1736–1795)
Length 6cm, Width 5cm, Height 6.5cm
Provided by The Institute of Qing History Renmin University of China

The white jade has some orange rind markings. It is carved in the round in the form of a lotus pod with a dragonfly on top of lotus seeds. The lotus pod and dragonfly also convey the meaning of a prosperous family having numerous progenies.

白玉俏色蜻蜓莲蓬

清乾隆（1736—1795 年）
长 6 厘米，宽 5 厘米，高 6.5 厘米
中国人民大学清史研究所提供

白玉质籽料，满金皮。随形琢碾，圆雕莲蓬形，玉皮作蜻蜓附于莲子之上，生动逼真。莲子凹凸有致，荷花含苞待放，荷叶蜷曲一侧，宁静又不失俏丽，浑然一体。莲蓬与蜻蜓皆多子，常暗喻多子多福。蜻蜓亦有青云直上、平步青云之寓意。

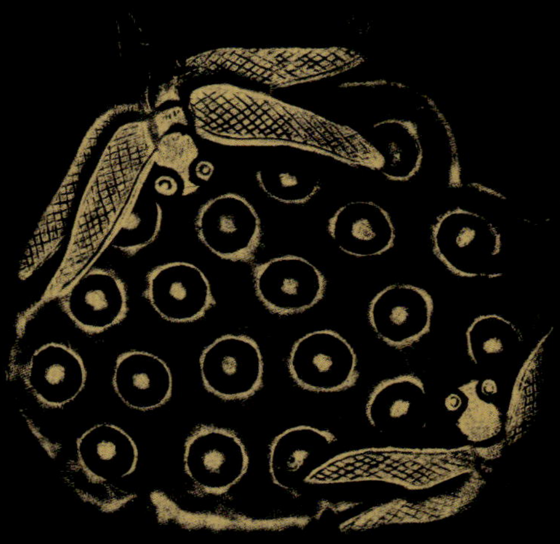

188 A celadon jade carving of lotus group

Qing Dynasty, Qianlong Period (1736–1795)
Length 11cm, Width 8cm, Height 4cm
The collection of the Summer Palace

The celadon jade bears some russet inclusions. It is carved in the form of lotus leaves and lotus pods. The lotus pods are full of seeds. This construes the propitious meaning of a family of numerous progenies.

青玉荷莲

清乾隆（1736—1795 年）
长 11 厘米，宽 8 厘米，高 4 厘米
颐和园藏

青玉质，略带黄皮。整料雕琢，底部巧妙雕刻荷叶，荷叶的边缘向外翻卷。器身雕琢莲叶包裹双莲蓬，莲蓬饱满，莲子凸出。寓意连生贵子、子孙满堂。

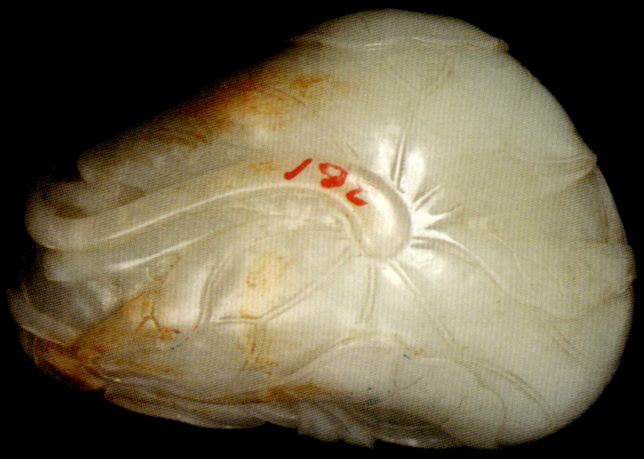

189 A white jade carving of lotus

Qing Dynasty, Qianlong Period (1736–1795)
Length 6cm, Width 4.3cm, Height 2cm
The collection of the Summer Palace

The white jade is carved in the form of a lotus pod with many lotus seeds. The lotus seeds allude to the concept of producing numerous offspring and descendants.

白玉莲蓬

清乾隆（1736—1795年）
长6厘米，宽4.3厘米，高2厘米
颐和园藏

白玉质。莲蓬里包含多个莲子，谐音『连子』，寓意连生贵子，有多子多孙，子孙满堂之意。

190 A white jade carving of a bean

Qing Dynasty, Qianlong Period (1736-1795)
Length 6.8cm, Width 5.8cm, Height 3.1cm
Provided by The Institute of Qing History Renmin University of China

The white jade bears some orange-red markings. It is carved in the form of a bean pod full of beans. The bean pod connotes the meaning of numerous progenies and a good harvest.

白玉豆荚把件

清乾隆（1736—1795 年）
长 6.8 厘米，宽 5.8 厘米，高 3.1 厘米
中国人民大学清史研究所提供

白玉质，带橘红色皮。圆雕扁豆，豆荚饱满，叶片翻转灵动，豆荚上细藤卷曲，生机盎然。豆角寓意多子多福，丰收富足，福泽延绵。

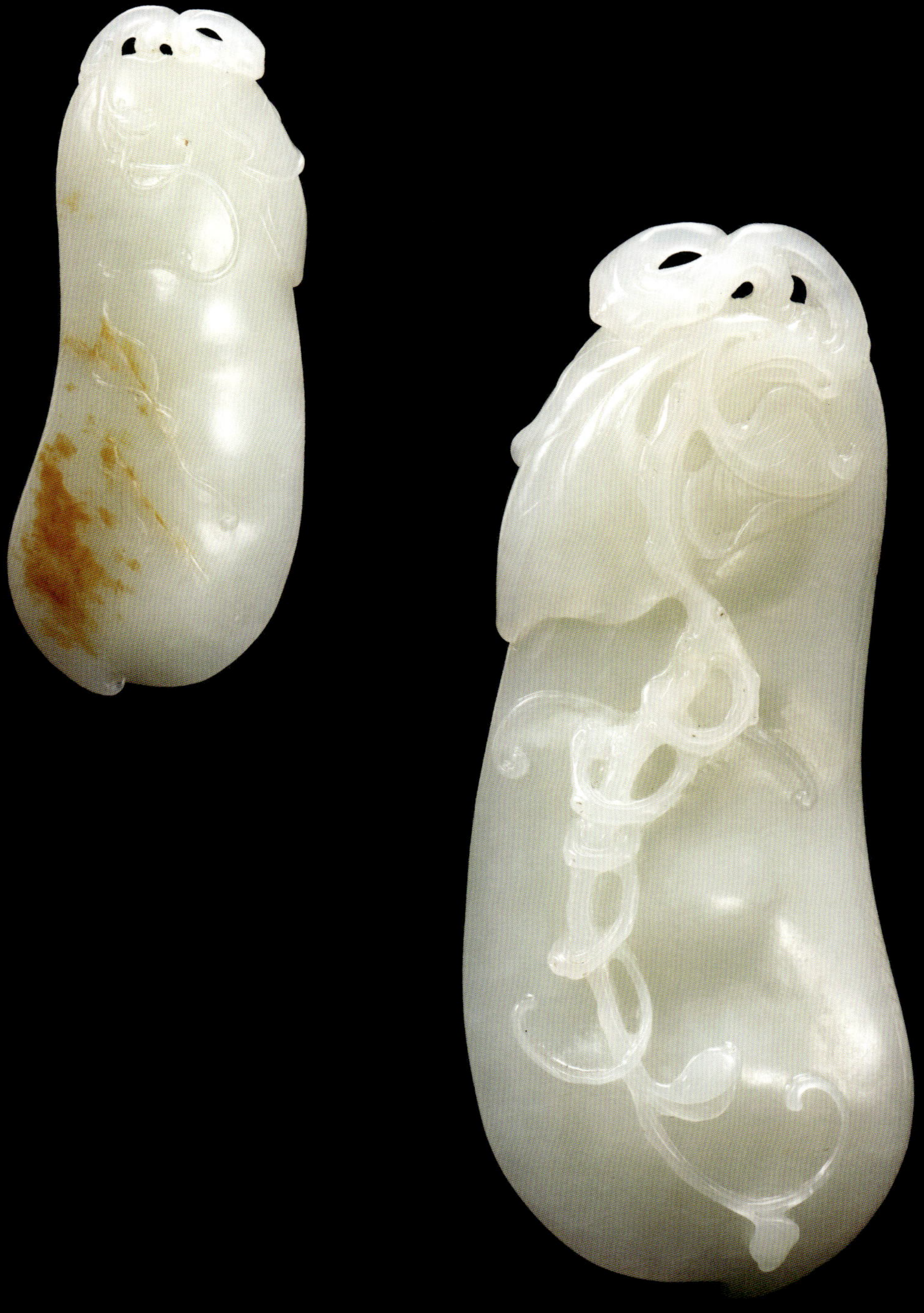

A white and russet jade carving of a lychee

Qing Dynasty, Qianlong Period (1736–1795)
Length 9.5cm, Width 3.9cm, Height 2cm
Provided by The Institute of Qing History Renmin University of China

The white jade has some orange rind markings. It is skilfully carved in the form of a succulent lychee. The lychee signifies good luck and great prosperity with numerous progenies.

雕荔枝一枚，洒金皮作叶片枝脉及表皮，白料作荔枝果肉，造型圆润饱满，叶片纹理清晰，富于变化。荔枝寓意大吉大利，多子多福。

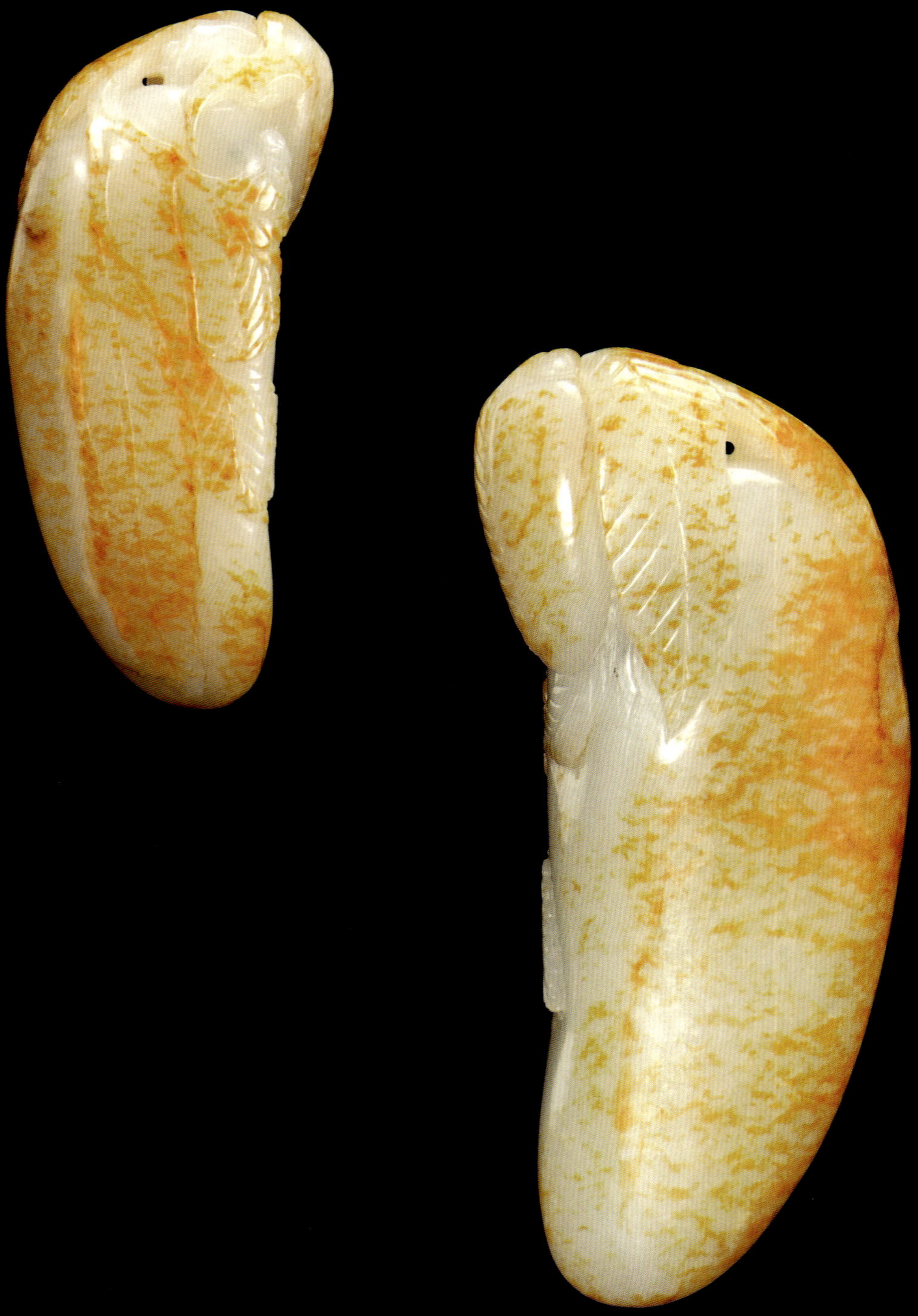

92 A white and russet jade carving of a finger citron

Qing Dynasty, Qianlong Period (1736-1795)
Length 6.8cm, Width 5.8cm, Height 3.1cm
Provided by The Institute of Qing History Renmin University of China

The white jade bears some russet inclusions. A succulent fingered citron (also called Buddha's hand) is carved in the round with a longhorn beetle resting on the fruit. The underside has an inscription of "Zigang". The fingered citron with the beetle connotes the meaning of "felicity and longevity".

白玉佛手天牛把件

清乾隆（1736—1795年）
长6.8厘米，宽5.8厘米，高3.1厘米
中国人民大学清史研究所提供

白玉质，间有糖色。立体圆雕，佛手造型饱满，层次丰富，茎叶翻转多变。巧作一天牛栖息于果上，枝下暗处阴刻『子冈』二篆字，以表工匠慕古之心。佛手，俗称佛手柑，因其形如人手而得名，被誉为果中之仙品，加上佛与『福』谐音，因此，佛手寓意吉祥幸福。天牛在远古时期被视为『神虫』，在古代代表铜钱，因此，有着财路亨通的吉祥寓意。天牛与佛手一起亦有『福寿齐天』之意。

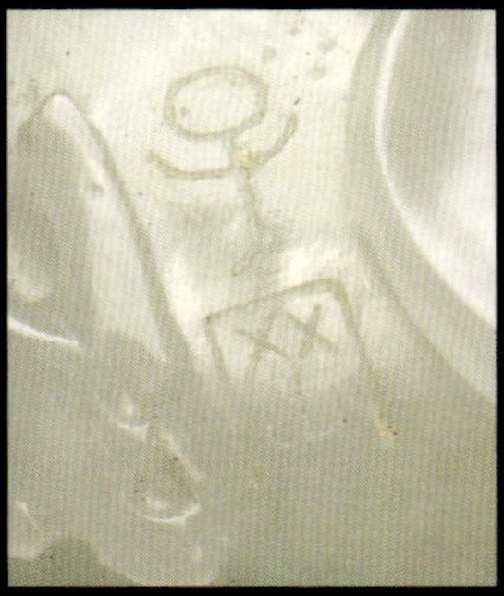

93 A white jade carving of finger citron

Qing Dynasty, Qianlong Period (1736-1795)
Length 6cm, Width 3.5cm, Height 10.4cm
The collection of the Summer Palace

The white jade has a greenish tone. It is carved in the form of a fingered citron. It came with an accompanying wood stand. The fingered citron often appears together with peach and pomegranate construing the concept of "Sanduo" (felicity, longevity and numerous progenies).

白玉佛手

清乾隆（1736—1795年）
长6厘米，宽3.5厘米，高10.4厘米
颐和园藏

白玉质，白中透青。圆雕成佛手。器身外侧凸雕盘绕枝叶为足。底配镂雕花枝木座。因『佛』与『福』同音，故佛手被当做吉祥物，常与桃及石榴一同出现，被称为『三多』即多福、多寿、多子。

194 A white jade carving of finger citron

Qing Dynasty, Qianlong Period (1736-1795)
Length 6.5cm, Width 4.5cm, Height 2cm
The collection of the Summer Palace

The white jade is carved with two joining fingered citrons, one larger than the other.

白玉佛手

清乾隆（1736—1795年）
长6.5厘米，宽4.5厘米，高2厘米
颐和园藏

白玉质。整器圆雕，一大一小两佛手连接在一起。

195 A celadon white jade carving of finger citrus and pomegranate group

Qing Dynasty, Qianlong Period (1736–1795)
Length 9.5cm, Width 6.2cm, Height 11cm
Provided by The Institute of Qing History Renmin University of China

The pale celadon jade is carved in the form of a finger citron together with a pomegranate. The finger citron and pomegranate group often appeared in art subjects of the Qing period. The combination of the two fruits conveys the message of great happiness and fortune.

青白玉佛手石榴

清乾隆（1736—1795年）
长9.5厘米，宽6.2厘米，高11厘米
中国人民大学清史研究所提供

青白玉质，底部有糖色。随形圆雕佛手与石榴。佛手圆润丰盈，肌理清晰逼真。石榴一侧微开小口，露出丰硕的果实，几片枝叶蜷曲点缀其间，生机盎然。佛手和石榴的题材在清代宫廷中被广泛应用，在瓷器、绘画等领域也较常见。佛手橘形似佛手，有『福寿』的吉祥寓意；石榴多籽，符合了中国传统思想中多子多福多寿的精神寄托，因此，这二者结合在一起，具有福上加福，多福多子的吉祥寓意。

196 A finely carved white jade mushroom group pendant

Qing Dynasty, Qianlong Period (1736–1795)
Length 4.6cm, Width 2.5cm, Height 4cm
Provided by The Institute of Qing History Renmin University of China

The white jade pendant is carved in the form of a group of three mushrooms. The stems of the mushrooms criss-crossing one another. The group of three mushrooms alludes to the concept of "a virtuous gentleman" and a "pure and untarnished family" which is revered by the literati.

白玉蘑菇形坠

清乾隆（1736—1795 年）
长 4.6 厘米，宽 2.5 厘米，高 4 厘米
中国人民大学清史研究所提供

白玉质。随形圆雕三朵蘑菇，菌盖上下肌理精准写实。背面菌杆彼此交错相连，菌盖内侧纹阴刻线工整均匀，每一蘑菇均圆润饱满，向内包围成伞形，有聚福之意。蘑菇属于菌类，三朵蘑菇常暗喻『三生君子』『清白传家』。整件器物充满着回归自然、洁身自好、崇尚清苦生活的文人情怀。

197 A white jade carving of mushroom group

Qing Dynasty, Qianlong Period (1736–1795)
Length 6.3cm, Width 4.3cm, Height 1.1cm
The collection of the Summer Palace

The white jade is carved in the form of two mushrooms akin to the shape of lingzhi. This conveys the wishing of good luck and happiness, good health with long life.

白玉蘑菇

清乾隆（1736—1795 年）
长 6.3 厘米，宽 4.3 厘米，高 1.1 厘米
颐和园藏

白玉质。菇类似于古人创造的如意，灵芝的造型，代表着吉祥如意，健康长寿。

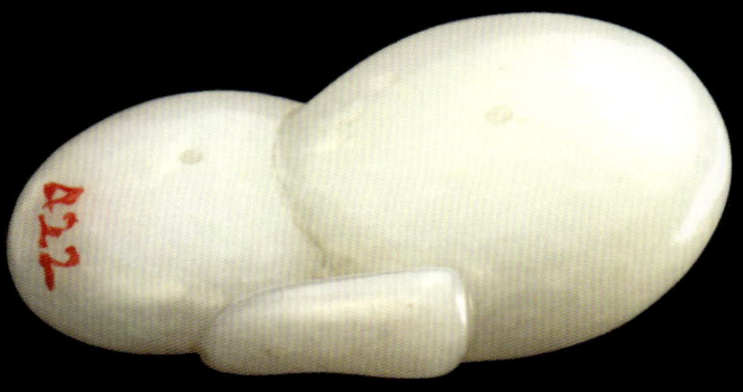

A white jade carving of pawpaw melon group

Qing Dynasty, Qianlong Period (1736–1795)
Length 6.5cm, Width 5.2cm, Height 3.1cm
Provided by The Institute of Qing History Renmin University of China

The white jade bears some light russet inclusions. It is carved with a pair of bilva melon with leaves. The bilva is a Sanskrit name for a sacred fruit belonging to one of the Buddhist Baruiwu (Eight Auspicious Objects). It also conveys the message of good friendship between the ancient scholars.

白玉木瓜摆件

清乾隆（1736—1795 年）
长 6.5 厘米，宽 5.2 厘米，高 3.1 厘米
中国人民大学清史研究所提供

白玉质，饰有琥珀色皮。依料圆雕，一对香木瓜体态圆润饱满，枝叶婉转繁茂。木瓜在佛教中属『八瑞物』之一，被誉为万果之中最为神圣的一种。不仅如此，木瓜还有着特殊寓意，早在先秦时期就有：『投我以木瓜，报之以琼琚』之说。代表着对彼此情谊的珍重，是古代文人表达友情时的馈赠佳品。

199 A white jade carving of "melons and butterfly" group

Qing Dynasty, Qianlong Period (1736-1795)
Length 9.7cm, Width 2cm, Height 6.7cm
The collection of the Summer Palace

The white jade has some russet inclusions. A melon is carved in the round with its vines together with a butterfly hovering on it. The melon with butterfly group signifies the prosperity of descendants.

白玉瓜瓞绵绵

清乾隆（1736—1795 年）
长 9.7 厘米，宽 2 厘米，高 6.7 厘米
颐和园藏

白玉质，略带黄皮。摆件随形而雕，呈瓜形，枝藤盘绕，蝴蝶游戏于瓜藤之间。『瓜蝶』即『瓜瓞』，典故出自《诗经·大雅·绵》『绵绵瓜瓞，民之初生』，寓意子孙昌盛兴旺发达。

A celadon withe jade carving of double gourd group

Qing Dynasty, Qianlong Period (1736–1795)
Length 3.6cm, Width 5.3cm, Height 7cm
Provided by The Institute of Qing History Renmin University of China

The pale celadon jade is carved in the round and pierced in the form of three little bottle-gourds with interlacing vines and leaves. The bottle-gourd has a seven-thousand-year history in China and many cultural allusions are developed around the gourd. It usually alludes to the very auspicious meaning of "a peaceful, happy and long life".

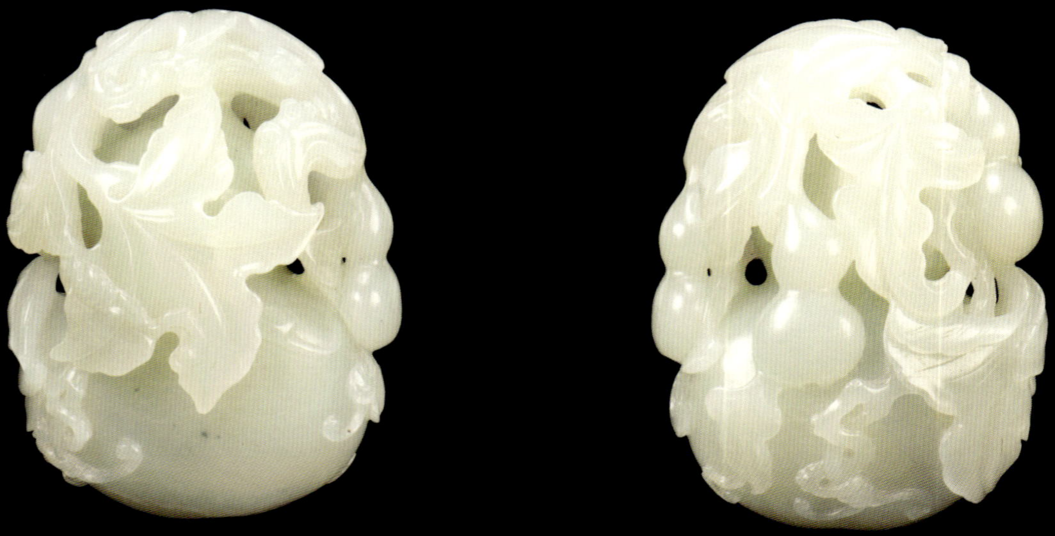

青白玉葫芦

清乾隆（1736—1795 年）
长 3.6 厘米，宽 5.3 厘米，高 7 厘米
中国人民大学清史研究所提供

青白玉质。随料圆雕葫芦形，镂空琢碾，饰以小葫芦三只，形态各异。四周叶片蜷曲交错，藤蔓蜿蜒其中，生机盎然，一片子孙满堂的热闹景象。

葫芦在中国有 7000 年的历史，形成了独特的葫芦文化：葫芦的枝『蔓』与『万』谐音，葫芦多籽，象征着『子孙万代』；葫芦谐音『护禄』『福禄』，暗喻『福禄双收』。道教亦视葫芦为法器，认为葫芦可以『聚气辟邪』。因此，在中国传统文化里，葫芦可谓是福禄寿齐全的吉祥之物。

201 A celadon jade carving of double gourd group

Qing Dynasty, Qianlong Period (1736-1795)
Length 6cm, Width 3cm, Height 7.5cm
The collection of the Summer Palace

The celadon jade is carved in the round in the form of bottle-gourd with surrounding vines and leaves. The bottle-gourd and vine rhymes with the Chinese word fulu and connote the meaning of numerous progenies with a happy and fruitful life.

青玉雕『福禄万代』

清乾隆（1736—1795年）
长6厘米，宽3厘米，高7.5厘米
颐和园藏

青玉质。圆雕呈葫芦形，藤蔓环绕。『葫芦』与『福禄』谐音，是富贵的象征。同时因葫芦藤蔓缠绵，结子繁多，枝蔓的『蔓』又与『万』谐音，故有祈求子孙万代、福禄双收的寓意。

202 A spinach jade carving of double gourd shaped screen with *"da ji"*

Qing Dynasty, Qianlong Period (1736–1795)
Length 21.8cm, Width 12.5cm, Height 0.7cm
The collection of the Summer Palace

The spinach green plaque is calved in the form of a bat and bottle-gourd with vines. The bottle-gourd is also gilt inscribed with the characters daji (great auspiciousness). The bottle-gourd connotes the idea of a prosperous life with numerous progenies.

碧玉雕花『大吉』葫芦形屏芯

清乾隆（1736—1795 年）
长 21.8 厘米，宽 12.5 厘米，高 0.7 厘米
颐和园藏

碧玉质。上部雕饰蝙蝠；周围浮雕葫芦及藤蔓；葫芦形牌上雕刻『大吉』二字，子口描金。『葫芦』与『福禄』谐音，寓意吉祥；葫芦多子，借喻子孙繁衍，多子多福，子孙万代。

大
吉

A white jade carving of nine lingzhi

Qing Dynasty, Qianlong Period (1736–1795)
Length 7cm, Width 5cm, Height 2.5cm
Provided by The Institute of Qing History Renmin University of China

The white jade bears some orange-color inclusions. It is carved with nine lingzhi in openwork. A bat is skillfully carved on the orange-color inclusion. This connotes the greetings of "birthday wishes for prosperity and long life".

白玉蝠纹九芝佩

清乾隆（1736—1795年）
长7厘米，宽5厘米，高2.5厘米
中国人民大学清史研究所提供

白玉质。留洒金皮。籽玉圆雕镂空，饰以形态各异的灵芝九朵。灵芝一脉相连，机理清晰，层次分明，肉质丰满，活灵活现。洒金皮巧雕一蝙蝠，精巧绝伦，画龙点睛。『九』是阳数最大，代表至高之极。九个如意即『九如』，有祈愿祝寿的吉祥意义。

204 A white jade carving of lingzhi brush washer

Qing Dynasty (1616–1911)
Length 8cm, Width 7.5cm, Height 3.1cm
The collection of the Summer Palace

The white jade bears some color markings and some cracks. It is carved in the form of a brush washer with two lingzhi mushrooms. The brush washer is a traditional object used in the scholar's study. The lingzhi also connotes the meaning of ruyi (in accordance to one's good wishes).

白玉灵芝洗

清（1616—1911年）
长8厘米，宽7.5厘米，高3.1厘米
颐和园藏

白玉质，有沁色、绺裂。玉洗以圆雕和透雕手法雕琢，中间挖膛为盛水池，用于涮笔。洗身内外皆光素，只在一端雕刻灵芝两株，一株向上生长凸出口沿，一株柄部向下延伸承托洗底。笔洗为中国传统文房用具之一，与灵芝搭配，取『如意』之意。

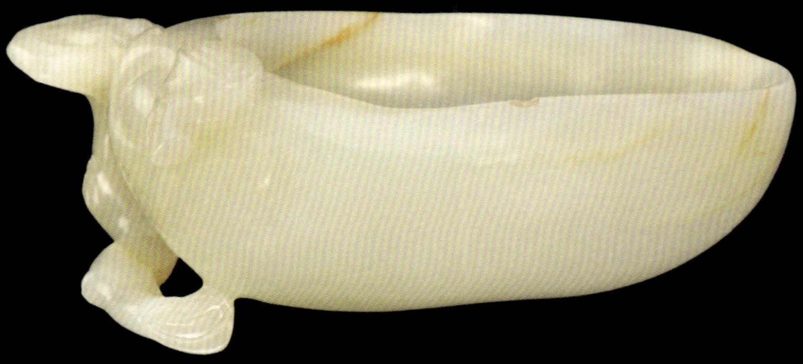

205 A white jade carving of lingzhi brush washer

Qing Dynasty, Qianlong Period (1736–1795)
Length 13cm, Width 9.5cm, Height 4cm
Provided by The Institute of Qing History Renmin University of China

The white jade brush washer has some yellowish rind marks. Nine lingzhi mushrooms of various sizes are carved in relief with interlacing stems on the outer wall and at the base. The brush washer with lingzhi signifies endless succession of happiness and prosperity.

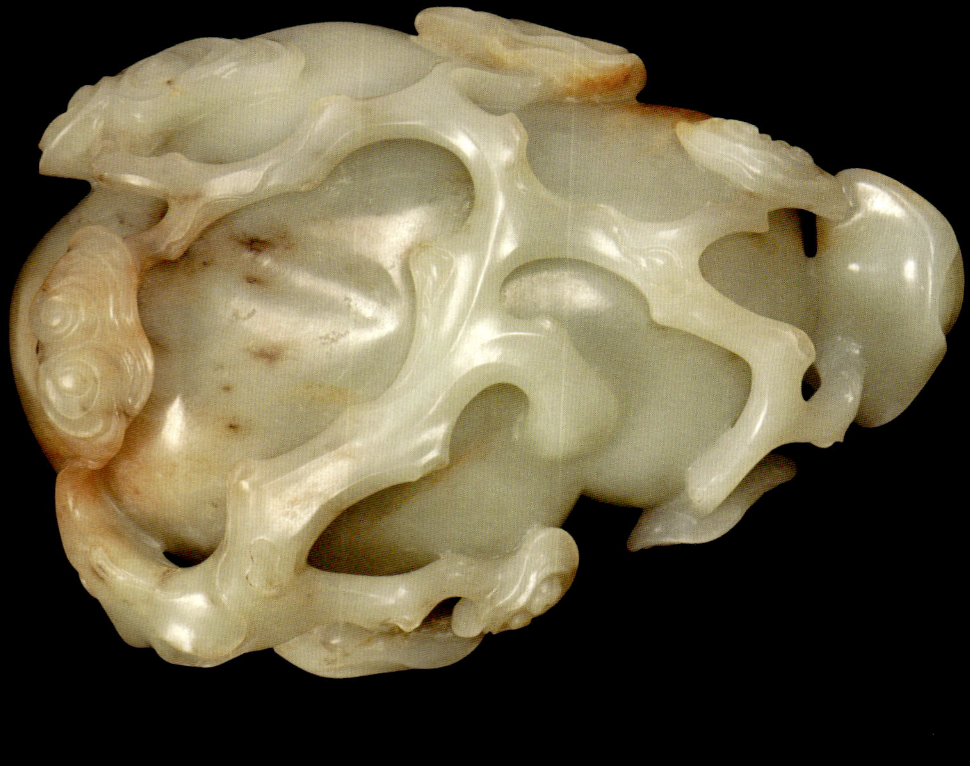

白玉如意灵芝形洗

清乾隆（1736—1795年）

长13厘米，宽9.5厘米，高4厘米

中国人民大学清史研究所提供

白玉质，留黄皮间有褐斑。整料圆雕如意形水洗，口沿打挖均匀，四周和底部镂空浮雕九只大小不一、形态各异的灵芝，盘根错节，彼此相连。如意的纹饰由来已久，其本就是由灵芝的形态演变而来，寓意吉祥如意，生生不息。

206 A jadeite *ruyi* with lingzhi

Qing Dynasty (1616–1911)
Length 27cm, Width 4.9cm, Height 3.5cm
The collection of the Summer Palace

The jadeite ruyi scepter bears some yellow, green and purple inclusions with some cracks. A larger lingzhi is carved at the top while the end part is carved with a small lingzhi tied with a yellow tasseled cord attachment. It connotes the meaning of "wishing for longevity".

翡翠灵芝如意

清（1616—1911年）
长27厘米，宽4.9厘米，高3.5厘米
颐和园藏

翡翠质，微带黄、绿、紫色，有绺裂。整料雕琢，灵芝形首，曲线形长柄；柄、尾雕饰小灵芝，尾系黄穗子。该器自成天然之趣，寓意长寿如意。

207 A white carving of group of pomegranates

Qing Dynasty, Qianlong Period (1736–1795)
Length 8.8cm, Width 5.7cm, Height 2.3cm
Provided by The Institute of Qing History Renmin University of China

The white jade bears some light brown inclusions. Two pomegranates are carved. The pomegranate conveys the message of "Fushou Sanduo" (more progenies, more happiness, and more of long life).

白玉『福寿三多』把件

清乾隆（1736—1795 年）
长 8.8 厘米，宽 5.7 厘米，高 2.3 厘米
中国人民大学清史研究所提供

白玉质，略带棕红色皮。随形雕石榴两颗，圆润饱满，裂开小口，有粒粒果实露出，构图生动巧妙。枝叶交错舒展，相映成趣，翻转多变而不失工整。石榴寓意吉祥，有多子多福多寿『三多』之美意。

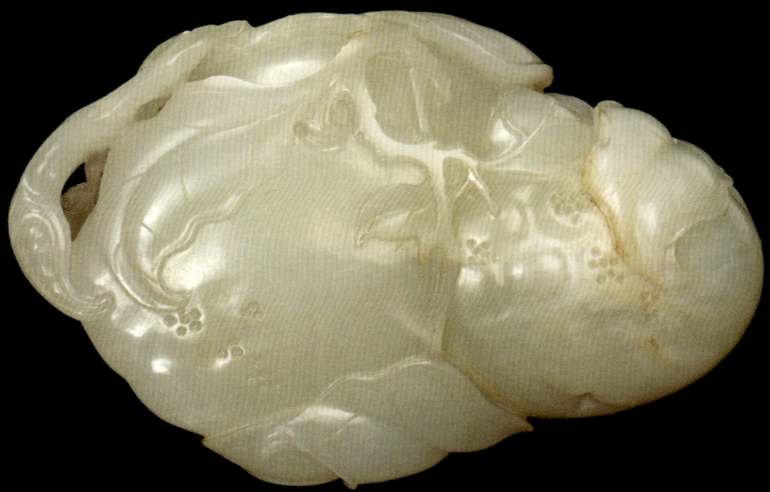

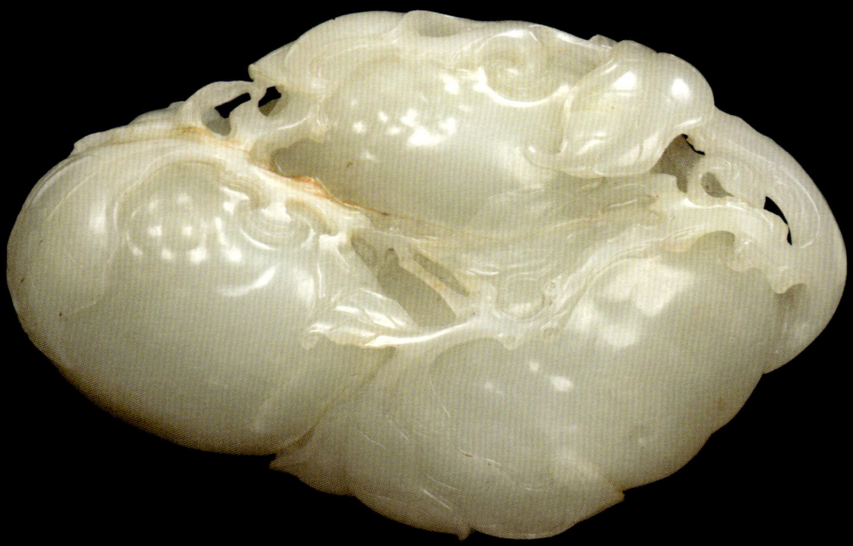

208 A pair of celadon jade carving of ruyi

Qing Dynasty, Guangxu Period (1875–1908)
Length 34cm, Width 8.5cm, Height 4.5cm
The collection of the Summer Palace

A pair of celadon jade ruyi scepters are calved with the same inlay of precious stones and materials such as corals, jadeite, lazurite and rose quartz. These precious materials then embellish objects like bat, fingered citron, pomegranate, and peach on the scepter. The backs of the ruyi scepters are carved with fingered citron, peach and pomegranate patterns signifying the concept of Sanduo ("three more") of "more progenies, happiness and long life".

青玉嵌百宝三多纹如意（一对）

清光绪（1875—1908年）
长34厘米，宽8.5厘米，高4.5厘米
颐和园藏

青玉质，成对。同料雕琢，云头形首，长柄；如意头及长柄镶嵌珊瑚、翡翠、青金石、芙蓉石等各种玉石，装饰出蝙蝠、佛手、石榴、寿桃；首、柄之间雕饰方胜纹；如意柄上青金石嵌饰出『南山千载瑞』、『沧海万年春』字形；如意柄末端雕饰蝙蝠纹，镶嵌彩石；如意背线刻佛手、寿桃、石榴纹饰，纹饰描金，即为三多。

209 A coral *ruyi* with peach and bats group

Qing Dynasty, Guangxu Period (1875–1908)
Length 50cm, Width 15cm, Height 15.8cm
The collection of the Summer Palace

The top of the scepter is embellished with carvings of two peaches, and bat while the handle is carved with peach, fingered citron, and pomegranate. Corals are believed by the people of the Qing period to be a symbol for longevity and had always been used as birthday gifts or for as display objects.

红珊瑚雕『福寿三多』如意

清光绪（1875—1908年）

长50厘米，宽15厘米，高15.8厘米

颐和园藏

红珊瑚质。头部由珊瑚枝拼接而成，饰双桃、蝙蝠，寓意『福寿』，如意柄雕刻桃、佛手、石榴，整体都体现『福寿』寓意。珊瑚，生长缓慢，寿命最高可达到五千年，在清代被认为是『长寿』的象征，常常被作为寿礼或陈设。

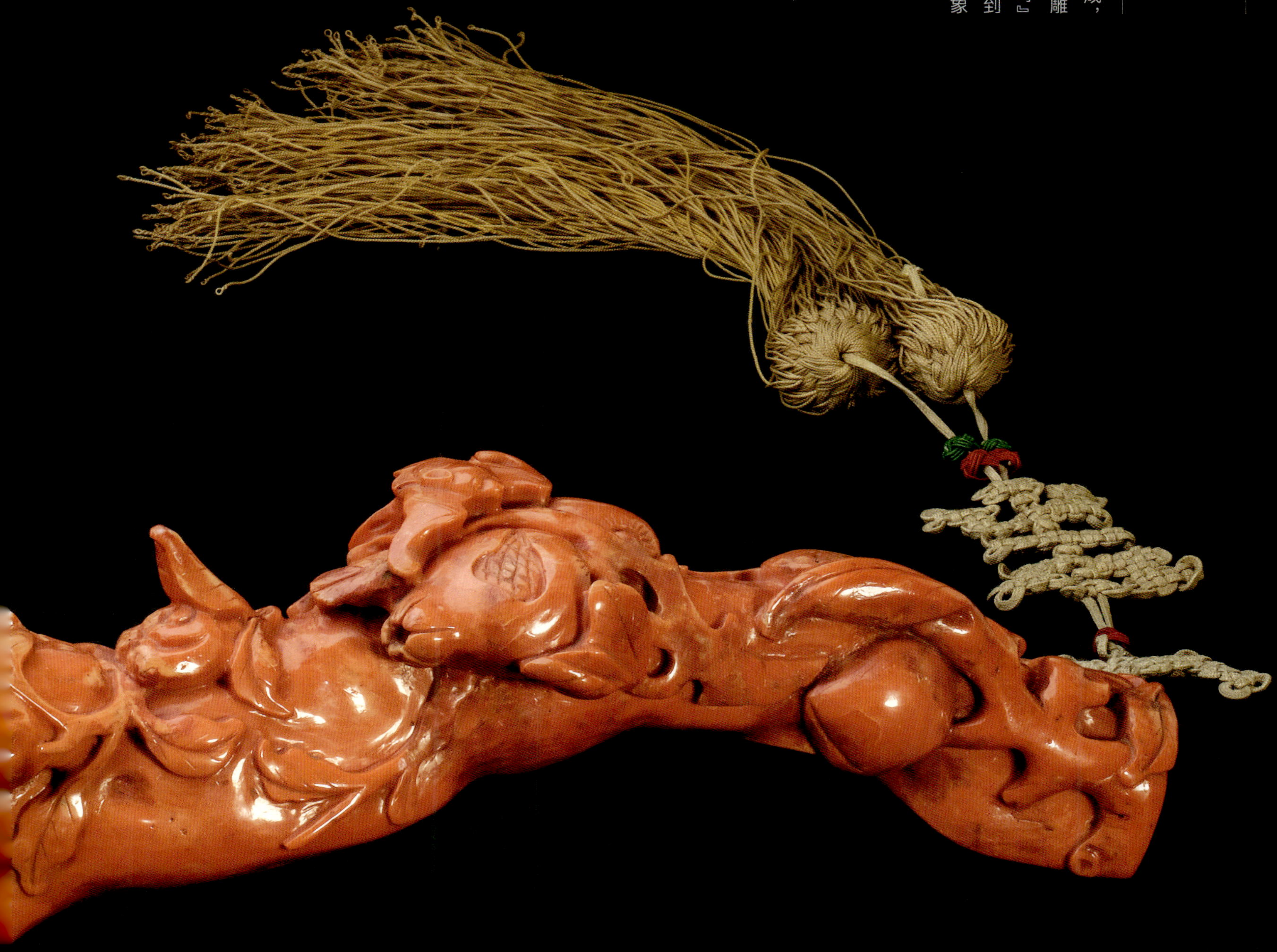

210 A white jade carving of pomegranate and cicada

Qing Dynasty, Qianlong Period (1736–1795)
Length 5.5cm, Width 4.5cm, Height 4cm
The collection of the Summer Palace

The white jade is carved with a succulent pomegranate with leaves and stem. The base has an accompanying wood stand. The Pomegranate conveys the message of numerous progenies with unending happiness and prosperity.

白玉秋蝉石榴

清乾隆（1736—1795 年）
长 5.5 厘米，宽 4.5 厘米，高 4 厘米
颐和园藏

白玉质。器形近似圆柱，小巧玲珑，不盈一握。顶部刻石榴，枝叶环绕，果实饱满。底部配木托和锦托。石榴子多而密，寓意多子，取子孙繁衍，绵延不断之吉祥寓意。

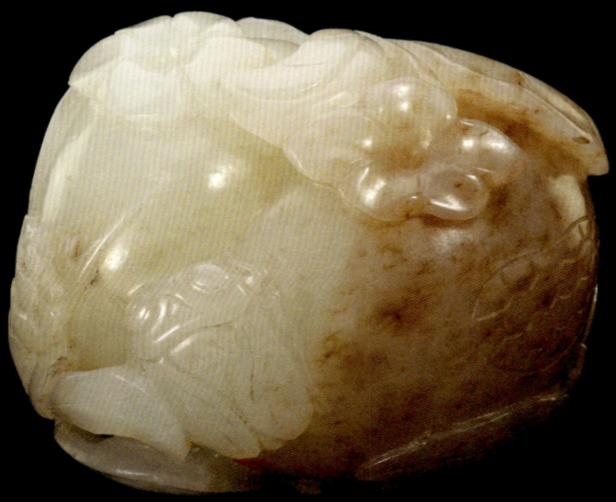

A white jade carving of pomegranate shape box

Qing Dynasty, Qianlong Period (1736-1795)
Length 8cm, Width 6.5cm, Height 4.3cm
The collection of the Summer Palace

The white jade is carved in the form of a box. The lid of the box is carved in shallow relief with pomegranate, stem and leave patterns. A cicada is also skillfully carved on the lid while the body is plain without embellishment. The pomegranate conveys the message of prosperity with numerous progenies.

白玉雕蝉石榴形盒

清乾隆（1736—1795年）
长8厘米，宽6.5厘米，高4.3厘米
颐和园藏

白玉质。器分上盖与盒身两部分，子母口上下扣合，合口平整严密。盒身饱满呈石榴形，盒盖顶部微凸，浅浮雕石榴、枝叶、鸣蝉纹，雕工精细，自然留取洒金色皮。盖顶纹饰表现细致，石榴成熟露出多子，枝叶环绕，鸣蝉闲憩。盒身光素，平底无纹。石榴多子，寓意子孙繁衍绵延不断，多子多福。

A white jade carving of persimmon with *ruyi* scepter

Qing Dynasty, Qianlong Period (1736–1795)
Length 6.1 cm, Width 4.5cm, Height 4.5cm
Provided by The Institute of Qing History Renmin University of China

The white jade has some orange-russet markings. It is carved in the form of a persimmon with layers of leaves on top and embellished with lingzhi and bat. It has a tassel cord attached to one side. This signifies "everything goes well with the coming of good fortune".

白玉灵芝蝠纹柿子

清乾隆（1736—1795年）
长6.1厘米，宽4.5厘米，高4.5厘米
中国人民大学清史研究所提供

白玉质，洒金皮。整料随形琢碾，圆雕柿子形，饱满圆润，叶片层叠其上，间有金皮俏色。灵芝与蝙蝠点缀其间，柿底饰如意一柄，系『卐』字绶带飘于一侧。寓意万事如意，福在眼前。

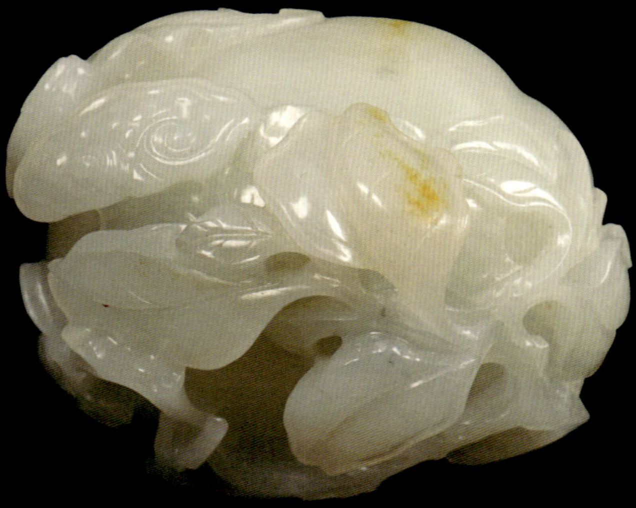

213 A white jade carving of "persimmon and lingzhi" group

Qing Dynasty (1616–1911)
Length 4.8cm, Width 2.1cm, Height 3.2cm
The collection of the Summer Palace

The white jade is carved in the form of a pair of persimmons with lingzhi. The name of this group of "persimmons with lingzhi" rhymes with the Chinese term Shishi Ruyi which means "Everything in Accordance to One's Wishes".

白玉雕『事事如意』

清（1616—1911年）
长4.8厘米，宽2.1厘米，高3.2厘米
颐和园藏

白玉质，雕双柿子及灵芝，双柿子象征『事事』，灵芝象征『如意』，合为事事如意，是中国古代传统吉祥纹样，寓意吉祥，表达了美好的祝愿。

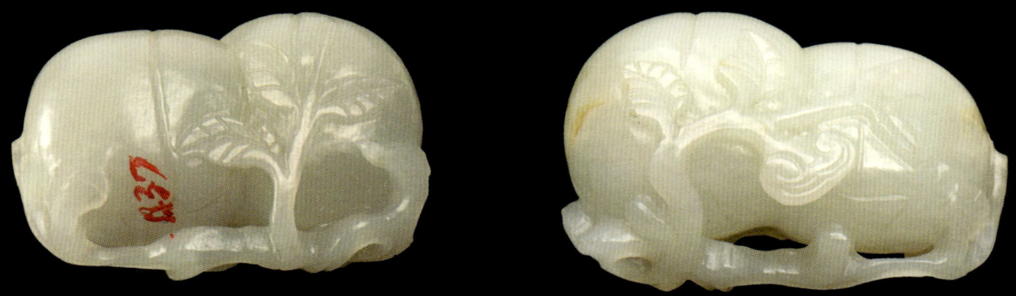

4 A white jade carving of "persimmon and lingzhi" group

Qing Dynasty (1616–1911)
Length 9cm, Width 3cm, Height 5.5cm
The collection of the Summer Palace

The white jade has some cracks and is carved in the round and in openwork with a sprig of persimmon and a lingzhi. This expresses the good wishes of the auspicious term "Shishi Ruyi".

白玉雕『事事如意』

清（1616—1911年）
长9厘米，宽3厘米，高5.5厘米
颐和园藏

白玉质，有绺裂。以圆雕和透雕手法，雕琢带枝柿子一枚，其下曲柄灵芝一棵。柿与『事』谐音，而灵芝则与如意外形相似，故取『事事如意』之美好祝愿。

215 A white jade carving of "peaches and bats" group

Qing Dynasty, Qianlong Period (1736-1795)
Length 7cm, Width 2.7cm, Height 6.6cm
The collection of the Summer Palace

The white jade is carved with double peaches and bats. The peach and bat are usually carved together to connote the idea of Fushou Shuangquan which means having both good fortune and longevity of life.

白玉『福寿双全』

清乾隆（1736—1795 年）
长 7 厘米，宽 2.7 厘米，高 6.6 厘米
颐和园藏

白玉质，雕双桃蝙蝠，桃代表寿，蝙蝠代表福，两者通常一起雕刻，寓意福寿双全。雕刻多只蝙蝠，也有『遍福』之意。

216 A white jade carving of two peaches with bats

Qing Dynasty, Qianlong Period (1736–1795)
Length 19.5cm, Width 9.5cm, Height 15cm
The collection of the Summer Palace

The celadon jade bears some russet markings. It is carved with a sprig of two peaches of different sizes with a bat clambering on the leaves. The peach and bat group conveys the meaning of Fushou Shuangquan which is very much revered by the Chinese.

青玉雕『福寿双全』

清乾隆（1736—1795年）
长19.5厘米，宽9.5厘米，高15厘米
颐和园藏

青玉质，略带黄皮。整料随形雕琢，一枝双桃，一大一小，桃叶上伏一只蝙蝠，下部桃枝盘绕，枝叶苍劲，叶片舒展灵动。桃寓意『寿』，蝙蝠谐音『福』，该器俏色巧雕，寓意福寿双全。

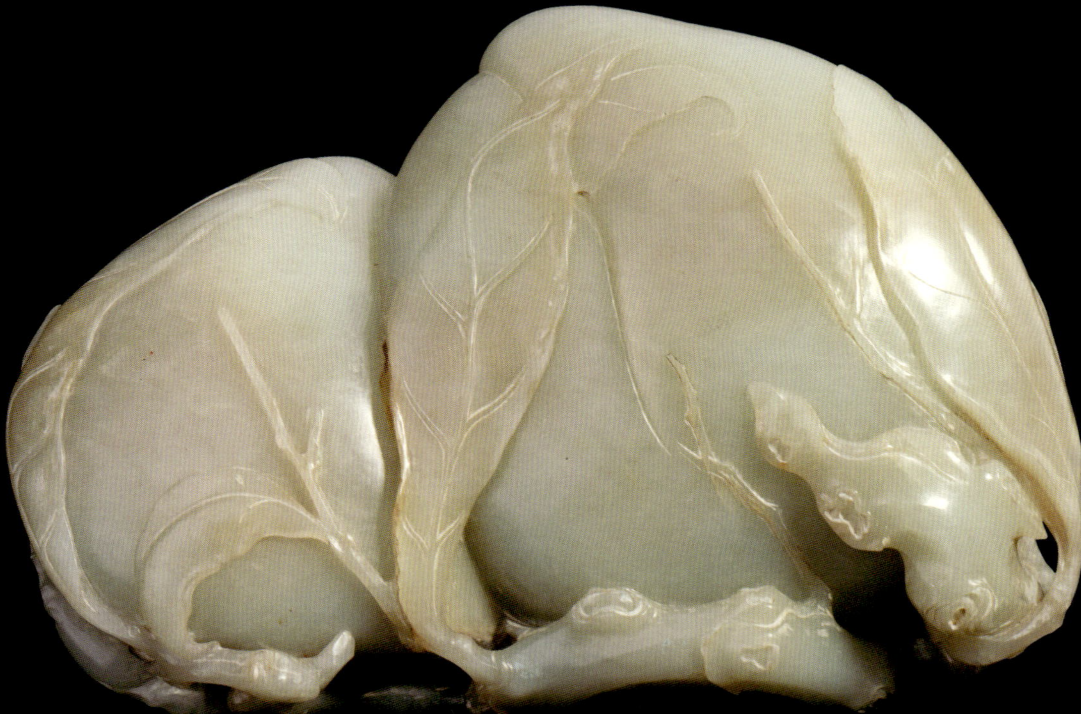

7 A white jade carving of "peaches and bats" group

Qing Dynasty, Qianlong Period (1736–1795)
Length 6.4cm, Width 4.8cm, Height 2.5cm
The collection of the Summer Palace

The white jade is carved with double peaches and bats. This is a standard carving alluding to the auspicious Fushou Shuangquan design of "having both good fortune and longevity of life".

白玉雕『福寿双全』

清乾隆（1736—1795年）
长6.4厘米，宽4.8厘米，高2.5厘米
颐和园藏

白玉质。以雕刻双桃蝙蝠为主，是典型的的福寿寓意文玩。桃是中国人心目中典型的『祈寿』寓意表现纹饰。所见仙桃纹饰多于与蝙蝠组合呈现，寓意『福寿』。

218 A white jade carving of peach and bat group

Qing Dynasty, Qianlong Period (1736-1795)
Length 6cm, Width 4.2cm, Height 2.5cm
The collection of the Summer Palace

The white jade is carved with the peach with prunus sprigs, bat and water-chestnut. The combination of these rhymes with the Chinese auspicious meaning of "Fushou Qimei" (equal good fortune and longevity of life).

白玉雕『福寿齐眉』

清乾隆（1736—1795年）
长6厘米，宽4.2厘米，高2.5厘米
颐和园藏

白玉质。整料雕琢，以寿桃为主体，折枝梅花附其上，梅枝上另附蝙蝠和荸荠。取寿桃『寿』意，取蝙蝠、荸荠、梅花与『福』、『齐』、『梅』之谐音，成『福寿齐眉』之意。

219 A white jade carving of peach and chilong dragon group

Qing Dynasty, Qianlong Period (1736-1795)
Length 7.2cm, Width 9.5cm, Height 3.3cm
Provided by The Institute of Qing History Renmin University of China

The white jade has some light russet and amber inclusions. It is carved in the round with two peaches of different sizes and lotus. A chi-dragon clambers on the peach. The smaller peach is carved with a lingzhi spray. This carving group is an auspicious display object to convey the message of "wishing high achievement for the son"and "blessing for longevity with numerous progenies".

白玉螭龙灵芝双桃

清乾隆（1736—1795 年）
长 7.2 厘米，宽 9.5 厘米，高 3.3 厘米
中国人民大学清史研究所提供

白玉质，间有糖色，俏琥珀皮色。圆雕大小两只蟠桃，大桃一侧饰以莲蓬，另一侧饰以荷花，桃身有螭龙攀附其上，大小桃枝叶相连，小桃一侧雕灵芝一簇。蟠桃寓意长寿，荷花与莲蓬寓意多子，螭龙即龙子，多寓意望子成龙，灵芝寓意长寿多福，此摆件充满了喜庆祥和之意。

220 A white jade carving of peach shape brush washer

Qing Dynasty, Qianlong Period (1736-1795)
Diameter 19.2cm, Height 10.5cm
Provided by The Institute of Qing History Renmin University of China

The white jade is carved in the form of a peach shaped brush washer with a lively sprig of eight peaches with curling leaves on the outer wall. The rim has a pair of bats. The "peach with bat" expresses the auspicious meaning of "good fortune and longevity" often used in the Qing palace.

白玉桃纹桃形洗

清乾隆（1736—1795 年）
直径 19.2 厘米，高 10.5 厘米
中国人民大学清史研究所提供

白玉质。籽料整挖而成，掏膛均匀，依料圆雕出桃形大水洗。外壁依次雕琢新枝幼桃八只，一派生机勃勃之景象；叶片丰富，翻转卷曲，衬托出大桃的沉稳持重。口沿处饰以一对蝙蝠，有福寿齐天之意。寿桃是中国传统文化中祝寿时的吉祥之物。此件白玉桃形洗便是宫廷中寓意福寿延绵、多子多寿的典型清代宫廷文房陈设。

221 A spinach jade carving of marriage bowl

Qing Dynasty, Qianlong Period (1736-1795)
Diameter 30.2cm Height 8cm
Provided by The Institute of Qing History Renmin University of China

This is a large washer carved with spinach green jade. It is flanked by two reticulated butterfly handles. Both the inner and outer walls are carved with many auspicious Buddhist objects together with the "Buddhist Eight Treasure" emblems. The washer has the connotation of good fortune and long life.

碧玉八宝纹『福寿常青』水洗

清乾隆（1736—1795年）

直径30.2厘米，高8厘米

中国人民大学清史研究所提供

碧玉质。选料大而完整，带有黑色碳点为典型新疆玛纳斯碧玉。整料掏出一水洗，口略外撇，底部内收，两侧出廓雕有双蝶耳，镂空浮雕蝴蝶一双，振翅欲飞。玉洗内雕山石，灵芝、万年青，及四只寿桃。画面布局饱满，枝叶灵动鲜活。外部依次雕刻宝瓶、宝盖、双鱼、莲花、右旋螺、吉祥结、尊胜幢、法轮佛教八宝的纹饰。此器寓意福寿绵长，吉祥如意。

222 A celadon jade carving of peach shape brush washer

Qing Dynasty, Qianlong Period (1736-1795)
Length 13.5cm, Width 13.1cm, Height 6.4cm
The collection of the Summer Palace

The celadon jade carries some russet inclusions. It is carved in the form of a peach shaped washer. The outer wall has stem and leaves carved in low relief with two bats. A monkey is carved climbing between the peach stem and the rim.

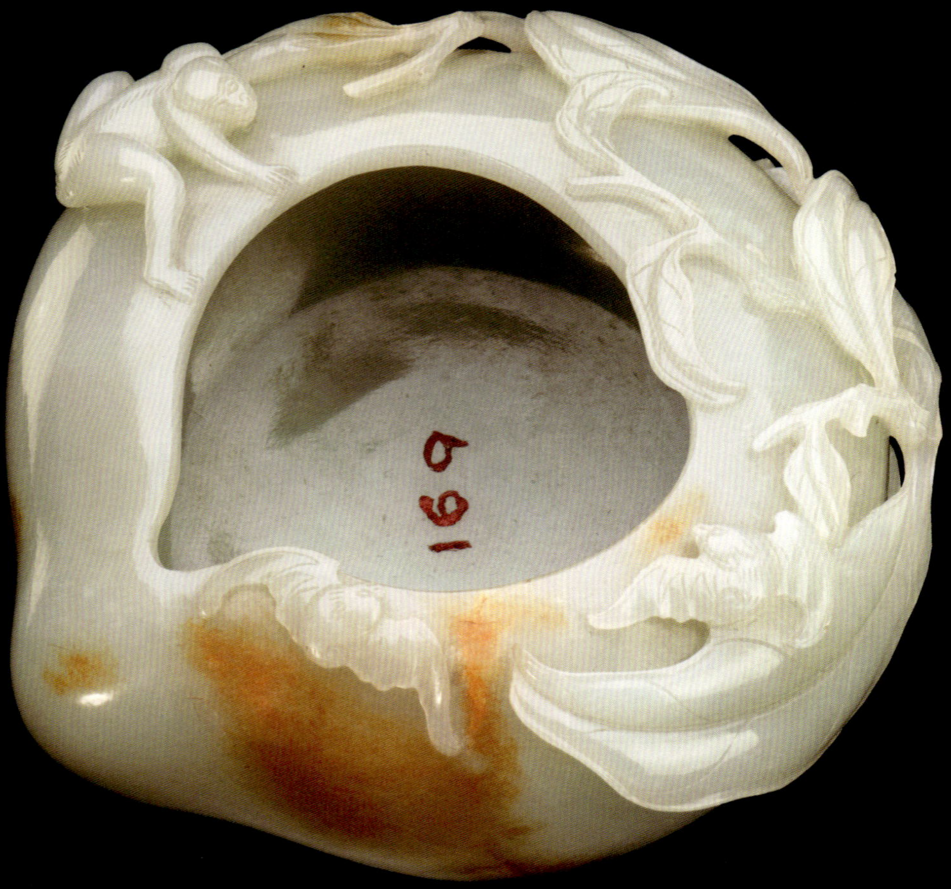

青玉『福寿』桃形洗

清乾隆（1736—1795年）

长13.5厘米，宽13.1厘米，高6.4厘米

颐和园藏

青玉质，带有少许黄皮。整料雕琢，俏色随形雕琢成寿桃形，挖膛，膛内光素；外壁浮雕枝叶，枝干粗壮，枝叶错落有致，单阴刻线琢出叶脉；洗口雕饰两只蝙蝠，翩翩飞舞；桃枝与洗口间雕饰一只爬伏灵猴，生动形象。

A white jade *ruyi* with bats and peaches

Qing Dynasty, Qianlong Period (1736–1795)
Length 40cm, Width 12cm, Height 5.5cm
The collection of the Summer Palace

The white jade scepter is carved with a cloud-shaped head in light relief with bat and peach. The long handle has lingzhi and floral patterns. The end of the handle has bat patterns with attaching tasseled cord. This construes the meaning of Fushou Wannian (longevity and happiness for ten thousand years).

白玉雕『福寿万年』如意

清乾隆（1736—1795年）

长40厘米，宽12厘米，高5.5厘米

颐和园藏

白玉质。整料雕琢，如意首为云头形，柄长条形。如意首采用浅浮雕技法，雕饰蝙蝠、寿桃纹；如意柄雕饰灵芝、如意花草纹饰，寓意『福寿万年』之意；柄尾饰蝙蝠纹，有象鼻孔，挂黄色穗子。

224 A coral carving of fishing felling farming and reading group

Qing Dynasty, Guangxu Period (1875–1908)
Length 37cm, Width 22cm, Height 39cm
The collection of the Summer Palace

This red coral is carved with the traditional landscape subject of Yuqiao Gengdu, the four different occupations (fisherman, woodcutter, rice-farmer, and scholar) in the old days. It also signifies the good life after retirement. The landscape includes the peach and pine trees which convey the message of longevity, and looks like a bonsai scene.

红珊瑚质。红珊瑚树枝干上雕刻渔樵耕读场景为主。渔樵耕读是古代农耕社会里，最典型的四个职业代表，也是中国古代劳动人民最基本的生存状态，象征着退隐之后的美好生活。另配以桃树、松树等长寿寓意植物。据光绪陈设档记载为玉华殿陈设，时名红珊瑚渔樵耕读盆景。

225 A white jade and wood handle *ruyi* with bats and peaches

Qing Dynasty, Qianlong Period (1736–1795)
Length 44cm, Width 10cm, Height 7cm
The collection of the Summer Palace

The head and tail of this scepter are made of white jade. The head is carved with cloud patterns and the tail part has inlaid of colorful stone peach and bat patterns. The wood handle has inlaid of the "Buddhist Eight Treasures". It connotes the meaning of good luck and propitiousness.

木柄百宝嵌福寿八宝纹如意

清乾隆（1736—1795年）

长44厘米，宽10厘米，高7厘米

颐和园藏

首、尾白玉质，木柄。云头形首，斧形尾彩石嵌寿桃、蝙蝠纹；中间木柄彩石嵌饰佛教八宝。盖、鱼、罐、花、螺、伞、长、轮。该器寓意吉祥。

226 A white and russet jade "peach and bat" group

Qing Dynasty, Qianlong Period (1736-1795)
Length 10cm, Width 9cm, Height 7.3cm
Provided by The Institute of Qing History Renmin University of China

This is white Hetian (Khotan) jade with some russet inclusions. It is skillfully carved in the round with two peaches with stem and leaves. There are two bats, one at the top and one at the bottom of the peaches. The double peaches with double bats connote the meaning of "Fushou Shuangquan" (having both good fortune and longevity of life).

白玉『福寿双全』摆件

清乾隆（1736—1795年）
长10厘米，宽9厘米，高7.3厘米
中国人民大学清史研究所提供

和田玉，留棕红色皮。选料硕大，立体圆雕。一双寿桃，圆润饱满，同出一枝，枝干蜿蜒曲折，桃叶翻卷缠绕，层次丰富，刀工爽利，雕刻力度极佳。上下两只蝙蝠遥相呼应，飞跃于寿桃顶端和底部，形态生动，造型灵动乖巧。双寿桃双蝙蝠寓意福寿双全，延绵不断。

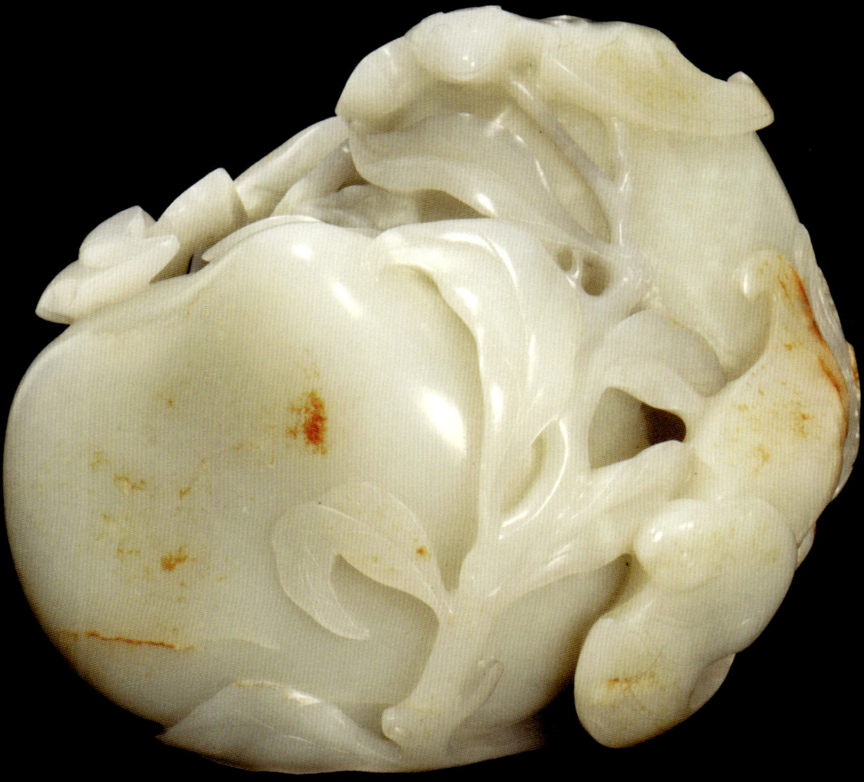

227 A white jade carving of water chestnut

Qing Dynasty (1616–1911)
Length 5.5cm, Width 2.3cm, Height 3.5cm
The collection of the Summer Palace

This white jade is skillfully carved in the form of a water-chestnut. The water-chestnut is prevalently depicted in Qing period jade carvings. It connotes the meaning of cleverness together with good fortune.

白玉菱角

清（1616—1911年）
长5.5厘米，宽2.3厘米，高3.5厘米
颐和园藏

白玉质。圆雕菱角，将其自然的形态清晰地表现出来。菱角题材在清代的玉雕中较为常见，寓意伶俐，有福至心灵、吉祥如意的含义，若与葱同时出现则寓意聪明伶俐。

228 A coral flower vase with Chinese leaf and grasshopper

Qing Dynasty, Guangxu Period (1875-1908)
Length 13.5cm, Width 5cm, Height 18cm
The collection of the Summer Palace

The red coral is expertly carved in the form of a Chinese cabbage with rolling out leaves. Two grasshoppers are delicately carved on top of the leaves.

红珊瑚蝈蝈白菜花插

清光绪（1875—1908年）
长13.5厘米，宽5厘米，高18厘米
颐和园藏

红珊瑚质。白菜利用珊瑚天然的枝状雕刻而成，菜叶呈左右翻卷状，菜身的纹理是阴线勾勒的手法制成。两只蝈蝈伏于菜叶之上，形态各异，栩栩如生。

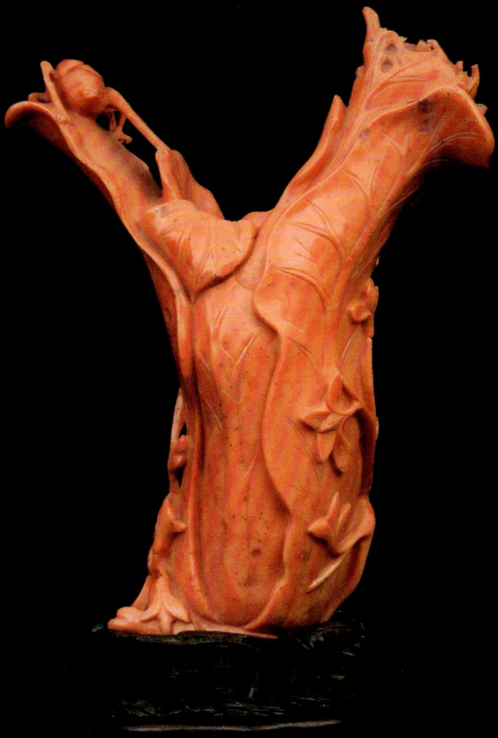

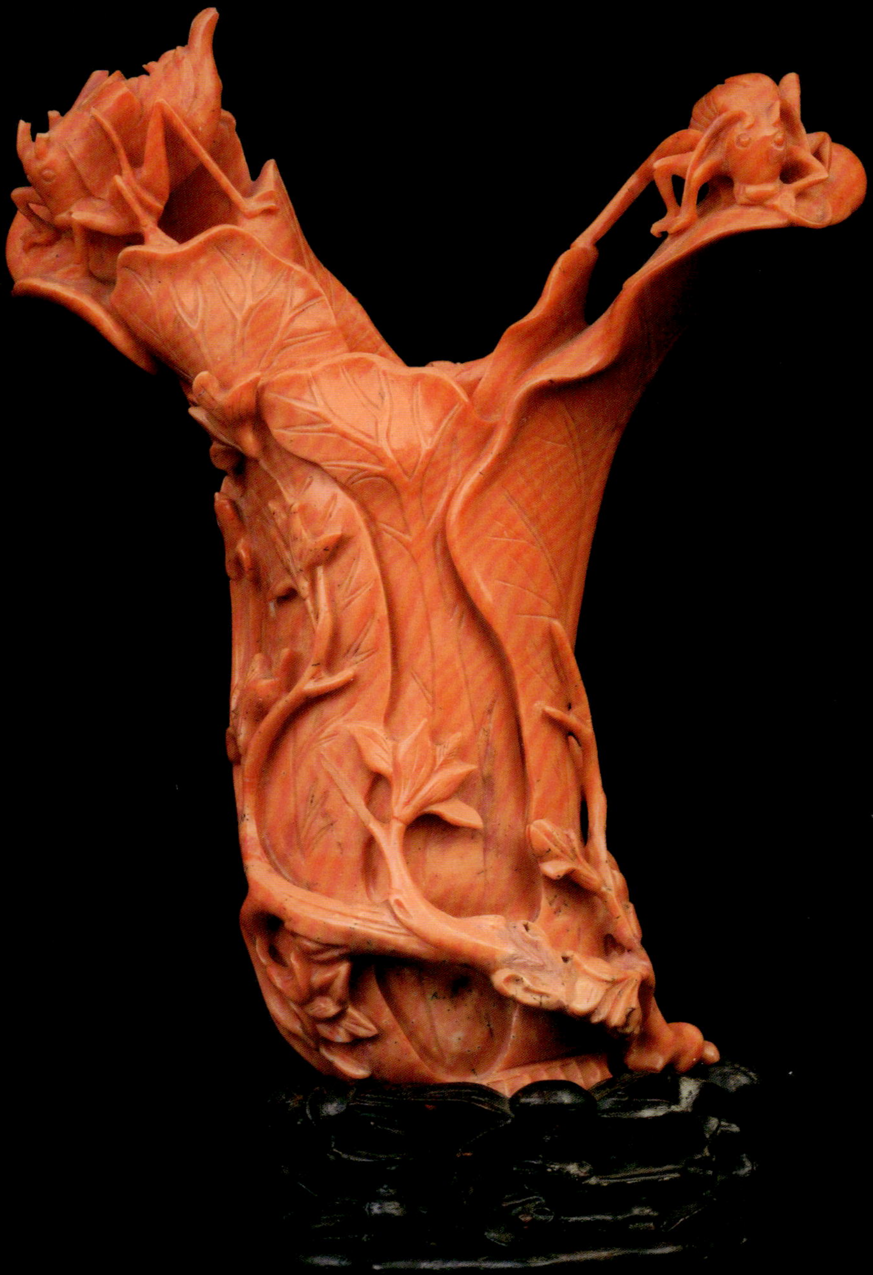

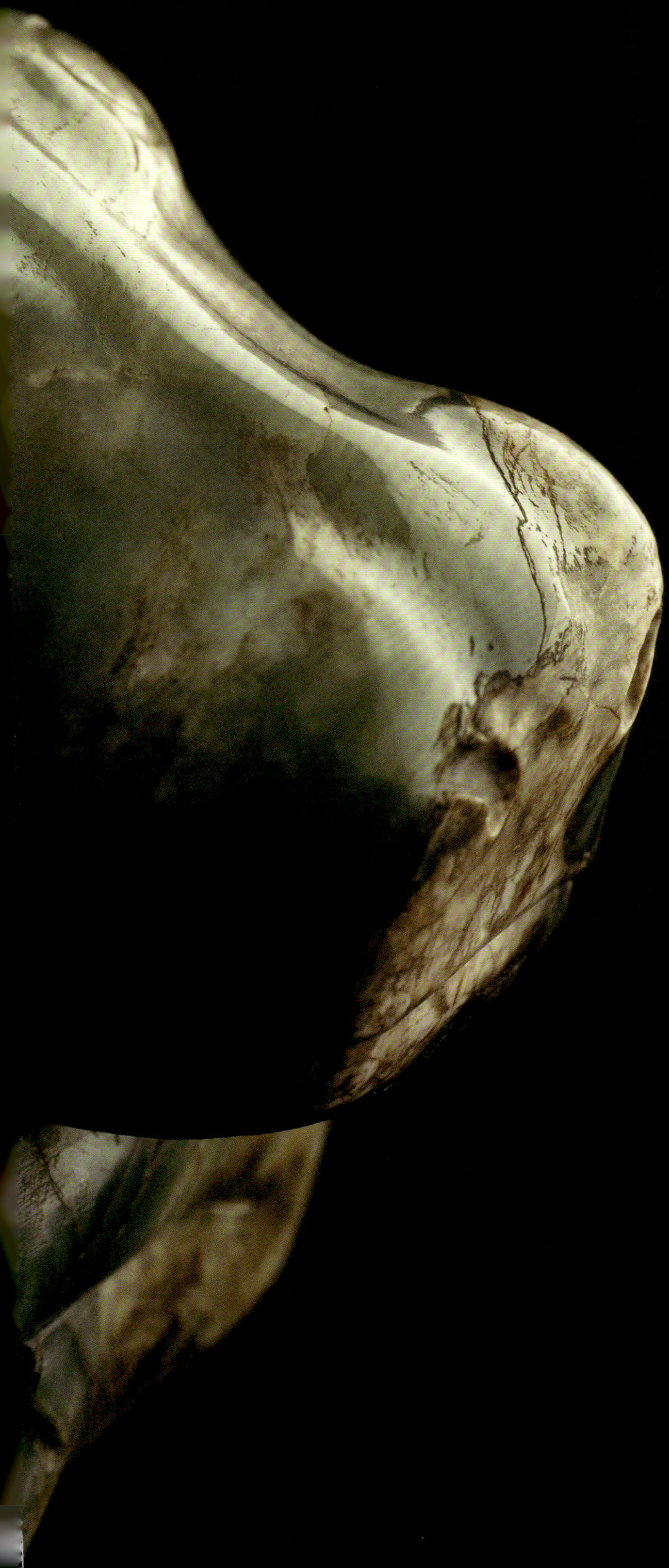

The most important and brilliant compositions in Chinese jade over the millennia are the jade carvings of animal subjects and themes. This reflects the Chinese people's endless and continuous affection for nature; love and respect of life; revere virtue and moral excellence; and the pursuance of a meaningful and prosperous life. These carvings also emanate the very remarkable artistic imagination and innovativeness with firm and persisting mental attitudes. The year 2022 marks the beginning of the second of the Chinese Two Centennial Goals and also the historical 20th National Congress of the Communist Party of China. With this exhibition we hope to continue the idea and concept of "Jade encompasses the virtue and benevolence in a gentleman (junzi)" with the great national spirit of perseverance to overcome hardship with a jade like enhancement of willpower in ensuring success.

动植物题材玉器，是中国数千年玉文化的重要组成部分和精彩内容，反映了中华民族绵延不断的热爱自然、敬畏生命、尊崇美德、追求幸福的人生观和价值观，精益求精、坚忍不拔的精神品格，以及丰沛卓越的艺术想象力与创造力。2022 年是实现中华民族伟大复兴的第二个百年奋斗目标的开局之年，及具有历史性意义的中国共产党二十大的召开之年，以此展致敬与赓续“君子比德于玉”和“艰难困苦，玉汝于成”的伟大民族精神。

Epilogue

The Qing dynasty Jade Exhibition jointly organized by the Institute of Qing History | Renmin University of China with the Beijing Summer Palace Management Office was the result of a long-term mutual close collaboration between the two organizations. The Institute of Qing History (IQH), as a higher academic institution, had also actively shouldered many social endeavors other than the academic researches. As it happens, during the last ten or more years, the Ministry of Education also emphasized the need for universities and other institutions of higher learning to actively take part and participate in social activities and societal interactions. In conjunction with this, the IQH and the Renmin University's History faculty, upon completing its required teaching and researching assignments, would also head toward the promotion of public and popular history and contribute more and more effort in carrying out these works to popularize the Chinese traditional culture. Such efforts would require a vast knowledge and deep understanding of these traditional fields. As such, some areas which were not originally within the traditional research would also require additional strengthening. In short, to actively participate in social and societal works popularizing the Chinese culture, it would require the participation of academic effort together with further development in the field of academic researches. To the IQH, the accomplishment of the history faculty is a long-term social responsibility and societal duty.

In the 1980s when the IQH was first established, senior scholars like Dai Yi, Li Wenhai, Wang Sizhi, and Wang Daocheng and others, utilizing the Summer Palace (Yiheyuan) with the Old Summer Palace (Yuanmingyuan) as an ideal starting point, heralded the IQH's research into the history of the Qing Dynasty imperial gardens. In the last decade, the IQH also amassed a team of researchers to collaborate with the garden-landscaping institutions of Beijing and other areas in the field of Chinese garden-landscaping research. The aim was to promote and enhance China's age-old cultural tradition of garden-landscaping. Through these mutual cooperation and collaborations, the research of Qing history has been vastly enhanced. It had also given a good opportunity for the IQH to participate more in social and societal projects. These projects also had given a favorable opening for the Summer Palace to work closely with the IQH. Over the years, the two organizations collaborated well to enhance the teachings and field studies together with holding and organizing various exhibitions and cultural activities, promoting the traditional Chinese garden-landscaping and propagating this unique Chinese historical culture. The impetus of these cooperations came from the mutual understanding of their historical mission and responsibilities.

The current study of the history of Qing dynasty falls mainly on traditional areas such as politics, ideology and culture. However, new areas such as the history of the daily culture, and physical quality of life are also gaining public attention to become the new ground of interest. With this in mind, our understanding and thoughts on daily culture and material quality of life had been vastly enhanced. The current exhibition on ancient jade hosted by the Summer Palace, together with other similar exhibitions hosted by other garden-landscaping organizations had all constituted tremendous good opportunities for our understanding and research into the material cultures such as the culture of jade.

The reverence and appreciation of Jade is an important constitution of traditional Chinese culture. A comparative study of the historical development of Chinese civilization with that of the West, the Chinese culture of jade could be easily recognized as truly distinctive. According to general accepted views in the history of Western culture, the development of human civilization went through three ages: the Stone age, the Bronze age and the Iron age. However, according to Chinese archeological evidences advanced by Mr. Zhang Guangzhi, the consensus reached within the Chinese archeological field is different. According to material usage, the Chinese pre-history civilization could be divided into four ages or periods. After the Stone Age, there was an additional Jade Age. Only after the Jade Age came the Bronze Age followed by the Iron Age. This had been fully proven in the many excavations from the Liangzhu culture and Longshan culture sites. The culture of jade has shown to be a very important ingredient in the traditional Chinese culture. The historical development subsequent to the Liangzhu and Longshan cultures, when compared to that of the Western civilization, had a very different path of development. It is this difference in the development path that propels us to a much deeper understanding of the significance of the Chinese civilization.

The Chinese jade culture has a stretch of continuance from the primeval pre-history until the Ming and Qing periods and had profoundly influenced the Chinese society. Until now we could still feel its effect and existence deeply. The various jade shapes and designs that we see today, if we carefully trace their origins and developments, would still render us into a deeper understanding of the Chinese culture and its characteristics. The jade culture of the Ming and Qing periods covered from the imperial courts to the society at large. As such, a deeper understanding of the Jade culture in the Ming and Qing dynasties would invariably enhance our research into the material and everyday culture of the two periods and the Chinese culture in general. Also, as the jade objects are invaluable cultural relics, many people would be highly interested or attracted to these jade objects. Appropriate exhibitions of jade culture and jade objects would also promote current popular and public culture making this a very meaningful societal activity. Upon the above reasons, the IQH is more than willing to participate in the various activities in public services. We will also continue to commit more academic strength into these research programs.

Zhu Hu

School of History Renmin University of China

December 2022

后记

中国人民大学清史所和颐和园管理处共同举办这样一场清代玉器展，是双方长期以来密切合作关系的延展。清史所作为一家高校学术机构，早从建所之日起，便主动担负了不少学术研究之外的社会服务工作。凑巧的是，最近十几年来，教育部也日渐强调，如今高校学科建设的任务和目标，除了通常的教学科研工作外，还要积极从事服务现实的社会工作。与此相适应，清史所以及人民大学的历史学科在完成教学科研任务外，以推动公共史学为龙头，为开展历史文化普及工作投入了越来越多的力量。这类普及工作需要广泛涉猎中国的传统文化，于是很多原本并不属于传统史学研究范围的内容，也需要加强相应的学术研究。总之，积极从事社会服务，弘扬中国优秀传统文化，既需要学术力量的参与，也要求学术研究的拓展。因此，对于中国人民大学清史所来说，发挥历史学的社会服务功能，是一项需要长期承担的、也是义不容辞的社会责任和义务。

从 20 世纪 80 年代起，也就是清史所正式建所后不久，本所的老前辈，如戴逸、李文海、王思治、王道成等先生，以避暑山庄和圆明园为抓手，开启了清史所对清代皇家园林史的研究。特别是最近十几年以来，我们集中了一批研究力量，与北京市以及其他地区的很多园林单位开展合作，共同研究中国园林文化，弘扬中国悠久的园林文化传统。这些合作研究，一方面使清史研究的内容得到了拓展，另一方面也使清史所得到了从事社会服务的良机。在开展这类合作的过程中，颐和园与清史所具有特别密切的合作关系。近年来，双方进行了多方面的合作，除了建设教学实习基地以外，还举办了各种各样的展览和文化活动推广园林文化，宣传中国特有的历史文化，其合作动力来自于双方同样具有的历史责任感。

对于清史来说，现在的研究当然还是以比较传统的政治、经济、思想、文化等方面的内容为主。但与此同时，日常文化史、物质生活史等新兴门类，引起了越来越多的人的关注，成为颇具吸引力的新方向。在这种方向的指引下，我们对于反映大众文化和日常生活的诸多方面，也都有了更多的认识和思考。颐和园举办的这场玉器展，以及其他园林单位举办的类似展览，便都成为我们了解和研究诸如玉器文化等物质文化史的良好契机。

众所周知，玉器文化是中国传统文化的重要组成部分。对照中国文明史和西方文明史的发展脉络来看，可以更加清楚地认识玉器文化的特质。按照西方文明史的通常说法，人类文明的发展一般经历三个阶段，即石器时代、铜器时代和铁器时代。但是按照中国考古学发现的证据，以张光直先生为代表，中国考古学界已经达成的共识，按照这种使用工具的标准，中国文明的发展可以划分为四个阶段，那就是中国在石器时代以后，其实还有一个玉器时代，玉器时代之后才是铜器时代和铁器时代。对此，从良渚文化和龙山文化以来的许多考古发现中，已经充分证明了这一点。

而玉器文化作为中国传统文化一个重要的基因，从良渚文化和龙山文化时代以降的历史发展过程中，与西方文明的发展相比，有了一个非常不同的历史走向。正是这样一个不同的走向，对于我们进一步认识中国历史文化的基因密码、认识中国文明形态的发展脉络，具有特别重要的意义。

这种玉器文化从远古一直到明清的延绵，对于中国社会的影响，到现在我们也完全能够深刻地加以体会。无疑，今天我们所看到的各种各样的玉器造型，倘若悉心追踪其源流，都可以构成对中国文明形态及其特质的深入认识。明清时期玉器文化覆盖了从皇室到大众的广泛社会层面，因此，深入认识明清时期的玉器文化，既有助于研究明清时期的物质文化和日常生活，也有助于历史研究的进一步发展。同时，鉴于明清玉器具有不菲的文物价值，社会大众对其有极大兴趣，所以适当展示这种玉器文化，对于当下大众文化建设，也是具有现实意义的社会活动。正是基于以上两种意义，清史所非常愿意参加这种社会服务活动，也会继续向这一研究方向投入学术力量，希望与各界朋友共勉。

朱浒

中国人民大学历史学院院长

中国人民大学清史研究所所长

2022 年 12 月

图书在版编目（CIP）数据

玉见生机 : 中国古代动植物题材玉器展 : 汉、英 / 北京市颐和园管理处 , 中国人民大学清史研究所编 . —北京 : 五洲传播出版社 , 2024.1
ISBN 978-7-5085-5108-1

Ⅰ . ①玉… Ⅱ . ①北… ②中… Ⅲ . ①古玉器 – 中国 – 画册 Ⅳ . ① K876.82

中国国家版本馆 CIP 数据核字 (2023) 第 173570 号

玉见生机——中国古代动植物题材玉器展

编　　者：北京市颐和园管理处
　　　　　中国人民大学清史研究所
译　　者：梅文超　李　娇
出 版 人：关　宏
责任编辑：邱红艳　樊程旭
文物摄影：杨京京
钤　　拓：平湖玺印篆刻博物馆
装帧设计：李猛工作室
出版发行：五洲传播出版社
地　　址：北京市海淀区北三环中路 31 号生产力大楼 B 座 6 层
邮　　编：100088
发行电话：010-82005927，010-82007837
网　　址：http://www.cicc.org.cn，http://www.thatsbooks.com
印　　刷：北京雅昌艺术印刷有限公司
版　　次：2024 年 1 月第 1 版第 1 次印刷
开　　本：787 毫米 ×1092 毫米　1/8
印　　张：59.5
书　　号：ISBN 978-7-5085-5108-1
定　　价：1980.00 元